ETHICS, TRUST,

AND

THE PROFESSIONS

This volume is part of a series
of publications resulting from the
Bicentennial celebration
of Georgetown University
(1789–1989).
The seminar
on which it draws was
sponsored and supported by
Georgetown University's
Bicentennial Office,
as well as by grants from the
Yamanouchi Pharmaceutical Co. Ltd.
and the
Helen V. Brach Foundation.

ETHICS, TRUST,

AND

THE PROFESSIONS

Philosophical and Cultural Aspects

Edited by

Edmund D. Pellegrino
Robert M. Veatch
John P. Langan

With the editorial assistance of Virginia Ashby Sharpe

GEORGETOWN UNIVERSITY PRESS
Washington, D.C.

4-15-10

Copyright © 1991 by Georgetown University Press
All Rights Reserved
Printed in the United States of America

Library of Congress Cataloging-in-Publication Data

Ethics, trust, and the professions : philosophical and cultural
  aspects : a Georgetown University bicentennial conference / edited
  by Edmund D. Pellegrino, Robert M. Veatch, and John P. Langan with
  the editorial assistance of Virginia Ashby Sharpe.
      p. cm.
  ISBN 0-87840-512-7 (cloth). -- ISBN 0-87840-513-5 (paper)
  1. Professional ethics--Congresses. 2. Trust (Psychology)-
-Congresses. 3. Confidential communications--Congresses.
I. Pellegrino, Edmund D., 1920- . II. Veatch, Robert M.
III. Langan, John, 1940- .
BJ1725.E765 1991
174--dc20   90-46368
                                                    CIP

Contents

Preface   vii
Acknowledgments   xi
Contributors   xiii

I. The Concept of the Fiduciary Relation
Daniel M. Fox
The Politics of Trust in American Health Care   3
Robert Sokolowski
The Fiduciary Relationship and the Nature of
Professions   23
Richard M. Zaner
The Phenomenon of Trust and the Patient-Physician
Relationship   45
Edmund D. Pellegrino
Trust and Distrust in Professional Ethics   69

II. What Does Trust Require?
Allen Buchanan
The Physician's Knowledge and the Patient's Best
Interest   93
Dan W. Brock
Facts and Values in the Physician-Patient
Relationship   113

Gilbert Meilaender
Are There Virtues Inherent in a Profession?   139
Robert M. Veatch
Is Trust of Professionals a Coherent Concept?   159

III. The Sociocultural Setting of the Professions
Samuel Gorovitz
Professions, Professors, and Competing Obligations   177
Eliot Freidson
Nourishing Professionalism   193
John Langan
Professional Paradigms   221

IV. Fiduciary Relationship: Several World Views
Rihito Kimura
Fiduciary Relationships and the Medical Profession:
A Japanese Point of View   235
Ren-zong Qiu
The Fiduciary Relationship between Professionals
and Clients: A Chinese Perspective   247
Hans-Martin Sass
Professional Organizations and Professional Ethics: A
European View   263

Preface

In 1789, when John Carroll founded his "Academy" in "George Town on the Potomack," the ethics of the learned professions seemed fixed for all time. In medicine, the Hippocratic Oath and ethic were accorded quasi-scriptural status. The ethics of law and ministry, while less explicitly stated, were equally durable. In the three professions, long-held traditions, bolstered by borrowings from the ethics of Christianity and Roman Stoicism and the ethos of the eighteenth century gentleman, made up what appeared to be an immutable canon.

That canon survived largely untouched until two decades ago. Now that canon has come under the most critical scrutiny ever, from a variety of directions. The educated public is alert to the enormous power of expert knowledge in a technological society and to the influence those who possess it can exert on our lives. The media have exploited the dilemmas of medical progress, the ethical lapses in professional behavior, and the sociopolitical implications of professional decisions. The rise of participatory democracy and moral pluralism have generated distrust of elitism and privilege. There is everywhere a growing demand for autonomy in decisions that affect our personal lives. Finally, ethicists have for the first time begun to challenge the way philosophical presuppositions have come to affect the traditional canons of professional ethics and practice.

The upshot is that the whole edifice of ethics in the professions has become problematic. Professionals themselves are confused about the nature of their obligation and the moral values that ought to govern their relationships with those who seek their help. It is difficult indeed to know what the ethics of medicine, law, or ministry will look like in

the twenty-first century. What seems certain is that a simple reasser-
tion of the traditional canons will not suffice.

A myriad of fundamental questions face us: Are the so-called
"learned professions" really different from the many other occupations and activities now laying claim to that designation? If they do
differ, are the differences of kind or degree? Are higher standards of
moral performance demanded of the "learned" professions? Are medicine, law, and ministry morally different from business, the crafts, or
other pursuits based in the cultivation of particular kinds of expertise?
Are the relationships with patients or clients to be understood as contractual, covenantal, or as commodity transactions? How are the legitimate self-interests of professionals and of patients or clients to be balanced while maintaining the moral character of the relationship?

These questions are of obvious significance to society as well as to
the professions. They call for the kind of formal philosophical examination to which, curiously enough, the ethics of the professions have
not been subjected until very recently. The essays in this volume address some of these issues from the historical, sociological, philosophical, ethical, and cultural points of view.

An indication of the searching nature of the current critique is the
amount of attention these essays give to the fiduciary relationship.
One would have thought this to be perhaps the most durable of the
elements in the traditional ethical canon. Yet the strength and diversity of opinions on the place of trust reveal how essential a rethinking of
the nature of the professions has really become.

Essential to any restructuring of professional ethics is a closer contact between philosophical ethics and the sociology and anthropology
of the professions as well as the different ways the professions are
seen in different cultures. The professions today operate across national and cultural boundaries. The ethical problems particularly are often
the same; but the differences in world view of lawyers, doctors, and
ministers from different cultures may yield different answers. These
differences and the presuppositions on which they are based require
more precise definition.

Few issues are more relevant to contemporary society than the nature and ethics of the professions. In a technologic, interdependent,
and knowledge-driven society, professionals exert unprecedented
power. Once outside the perimeters of our own expertise, we are all
vulnerable to the way the professions use their power. This is most
dramatically the case when we ourselves are in need of the services of
a physician, lawyer, or minister.

The professions are also powerful shapers of our culture and mores. Policy makers are dependent upon their knowledge. Opinion makers draw on them for their metaphors. The general public looks to them for authoritative answers to the complex social and cultural issues of the day. Yet, everyone is concerned about the parlous state of professional ethics. They remember the lawyers of Bhopal and Watergate, the physicians of Auschwitz and medicare fraud, and the ministers of the electronic church. We need not be confirmed cynics to approach professional relationships with trepidation today.

Similar questions have, of course, occurred in the past. What is different today is that the ethical ground rules are changing drastically. Practices that would have been condemned in years past are now defended and legitimated by creditable thinkers. What it is to be a profession is now an open question. Without the traditional moral standards by which to judge professional performance, we are all increasingly uneasy in relationships which paradoxically demand the highest degrees of moral integrity.

These essays are intended to stimulate discussion between and among the disciplines and the professions about what it is to be a profession today. This is a particularly pertinent enterprise for today's universities, whose professional faculties are charged with the intellectual and moral formation of tomorrow's doctors, lawyers, and ministers.

John Carroll would probably be surprised to learn that the immutable framework of the ethics of the professions should be in such a troublous state. He would not be surprised and indeed would be pleased to see the subject engaged by the "Academy" he founded on the Potomac two hundred years ago.

EDMUND D. PELLEGRINO
ROBERT M .VEATCH
JOHN P. LANGAN

Acknowledgments

The editors wish to express gratitude for generous grants from the Yamanouchi Pharmaceutical Co. Ltd. of Japan and the Helen V. Brach Foundation which made this conference possible. We are also deeply indebted to Mrs. Marti Patchell, Assistant to the Director of the Center for the Advanced Study of Ethics at Georgetown, for her indispensable assistance in planning, organizing, and running this Bicentennial Conference. Likewise, the assistance of Virginia Ashby Sharpe has been crucial in editing and collating the entire manuscript. Finally, we are grateful for the support of Father Charles Currie, S.J., Director of the Bicentennial Celebration of Georgetown University, through every phase of the project.

Contributors

Daniel W. Brock, Ph.D. is Professor of Philosophy at Brown University, Providence, R.I.

Allen Buchanan, Ph.D. is Professor of Philosophy at the University of Arizona, Tuscon.

Daniel M. Fox, Ph.D. is Professor of Humanities in Medicine at the State University of New York, Stony Brook.

Elliot Freidson, Ph.D. is Professor of Sociology at New York University, New York.

Samuel Gorovitz, Ph.D. is Dean of the College of Arts and Sciences at Syracuse University, Syracuse, N.Y.

Rihito Kimura, J.D. is Director of the Asian Bioethics Program at the Kennedy Institute of Ethics, Georgetown University, Washington, D.C., and Professor of Bioethics and Law, Waseda University, Tokyo.

John Langan, S.J. is the Rose F. Kennedy Professor of Christian Ethics at the Kennedy Institute of Ethics and a Senior Fellow at the Woodstock Theological Center, Georgetown University, Washington, D.C.

Gilbert Meilaender, Ph.D. is Professor of Religion at Oberlin College, Oberlin, Ohio.

Edmund D. Pellegrino, M.D. is the Director of the Center for the Advanced Study of Ethics and the John Carroll Professor of Medicine and Medical Humanities at Georgetown University, Washington, D.C.

Ren-zong Qiu is a Visiting Scholar at the Program for Medical Ethics at the University of Wisconsin, Madison.

Hans-Martin Sass is Director of the European Bioethics Program at the Kennedy Institute of Ethics, Georgetown University, Washington, D.C.

Reverend Robert Sokolowski, Ph.D. is Professor of Philosophy at The Catholic University of America, Washington, D.C.

Robert M. Veatch, Ph.D. is Director of the Kennedy Institute of Ethics, Georgetown University, Washington, D.C.

Richard Zaner, Ph.D. holds the Anne Geddes Stahlman Chair in Medical Ethics in the Department of Medicine, Vanderbilt University, Nashville, Tenn.

I.

The Concept of the Fiduciary Relation

DANIEL M. FOX

The Politics of Trust
in American Health Care

I. Introduction

The history of relationships between physicians and patients is a subject about which considerably more is written than is known systematically. There is little firsthand evidence about how the participants in medical encounters have behaved under different circumstances and different times. Nevertheless, "trust has always been a problem in the medical relationship," Edmund D. Pellegrino said, commenting on an earlier draft of this paper, because "merely being ill leads to resentment."

Most of the scholarship on medical encounters, past and present, describes them as revealing the attitudes about medical knowledge, social class, race, gender, family, community, and work particular to a time and a place. Medical encounters appear to be special cases of more general characteristics of a society.[1]

A constant in this history is concern among physicians regarding threats to what they claimed to be their proper relationship with patients. The great texts in the history of medical ethics are most useful to historians of social and political affairs as records of medical discontent, and often of idealizations, and even minority opinions about how physicians and their patients ought to behave.[2]

On the basis of this historical evidence, I will argue in this paper that concern about the fiduciary relationship between physicians and patients in the contemporary United States reveals a great deal about pressures for and against fundamental changes in the health polity. In particular, I will argue that concern about the fiduciary relationship is the result of a shift in the fundamental premises of our health policy and the relative political weakness of countervailing premises. Moreover, the medical profession and the institutions it dominates have been heavily involved in bringing about this change in the premises of health policy.

Before laying out my argument in detail, I will describe what I mean by health polity and health policy. The unconventional phrase "health polity" encompasses more individuals, institutions, and ideas than the words that are ordinarily used to describe health policies and politics. The *Oxford English Dictionary* defines polity as "a particular form of political organization, a form of government...an organized society or community." I use the phrase health polity to describe the ways in which a community, in the broad sense of this definition, conceives of and organizes its response to health and illness.[3]

"Health policy," in my formulation, is the polity's systematic and ongoing activity of decision making regarding what resources ought to be allocated to the polity and how they ought to be distributed. The story of policy is recorded in what is done (or not done) by the leaders of the polity. Health policy is constantly changing as a result of three interacting influences. The first is *ideas* about science, medicine, illness, class, race, gender, and social obligation, to name just a few. The second is *interests*, that is, whatever the leaders of groups within the polity perceive as good for their members. The third influence is *illness* or, more precisely, the epidemiological situation, that is, whatever are perceived to be the major events accounting for morbidity and mortality.[4]

To support my claim that contemporary concern about the fiduciary relationship is a result of changes in the polity that are revealed in the history of policy, I argue (1) that fundamental *ideas* about the purpose of the health polity have been in active change for the past half century, (2) that this change has driven the behavior of major *interest groups*, and (3) that changing ideas and interest group behavior help to explain apparent irrationalities in how we have addressed *illness* or the epidemiological situation. Finally, I speculate about the impact of these changes on the health polity's current perception of the fiduciary relationship. My strategy is to describe the health polity at four points in time, each twenty years apart.[5]

II. The Health Polity in 1929

The institutional map of the health polity sixty years ago was relatively simple. Physicians, the most visible participants in the polity, were organized in county and state societies that had federated into the American Medical Association a generation earlier. Hospitals were growing in size and number and would continue to do so despite the hard times of the next decade. There was a consensus that medical progress began in laboratories, was translated into practice, and was best taught in teaching hospitals affiliated with medical schools. Most physicians practiced alone or in very small groups and were paid fees directly by their patients. The exceptions were the few physicians who were employed by large industrial corporations, those who worked for salaries in charity or government clinics for the poor, or those who were paid by mutual benefit societies. Government health policy was implemented at mainly state and local levels, in areas such as licensure, sanitation, infectious disease control, medical care for the poor in clinics and public hospitals, and custodial care for the mentally ill and disabled. The federal government had just abandoned a direct service program for poor mothers and children as a result of objections from organized medicine and the Roman Catholic church. Federal programs took care of seamen, Native Americans, and veterans. The Public Health Service supported state health departments and had a small, highly regarded research capacity.

Most employers and labor leaders did not consider themselves to be part of the health polity. Many employers were concerned about work-related illness and injury, but only a few conceived health care more broadly. Organized labor concentrated its energies on winning and maintaining the right to bargain about wages, working conditions, and job stability. There were exceptions, however. A few life insurance companies paid close attention to health policy, as an outgrowth of their desire to reduce claims. The pharmaceutical industry, along with organized medicine, advocated public regulation of drugs and drug prescription in order to drive so-called quacks and their remedies from the market. A few labor unions were involved in the politics of recently enacted statutes to compensate workers for on-the-job injuries, and others offered their members medical care.

There were signs of ferment. A small group of influential people in the health polity were routinely calling attention to a major change in the causes of mortality: for the first time, chronic diseases were responsible for more deaths than infections or injuries. The members of this group included state public health officials, statisticians working for life insurance companies, and laboratory scientists. Two years earlier, the ten leading philanthropic foundations had begun to finance what would be a six-year study of the costs and organization of medical care. The purpose of the inquiry was to recommend new health policies, especially to pay the medical care costs of people with low incomes. Leaders of the American Medical Association accepted appointment to the study's steering committee. They were concerned not only about physicians' incomes and health care access for the poor but also they wanted to make certain that proposals for insurance pools organized by the states, which the AMA had helped to defeat a decade earlier, did not resurface.

Much of this detail will be familiar to anyone who has read even cursorily in the history of twentieth-century health affairs. I adduce it as a reminder of how people thought about the health polity on the eve of what was to be six decades of wrenching change. What stands out in the year 1929 is that most of the people who paid for care were not represented by organizations in the polity. The exception was state and local, and to a lesser extent the federal government, which paid for the care of the very poor and special populations. Further, most of the people in the polity conceived of the financing of medical care as a matter outside conventional policy. Insurance, both mandated and private, seemed safely off the agenda. Payment by patients for physician and hospital care was conceived as only incidentally an economic transaction; business systems, for instance, were rudimentary and many doctors and hospital managers were pleased to keep them that way. There were a considerable number of proprietary hospitals, but most of them were small and were owned by doctors in communities where government or philanthropy, for various reasons, had chosen not to build them.

In sum, the situation of the health polity in 1929 was as follows: There was broad consensus on leading *ideas* about scientific progress, its causes and dissemination; about the goals and limits of public policy and what leading groups would do to further or protect their *interests*. Although there was broad consensus that the *epidemiological situation* appeared to be changing, there was not much clarity about the implications of the increasing prevalence of chronic disease. A few individuals wrote notable essays about the fiduciary relationship during this period—the most famous being Francis Peabody and Richard C. Cabot of Harvard—but it hardly seemed to be a significant issue for the health polity.

III. The Health Polity in 1949

Enormous changes in the health polity occurred in the next twenty years such that a person who was in college or medical school in 1949 would have a very different perception of ideas, interests, and the epidemiological situation than his or her teachers had. For example, most medical care was now paid for by third parties. For fifteen years, enrollment in voluntary insurance had grown. During World War II, with incentives to employers to pay part of the cost, third-party insurance had become the major source of income for hospitals. After the war, health care became a major issue for unions as well, legitimized by the law of collective bargaining. By 1949, government, on all levels, had become a much more significant actor in the health polity. The federal government was providing social insurance for the aged and, along with states, income to the poor and disabled. Moreover, the federal government was subsidizing hospital construction and had for over a decade been spending considerable money, through the states, on medical care for women and children. The veterans' medical care program had grown enormously. The extramural research program of the National Institutes of Health was begun in 1945. Mandatory health insurance was very much on the agenda of a president just one year past reelection. The states were making large commitments to build new medical schools and hospitals.

Medical politics had changed as well. From the 1930s, specialty societies competed successfully to represent the interests of the members. Geographic medical societies (county, state, and the AMA) had considerable power, and would claim to use it with devastating effect in national elections, but there was also evidence of decline. Perhaps most important, the federal courts convicted organized medicine of violating antitrust laws by impeding the growth of large prepaid group practices. More important than decline was a change in the function of county and state societies. They were most useful to their members as negotiators with government agencies and insurers and, in many instances, as managers of payment systems. Even the AMA was more overtly concerned about the business of medicine. Its staff economists, alone among American social scientists of the time who studied the health polity, wrote about medical care as a commodity that, like other consumer goods, was sold in local and regional markets.

These changes in the polity, though much remarked on, did not seem particularly ominous because there was consensus on what seemed to be larger issues. Most important for the coherence of the polity, there was agreement about how to maintain, even increase, the progress of medical science, and there was no audible doubt that this progress would benefit the health of the public. Most of the health policy that had been enacted since the 1930s strengthened the ideas about progress that the polity held in 1929. Medical progress began in laboratories, was tested and communicated in teaching hospitals, and was then disseminated down a hierarchical pyramid of institutions and professionals in geographic regions. This reading of the history of medicine since the nineteenth century guaranteed the integrity of the fiduciary relationship between physicians and their patients. These ideas not only justified the increasing resources allocated to the health polity, they also justified the specific policy choices made by the federal government in medical research and the construction of facilities, and by states and cities in financing medical education and treatment of the poor in public and voluntary teaching hospitals.

Nevertheless, the health polity—and with it, comfort with the fiduciary relationship—had serious problems. These problems were a result of two interrelated factors. The first is familiar: difficulties in the financing of medical care created by the rational political behavior of interest groups. The second has had almost no attention to date: the pressure of the epidemiological situation on the financing policy created by the rational behavior of interest groups. The combined weight of these problems, which have yet to be resolved, has created and continues to create enormous dilemmas for the health polity, and especially for the fiduciary relationship.

Health policy, in any country in any year, is the result of the interplay of ideas, interest, and illness. In the United States since the 1930s, compromises that resulted from the action of interest groups acting on strongly held ideas have created financing policy that has been influenced, but not driven, by illness, what I have called the epidemiological situation. Whatever one's private opinion about the adequacy of financing policy since the 1930s, it has been the result of the politics of interest groups. The politics was driven by ideas about the primacy of physicians and hospitals in health care, about the virtues of fee for service medicine, and about the special virtues of private action (and the inherent problems of government management). Interest groups whose calculated political behavior reflected these ideas have, for six decades, dominated health policy. In the late 1940s, they appeared to be triumphant. The nation's health financing policy had several components: commercial and nonprofit (Blue Cross) health insurance for working-age adults and their dependents, paid for by employers and employees with a considerable public subsidy through income tax exclusions and deductions; federal and state subsidies (direct and through tax expenditures) for capital to construct hospitals; and categorical public welfare programs for the poor and the disabled.

The groups in favor of this policy included organized medicine, hospital leaders (who included, at that time, the major religious denominations) and their associations, and the insurance industry (and with them, banking and service industries). Although industrial leaders and their associations were not actively involved in the politics of health care financing, they were generally happy to support the view of people they regarded as their social peers. Arrayed against this formidable coalition were some of the national leaders of industrial labor unions, advocates for children and the elderly, liberal social reformers and, after 1948, President Harry Truman; all of these urged a national health insurance scheme. Many labor leaders were ambivalent about national health insurance and preferred to deliver health benefits to their members as evidence of their prowess at collective bargaining. After the defeat of several key liberals (including the majority leader of the Senate) in the elections of 1950, national health insurance was presumed to be politically dead.

The triumphant policy for financing health services made it difficult to address the growing pressure of chronic disease and disability on the health polity. This is a long and complicated story that is usually ignored because it involves technical issues of insurance rating and underwriting. To put the issue in simplest terms: an insurance system based on groups of employees and paid for by contributions from them and their employers is highly sensitive to financial pressure created by long-term illnesses among members of each group. Groups of older and sicker workers have higher premiums than younger ones. In a competitive insurance market, firms take advantage of this situation by offering cheaper policies to groups whose members are willing to forgo benefits. Younger and, in the main, healthier workers, their unions and their employers are eager to take advantage of lower insurance costs which translate into higher real wages.

As a result, under our financing policy there was (and remains) considerable incentive to transfer the burden of the most expensive health care to other payers. In the United States of the 1940s and 1950s, this meant restricting growth for coverage of physicians' services, home health care and nursing home care, capping hospital visits, and forcing many people with chronic illness (mainly retirees but also younger people) to get their health care from underfunded public welfare programs. These financing policies coincided with rising unit costs for hospital and medical services. Medical care was becoming more intensive—in labor and equipment—and thus more expensive. More people with more chronic diseases used more units of services. Insurers, in a competitive market, had incentives to control costs. Hospitals and physicians, beneficiaries of the creation of private health insurance in the 1930s and 1950s, now found themselves the antagonists of the payers.

I have, of course, oversimplified the situation. During these years, the pressure of rising unit costs multiplied by the increasing prevalence of chronic disease brought incremental change in our financing policy. Insurers gradually covered more hospital days and more long-term care, and shifted costs from retirees to younger workers. The insurance industry invented major medical coverage around 1950 to pay the catastrophic costs of illness. Federal and state expenditures for the poor and the disabled and, a growing category, the medically indigent, gradually increased. Ideas and interests were accommodating the epidemiological situation.

Despite the gradual accommodation, however, financing policy strained the fiduciary relationship between physicians and patients. In the past, physicians had frequently taken patients' financial circumstances into account when giving advice. Now they were under a new set of pressures. They had strong incentives to minimize their patients' out-of-pocket costs while maximizing their own reimbursement from third parties. At the same time, they were increasingly under competing pressures from hospitals, who were being urged by insurers and state welfare and regulatory agencies to reduce the hospital services (notably diagnostic tests, and days) that they ordered. These matters are complicated, but for the purposes of this paper it is sufficient to generalize that patients and payers were increasingly expecting physicians to make explicit economic calculations as part of their treatment decisions.

Nevertheless, there was still general agreement in the polity in the 1950s that medical care was special—that it was not like other goods and services produced and consumed in the American economy. This agreement, this central organizing idea in the health polity, gradually eroded, mainly as a result of the effects of conflicts among interest groups around financing policy.

IV. The Health Polity in 1969

Changes in financing policy in the 1960s placed further strains on the fiduciary relationship. In outline, these changes are familiar, since they have driven health financing ever since. But I interpret their significance somewhat differently than many of my colleagues.

I call these changes in health care finance the compromise of the 1960s. On the eve of the compromise we had the financing policy I have described in the preceding paragraphs. This policy, as I have argued, responded to strongly held ideas and the interests of powerful groups. As a result of this financing policy, however, the major pressures created by the epidemiological situation—the growing burden of chronic disease and disability—were addressed only indirectly. The compromise of the 1960s was an accommodation of existing ideas to new perceptions of interest, to new actors, and to the relentless pressure of chronic illness. Like all successful compromises, it left most of the people who accepted it, even those who brought it about, only partially satisfied.

The ideas that were accommodated in the compromise of the 1960s are familiar from earlier sections of the paper: Medical progress is benign, if expensive. More of it ought to be available to more people, but in circumstances that preserve the relationship between work and entitlement, and maintain the private and nonprofit markets in insurance and means-tested programs for the poor and the medically indigent.

During the 1960s, the salience of new interests was magnified by our political institutions. The most evident new interest group was the elderly—both people over age sixty-five and working-age adults—who were eager to avoid the direct cost of health care for their parents and for retirees in their employee insurance groups. Other groups, which consisted primarily of Blacks and Hispanics, mobilized around access to rights and opportunity, which included health care. These groups were strongly supported by national leaders of the labor movement. Political institutions were uncommonly receptive to the claims of these groups in the mid-1960s. The election of 1964 created a mandate for a president with a liberal agenda and returned a Congress more liberal than any before or since.

Equally important, a shift had occurred in the array of interests within the health polity. As a result of rising costs and the increasing pressure from insurers and state government to restrain their growth, hospitals' interests diverged from those of many organizations of physicians. The hospitals were now eager for public funds to pay the costs of their most expensive patients—the elderly and the poor suffering the acute interludes of chronic disease. Many physicians, particularly those in academic medicine, many surgeons and those in the hospital-based specialities, shared this interest. The membership of the AMA had dropped by a quarter over the previous decade.

The compromise of the 1960s—really the years 1965-1967—had four elements. The first was Medicare, social insurance for the elderly which spread the cost of the most expensive patients to the paychecks of everyone who worked at a regular job. The second element was an agreement to maintain the existing structure of private and nonprofit insurance by using that sector to administer Medicare and by a consensus among the most powerful congressional leaders that health insurance for the elderly was not the first installment (as many liberals wished) on national health insurance for everyone. The third element of the compromise, which followed from the first two, was to ignore the problem of paying for the management of chronic illness; that is, for long-term care outside hospitals. The officials of the executive and legislative branches of government who created Medicare insisted that it was a program to pay only for acute care (this, despite the fact that it paid for more nursing home and home health care than any private insurance policy in history). The final element, hardly debated at the time, was agreement that the remaining poor, disabled, and medically indigent would still receive means-tested care. The new Medicaid program consolidated, rationalized, and increased the federal subsidy to the states for means-tested care.

The consequences of the compromise of the 1960s have, over two decades, created the problems in the fiduciary relationship that distress many contemporary critics of American medicine. In oversimple terms, a direct (and certainly unanticipated) result of the compromise in action was to create enormous pressure to change the fundamental organizing idea of the health polity: the notion that health care, and therefore the people who provided it, was not a commodity but rather a calling (to some) and a collective good or social utility (to others).

V. The Consequences of the Compromise

The unanticipated effects of the compromise of the 1960s occurred mainly because either undoing it or making a new one was politically impossible, at least through the end of the 1980s. These effects were intensified, moreover, by problems in the general economy and their impact on business and government.

The consequences of the compromise are familiar. Because Medicare reimbursed hospitals and physicians generously (as a deliberate policy to cement their loyalty to the program), it fueled a general inflation in health care costs. Moreover, both Medicare and private insurance contained what, in the 1970s, economists labeled perverse incentives, to use (even to overuse) the most expensive acute care services. In addition, Medicaid, because it was an open-ended program rooted in the philanthropic tradition of paying for services used by the poor (as opposed to the logic of insurance underwriting) quickly and unexpectedly became the major source of support for long-term care for the elderly and the chronically disabled.

The costs of health care to everyone, but especially to government agencies and employers, were increasing rapidly at a time when the prosperity of the quarter century after World War II had been replaced by inflation and recession. By the mid-1970s, the problems of paying, and thus of containing, these costs had become the dominant issue in the health polity.

In theory, the problem of cost escalation in health care could have been solved (as it had been in Western Europe) by creating a public-private national health insurance system that spread the cost more equitably across the population and imposed rigorous controls on utilization. Throughout the 1970s various influential liberals promoted this solution (including Jimmy Carter in the presidential campaign of 1976). But proponents of national health insurance could not mobilize significant interest group support. Moreover, the most significant supporters of similar plans in the past, the national labor organizations, were rapidly losing power in the workplace and thus in national affairs.

By the late 1970s, a new idea—the notion that medical care was a commodity—was acquiring new adherents who believed that it was the key to controlling medical care costs. A few economists and ideologues of the political right had for many years advocated reconceiving the health polity as a sector of the economy. Their goal was either analytic or political or both. The analytical goal was to understand better the behavior of people in relationships in which buyers and sellers are, in economists' language, "asymmetrically informed." Some of them had as a political goal preventing the expansion of, or rolling back, a collectivist welfare state, which they believed to be dysfunctional. Others were offended by the monopoly power exerted by doctors and their allies in the hospital industry, whom they regarded as aggrandizing themselves by taking advantage of the idea that medical care is a special, collective good.

Whatever their motives, they proposed policies which, whatever else they did, were supported by effective coalitions. Some of the policies were regulatory; others sought to increase competition. The policies themselves are familiar, and need not be detailed here. State governments, encouraged by the federal government and by the insurance industry, devised regulations that reduced or limited expensive overcapacity in hospitals. All payers imposed controls on utilization by patients—but really by physicians ordering hospital stays—through either preadmission screening or postadmission audits. To promote competition, the federal government and insurers—acting at the request of employers—encouraged health maintenance organizations and various forms of discounting (generally called preferred provider arrangements). Diagnosis-related groups (DRGs), the most celebrated innovation, are a regulatory strategy designed to promote competition to conserve resources within hospitals.

These strategies were implemented because the constituency supporting them was the most powerful ever assembled in the health polity. For the first time, employers took a vigorous interest in health care financing. Before, they had supported their natural political allies but always with the knowledge that they could pass on increases in the cost of health benefits to the people who bought their goods or services and to their employees. Now their products were suffering in international price competition and their employees were increasingly disadvantaged by inflation. Insurers embraced the strategies because employers demanded that they control costs. The federal government and the states endorsed them—even before the Reagan administration—as a way to limit budget deficits. Hospital leaders endorsed the cost-containment strategies, though often with reservations, because they saw them as the only way to prevent even more onerous regulation by the federal government and because many of them were attracted ideologically to a business point of view.

Physicians were conspicuously absent from the cost-containment coalition. The economizers—my term for the members of the coalition who regarded health care as a commodity and set out to influence its supply and demand through regulatory and market mechanisms—did not need active support from physicians.[6] Moreover, they knew they could count on their passive support; on physicians' desire to continue to be paid as handsomely as they had been as a result of the compromise of the 1960s. Whatever the long-term results of the idea that medicine is a commodity that is supplied to demand by economic actors, in the short run it correctly predicted the behavior of most members of the medical profession. That this behavior was often accompanied by laments and snarls would, to an economizer, be regarded as beside the point.

These events of the recent past provide the context, and the stimulus, for much of the contemporary concern about the future of the fiduciary relationship between physicians and their patients. If health care is a commodity, then it is prudent for buyers to beware of sellers, especially if they might have a personal stake in withholding care. If it is a commodity, then it is appropriate to formulate decisions on the basis of the economizers' models of cost-benefit and cost-effectiveness analysis. Informed consent to transactions does not mean quite the same thing as it does in relationships in which physicians are presumed to be advocates for patients. The traditional assumptions of medical ethics need to be reexamined in a society in which we take as natural descriptions of the health polity such economizers' concepts as provider, consumer, industry, sector, market, and price. The array of health services in the future will be very different if the response to the epidemiological pressure of chronic disease is based on notions of efficiency and productivity rather than considerations of collective welfare.

VI. The Health Polity in 1989

Contemporary histories properly have inconclusive endings. It is malpractice among historians to claim that because we have grounded hypotheses about the past we have some insight into how events in the present will affect the future. Contemporary historians carry the additional risk that many people will read their narratives as polemics. Such ascriptions of intent are projective tests when historians have done their job properly.

My purpose is to take no sides. Nevertheless, some readers will believe that I have argued that the assumptions of the economizers threaten the integrity of the fiduciary relationship between physicians and their patients. Others will infer the opposite, that I am delighted by the bashing that the medical profession has experienced in recent years. Both interpretations could, I hope, be sustained by a selective reading of this paper. It is always too early to tell the course of history—which is a major reason why historians rarely are recruited to exercise power. Thus I can invent two plausible scenarios about the near future of policy to finance health care. Each scenario would have a different effect on who worries about what issues in the fiduciary relationship.

According to the first scenario, there will be a major reorganization of health financing policy over the next decade. Large employers, especially in "smokestack" industries, want to spread the costs of health care for an aging labor force to other parts of the economy in order to be more competitive with firms in other countries that do precisely that. Led by the Chrysler Corporation and eagerly supported by industrial unions, American business will form a coalition that can, finally, create a national health insurance system. The coalition will also recruit the same political interests that supported the expansion of Medicare coverage in 1988 and several innovations in Medicaid during the Reagan administration. This system will be managed, in part, by the insurance industry, but without the profits handed to them in the 1960s when they became fiscal intermediaries for Medicare. The insurance industry will gladly trade the certain return of management fees for the precarious and low profits of writing health insurance in an era of rigorous cost containment. Moreover, as part of this reform, the problems of the uninsured and underinsured will be solved, using one of several mechanisms, including major changes in the Medicaid program. The coalition supporting this scenario will also address the problem of financing long-term care. As a result of these events, we will have universal health coverage supported by both premium and tax dollars. Our system will most closely resemble that of Canada.

The second scenario extrapolates current policies into the foreseeable future. Instead of promoting a national program, business will decide that it is more cost-effective to increase its pressure to reduce demand for health care and the supply of people and facilities who provide it. This decision will be influenced by the national budget deficit, that is, by the political difficulty of financing more care, especially for the management of chronic illness in children, the elderly, and people of working age, without huge public subsidies that will require new taxes. Health care will be regarded as a commodity for people who are covered and as a residual and minimal public service for those without insurance or those who have exhausted their benefits.

These scenarios would have strikingly different effects on what people worried about in the fiduciary relationship. In the first, the major concern would be about problems of gatekeeping and methods of rationing scarce resources. The second would amplify current issues; in particular, the competing economic interests of physicians and payers, on one side, and patients on the other.

Most likely neither scenario will be followed. The history of the fiduciary relationship, as of everything else, has never been predictable. It is likely, however, that ideas, interests and illness will continue to determine the behavior of the institutions in the American health polity.

Notes

1. For a review of pertinent literature, with citations, see Daniel M. Fox, "The Politics of Physicians' Responsibility in Epidemics: A Note on History," *Hastings Center Report* 18 (1988):5-10, reprinted in Elizabeth Fee and Daniel M. Fox, eds., *AIDS: The Burdens of History* (Berkeley: University of California Press, 1988), 86-96.

2. For a particularly revealing analysis of the relationship between ethical texts and medical behavior, see Darrel W. Amundsen, "Medical Deontology and Pestilential Disease in the Late Middle Ages," *Journal of the History of Medicine and Allied Sciences* 32 (1977):403-21.

3. For a more extensive description of my use of the phrase health polity, see Daniel M. Fox, "AIDS and the American Health Polity: The History and Prospects of a Crisis of Authority," *Milbank Quarterly* 64, supplement (1986):7-33, revised and reprinted in Fee and Fox, *AIDS*, 316-43.

4. For a recent assessment of these interacting influences, see the papers in the special supplement to the *Milbank Quarterly*, entitled *Disability Policy: Restoring Socio-Economic Independence, Milbank Quarterly* 67, supplement (in press).

5. Most of the description that follows is based on a rich secondary literature or on my reading of primary sources which I have cited in other publications. Key secondary sources include Daniel M. Fox, *Health Policies, Health Politics: The Experience of Britain and America, 1911-1965* (Princeton: Princeton University Press, 1986) and Rosemary Stevens, *In Sickness and in Wealth: American Hospitals in the Twentieth Century* (New York: Basic Books, 1989). Most of the earlier secondary material is summarized in Paul Starr, *The Social Transformation of American Medicine* (New York: Basic Books, 1982). Much of the material on chronic disease and the incentive system of voluntary health insurance is in the publication cited in note 4 above.

6. I use the term "economizers" to make plain that I am not talking either about economists or about the application of economic analysis to the data of health affairs. Rather, I am talking about political behavior that converts the units of economic analysis into the goals of public policy. Economists need not (and in many instances, especially in other Western countries, do not) make political judgments solely on the basis of economic analysis. Considerable economic analysis has, moreover, been used to justify employing other models for health policy than the one I call "economizing." I initially addressed these ideas in *Economists and Health Care* (New York: Prodist, 1979) and have returned to them recently in "The Politics of Knowledge: Research and Health Policy in the United States," in *Proceedings of the Second Annual Health Policy Conference*, McMaster University, 1989 (in press).

Discussion

Dr. Buchanan: I would like to go back to a remark you made very early about different ways of doing historical analysis of the health polity. You mentioned as an example Paul Starr's book and said that it, like many others, proceeds on the assumption that the question one is trying to answer in a historical analysis is: Why is the U.S. different? Why doesn't it have national health insurance at least, if not a national health service? I agree that that is a working assumption for many such writers.

Then you said that you thought that this was the wrong way to go about it. In a minute I would like some amplification on what you think was wrong and what kinds of good results you can get if you don't make that assumption or that you miss if you do make it. It seems to me that Paul Starr, for one, is somebody who is very up front about this. He does have a normative axe to grind. He doesn't view himself as a historian anyway. He views himself as a political scientist/sociologist, or a political sociologist.

I am very interested to know what kinds of questions you think get neglected by taking the normative approach, even if one takes it self-consciously and straightforwardly.

Dr. Fox: Let me first say that I never pay attention to the labels people give themselves. I like to look functionally at what they do, and when I use economic or sociological theory, I expect to be taken to task when I misuse it. When somebody says, "I am a sociologist," and uses the historical method, I feel perfectly competent to say: "Have you thought about this or have you thought about that?"

In summary form, the difference between the method that I urge and the normative method is not in advocacy because, as you may know, I am doubly trained in history and public administration. As a public administrator, I am happy to tell you where I am. It is not an issue of advocacy. I take as my first goal, when I am doing historical research, to try to figure out how the world looks to contemporaries at the particular moment before me, what was important to them, what they felt, and what their values were, rather than to impose on that set of contemporaries my own present-day concerns or my own present-day politics.

In practical terms, this approach has led most people who practice history in the twentieth century to a lot of unexpected and interesting findings. Perhaps in the context of the talk I just gave, the simplest example is that when I went back and looked at what mattered to contemporaries in the formulation of United States health policy in the half century before 1965, I discovered that ideas mattered and that ideas drove the behavior of interest groups in ways that nobody had taken into account.

When the people who proposed, advocated, made, and carried out health policies said that new knowledge begins in laboratories, it is tested and disseminated from teaching hospitals, and then it flows down a pyramid-like shape out to the community, they believed it, and it was central to health policy and, until the 1960s, it was more important than how you paid for health care. So to me, respecting contemporaries, respecting the source is crucial. It is an enormously liberating activity.

Fr. Sokolowski: I have a philosophical question. In your last paragraph you say that "ideas, interests, and illness will continue to determine the behavior of the institutions in American health polity." In other words, this constellation is not likely to change.

Dr. Fox: I suppose that this really is a normative statement, or rhetorical.

Fr. Sokolowski: In a way, though, it is different from a normative statement because if you do have a kind of dimensional analysis, like force, mass, and acceleration in physics, you know, you could say that you are analyzing in a way that is different. It is not normative, it is structural.

Dr. Fox: I guess the more accurate statement is: as long as we are stuck with the political institutions we have in this country, there is a high probability that those will be the three interacting forces.

Fr. Sokolowski: I think it would be very interesting to take those three factors and apply them to other technological developments, such as nuclear energy. There is the same constellation at work. Or now child care, which is sort of a nascent area in government policy. Would you want to claim that those factors are transportable beyond the medical model?

Dr. Fox: I would like to hear other people do it. In my work I have extended this analysis to disability policy, but I am hesitant to go beyond that.

Fr. Sokolowski: Teaching would be another very interesting example—especially on the lower levels.

Dr. Fox: What would be the equivalent of the epidemiological situation?

Fr. Sokolowski: Illiteracy and things like that.

Dr. Brock: You stress the coming acceptance in the last couple of decades of the view that health care is a commodity, but I wonder how much you want to say that that implies as well the giving up of the view that health care is special.
A striking thing about the eighties, it seems to me, is that over the last decade there has been an increasing public awareness of the numbers of people in this country who don't have health care and an increasing sense that that is a bad thing. So, to many analysts, it now looks perhaps more likely than it has at any other point in the last decade that we might actually do something about the problem.

Now, it seems to me that that acknowledgment of the problem as a problem does seem to hinge on the assumption that health care is special.

Dr. Fox: Although there are—to oversimplify—people who believe that you ought to be compassionate about the thirty-seven, soon to be forty-five, million uninsured in this country, the major driving force behind any of the reforms in the fifteen states that have done something is the cost of the uninsured to business, to taxpayers, and to hospitals. Nobody is talking about the problem in the context even of the sixties compromise.

The sixties compromise was the quickest piece of the compromise to go through Congress. It was agreed that to take care of the equivalent population we merely needed to put some more money into our traditional charity model, called Medicaid. Nobody is talking very seriously about the Medicaid option today because we have recognized that our philanthropic tradition has a plastic edge in terms of responding to people's needs, not considering them as consumers. As a result, Medicaid not only takes care of our long-term care but it takes care of more than fifty percent of our disabled. That is a literal fact. To me, the fact that no one is even talking about charity is an example of why the concern about the uninsured and underinsured is tied up in commodity language.

Dr. Brock: If health care hadn't all along been viewed as different from other commodities, then we never would have had a problem about the cost of the uninsured. They simply would not affect services.

Dr. Fox: Absolutely. We wouldn't have cared. That is exactly my point. It is consistent with my point, yes.

Dr. Gorovitz: If I could just add a footnote to that, nor does anyone collectively worry about the total cost of Mercedes-Benz's purchased. It is not just a balance of payments issue. No one is saying that we are spending too much of our gross national product on Mercedes-Benz's or televisions or bowling, any pure commodity.

Dr. Fox: But we are talking about an industry in which the major purchaser is using tax dollars, unlike Mercedes. I think if medicine were ever commodified to the point that tax dollars were not an issue, you would see it getting paid about the same attention as part of the gross national product as the other leading industries, say construction or education.

Dr. Brock: You still have the insurance phenomenon, which would make people worry about whether they were buying health care that is worth its cost.

Dr. Fox: I recently have taken a piece of this argument internationally and because most people that I work with in Western Europe just assume normally that all their thinking about health policy should proceed from the collective welfare and distributive justice model, with varying degrees of social conflict, they are quite surprised to discover that there are serious people in the United States who want to have a more rigorous commodity view of the world.

Dr. Buchanan: Just briefly, I would like to add a word of caution about this dichotomy between treating health care as a commodity and not treating it as a commodity.

I like Dr. Fox's point about whether health care is special or not as being more helpful because part of what people object to, or at least associate with the commodity approach, is the idea of using cost effectiveness in their analysis, using standard tools of neoclassical economics models of rationality as maximization. It is clearly a mistake to reject that kind of methodology. The point is to make use of that methodology in the service of the proper recognition of the special quality of health care.

The consumer choice health plan in one sense creates consumer choice health care economics and the economic policy of rationality. On the other hand, it doesn't treat it as a commodity in the sense of getting something to which there are no entitlements or which is a good, just like video recorders or other kinds of things.

What I am worried about is people who say: look, health care is special, it is not a commodity, therefore we shouldn't be paying attention to economic analysis. The proper thing to do is harness the economic analysis for the appropriate goals, and as people are pointing out in Western Europe now, too, unless this is done, all of the good distributive justice programs and goals will go up in smoke because no one will be able to pay for it or no one will be willing to pay for it.

Dr. Meilaender: I wanted to return to your set of ideas, interests, and epidemiologic situation and just ask two questions.

The first I imagine is a very simple-minded question, but what is the fiduciary relation? Is it an idea? Is it an interest? It is not an epidemiological situation, but how does it relate to that set of three interwoven concerns?

Second, I was not always clear on how we got from one of your time slices to the next. For instance, can you explain in more detail how a shift takes place in the role that ideas play?

Dr. Fox: Yes. First, the toughest part of writing this paper was deciding what I thought the fiduciary relation was for the purpose of this paper. It is not a way I comfortably think, and I decided to take the easy way out by assuming that it is a set of ideas about the relationship of doctors and patients in the medical encounter, and that my source material would be what people said about the encounters. So it is a very empirical, oversimple definition.

My use of a construct of ideas, interests, and epidemiological situation is a device. It is a way of oversimplifying, a way of presenting, a way of saying: well, things are more complicated than they look. In my view of the history of health policy, all three are always there, you can't sort them out, and it is not possible or desirable to say that at one point in history one or the other of the three was more important.

Dr. Meilaender: You did say that at a certain time people took certain kinds of ideas seriously, and I took the implication of that to be that something shifted and they didn't play the same role after a certain period of time.

Dr. Fox: Well, ideas change. In other words, the central idea that I was trying to talk about in this paper was the notion that medical care was special and that what was tied to it, as a set of ideas about how you organized a health system and how you thought about entitlements for various people who received care, has taken a perceptible shift to the commodity view.

ROBERT SOKOLOWSKI

The Fiduciary Relationship and the Nature of Professions

I. Introduction: Formal Knowledge as the Distinguishing Feature of Professions

It has not proved easy to determine what a profession is. There is no problem about the existence and definition of skills and arts: clearly, some people know how to repair refrigerators, or treat sick animals, or cut hair, and the like. They have cultivated these skills and hence are obviously different from people who cannot do such things well. If the people who have the skills also understand what they are doing, if they have knowledge as well as skill, if they can teach and explain as well as perform, they can be said to possess not only a skill but an art, a *technê*.[1] When people who possessed certain arts formed associations to protect, promote, and teach their art, they were said to form guilds. Arts and guilds are not controversial; they are easy to identify. What more is needed? Is it truly necessary to introduce professions? Why not stay with the arts of medicine and law, and the guilds of doctors and lawyers? Is the distinction between a *technê* and a profession a genuine distinction, or does one term of the distinction, the profession, get absorbed into the other, the art, when we think precisely about the issue? How is a profession different from an art, how is a profession different from a guild?

Some twenty-five years ago, Bernard Barber[2] provided four features that an occupation must have if it is to be considered a profession: general and systematic knowledge, orientation to community interest, self-monitoring through internalized codes of ethics, and rewards that symbolize accomplishments in work and that are sought

as ends in themselves. A few years later, G. Harries-Jenkins[3] supplied
a list of six elements of professionalization, then went on to subdivide
these elements into no fewer than twenty-one subelements.

The debate has continued, and recently John Kultgen (1988) concluded his book *Ethics and Professionalism* [4] with the claim that the distinction between professions and other occupations is, in fact, now a
genuine distinction. In a chapter entitled "Professionalism without
Professions," he claims that professionalism is a way of being and acting that can be achieved in any occupation. He says that "the ideal of a
professional is that of a person dedicated to providing proficient service to those who need it."[5] He describes the various virtues, both moral and intellectual, that a dedicated professional must have; he observes that such virtues can be "deliberately pursued and cultivated";[6]
and he claims that all these virtues "are relevant to features of work as
such, not just features of particular kinds of work."[7] Since practically
everyone provides some sort of specialized labor, each person, he says,
contributes something to society and ought to shape his or her contri-
bution according to professional ideals. Even apparently menial and
routine tasks involve some specialization; and if there are forms of
work for which the professional virtues seem hardly to be required,
societies should organize these occupations in such a way that greater
professionalization can be realized in them: "The challenge is to alter
the conditions of other kinds of work so as to foster greater self-
development and self-expression and to provide conditions in which
workers will know and approve the products of their labor."[8] Kultgen
maintains that professionalism must be universalized and observes
that the term "profession" has suffered extensive "semantic hemor-
rhage"[9] as more and more occupations have laid claim to it. Thus, in
the terms we used to introduce our question, Kultgen's position would
imply that professions do not differ in principle from skills and arts.

Kultgen's proposals have much in common with the encyclical
Laborem exercens of Pope John Paul II.[10] In his encyclical, the Holy Father does not discuss professions as such, but he does extend the concept of work to cover many different kinds of human performances:
"Work means any activity of man, whether manual or intellectual,
whatever its nature or circumstances; it means any human activity
that can and must be recognized as work, in the midst of all the many
activities of which man is capable and to which he is predisposed by
his very nature. . ."[11] The pope unifies the concept of work not in
terms of the activity that is done but in terms of the one who accom-
plishes it, the human subject whose dignity, rights, and duties must
everywhere be respected.

The recent book by Eliot Freidson, *Professional Powers*,[12] may be taken as a counterpoint to Kultgen's work. Freidson distinguishes where Kultgen identifies. Freidson's aim is to "emphasize analytical description over abstract theorizing."[13] He provides a highly differentiated view of the professions, distinguishing not only the variety of professions themselves but also the variety of roles found within each profession: the roles of practitioners, administrators, teachers, and researchers. He comments in detail on the various ways professionals exercise power but also stresses the limits of such power, and he criticizes large-scale generalizations, such as the claim that professionals constitute a single new class in our social order or that professionals who are self-employed enjoy greater autonomy and success than those who work for others. He takes the concept "profession" as a historical concept, "an American social category for distinguishing a group of occupations,"[14] but he acknowledges that the concept can apply, with adjustments, to groups of people in other modern countries. Although Freidson stresses detail and variety, he does claim that the professions can be distinguished from other occupations. They are so distinguished, he says, by virtue of the "formal knowledge" they possess, apply, protect, and develop.[15] Members of the professions are the "agents of formal knowledge."[16]

The formal knowledge that is at the core of professions is, Freidson says, specialized knowledge, different from what most people know; it requires extensive education and training. It is the knowledge "shared by particular groups of people who perform activities on a regular basis that other people do not."[17] However, it is not just specialized knowledge, which has been found in all civilizations and can be found in the arts; it is specialized knowledge that, in the modern West, has taken on a distinctive character or structure, one that Freidson calls "formal." It has been shaped into systematic theories that explain facts and justify actions. It involves hypotheses, axioms, deductions, and models. Freidson says it is knowledge characterized by rationalization, a term that he takes from Max Weber and defines as "the pervasive use of reason, sustained where possible by measurement, to gain the end of functional efficiency."[18] He observes that "rational" knowledge and action are realized in or associated with contemporary natural science, technology, economic and institutional management, and social organization. He also states that such knowledge does not apply itself; it exists in and is developed by "human agents or carriers."[19] We might say that the formal knowledge is both embodied and applied in and through the professional.

II. Prudence and the Distinction between Art and Profession

Let us assume that Freidson is correct in isolating the possession of a certain kind of knowledge as the distinguishing feature of a professional. The knowledge in question, furthermore, is useful knowledge, the kind that can be applied to situations to bring about a desired result. Not all knowledge is useful in this sense; there is a kind of speculative or theoretical knowledge that can be very important for us without being practical and useful. There is some knowledge that is simply about the way things are and the way things have to be, about essentials and necessities; and our response to such knowledge may not be to put it to our use, but simply to recognize that things are that way and that there is nothing we can do about it. The patterns of time, for example, are essential and necessary; the future becomes the past through the present. It is not strictly speaking useful for us to know this, not in the way it can be useful to know the intricacies of the tax laws or the symptoms and causes of arthritis, since we cannot do anything about or with the passage of time. Such knowledge is too basic to be useful; it expresses what we must simply take as it is, not what we can use in modifying the world.

But not all useful knowledge ought to be called professional knowledge. A good automobile mechanic may know a lot of useful things about cars, but we would not, I think, want to call him a professional. One reason for our reluctance has already been provided by Freidson. The mechanic's knowledge is not formal and systematic enough to become the basis of a profession; his knowledge is tied to the particularities of the automobile. If he knew not only a lot about cars, but also a lot of physics, mathematics, mechanics, metallurgy, chemistry, and electromagnetics, and if he could apply all this knowledge to the automobile, then he would be not just a mechanic but an engineer. He would not only know that certain things are true about cars, but would also know why they are true, and he would be able to trace the "why" through several layers of explanation. He might or might not be a better mechanic because of all this, since auto repair deals with this particular car and not with theory and explanation, but he would be able to do certain things that a mechanic could not do. He might, for example, be able to help in developing new synthetic materials for automobile engines.

When we say that the knowledge of the professional, though still practical, is more formal and abstract or general than that of the mechanic, we do not mean that the professional's knowledge departs from the world and expands into mere words or textbooks. To be more formal and abstract or general means to have a wider range, to work within a more comprehensive context and with more materials. The mechanic may know that the terminals of the battery must be kept clean and that batteries run down after three years or so, but the engineer can see the car battery as an instance of the same forces that are at work in radios, lamps, generators, and bolts of lightning. Because the engineer's knowledge is so wide-ranging, he or she can see other ways of doing what is done with a battery. Because, for example, a doctor's knowledge of medicine is so wide-ranging and because she knows why certain things happen, she can think of many different ways of treating the headache that I have been trying to treat with aspirin. One feature of the knowledge possessed by professionals, therefore, is its formal and wide or expanded character.

But if knowledge, even formal knowledge, is the only distinctive feature of the professional, it is still not clear how a profession can be distinguished from an art; *technê* was also defined classically as skill with understanding. The distinction can be sharpened by noting another important aspect of professional activity. If I go to an automobile mechanic, all I entrust to this person is my automobile, but when I approach a professional, I subject something more than a possession of mine to the professional's expertise: in a distinctive way, I subject myself and my future to his or her assessments and to his or her judgment. Using the word "prudence" in the classical sense, the sense given to it by Aristotle as a person's ability "to deliberate about what is good and expedient for himself" in a way conducive to the good life in general,[20] I submit my own prudence to that of the professional. In a limited way, I hand over the steering of my life to this person. I let him or her take over not just one of my things, but my choices and activities themselves. I must do so, because I have wandered into an area of life in which my own knowledge does not equip me to steer by myself. Someone fell on my sidewalk and broke an arm and is suing me; I have developed severe headaches and blurred vision; I need to learn Russian because I will be stationed in Moscow. For a while I must do what someone else says I should, not what I simply decide to do myself. In engaging a professional, I do not abandon my own prudence; I do not delegate my prudence to someone else, but I do blend my prudence with that of the professional, or the professional's with mine.

It is true that the professional assumes responsibility for only a limited part of the client's life and that the client remains the ultimate agent in the relationship. As a client, I could always stop the transaction in question. But within that limited domain and with the importance that the domain may involve (my mental or physical health, my familial relationships, my legal standing), the professional deals not merely with my possessions but with me. If I go to a mechanic or to a dry cleaner, even one that provides "professional dry cleaning," I hand over my car or my jacket to someone else, but in dealing with a doctor or a lawyer or a teacher, I submit myself to be determined in my future condition by the one I consult; if I hire an architect to build a house for me, I am entrusting to that professional the design of part of my future life. This blending of my own prudence with that of the professional shows how knowledge can be common and shared even when it is practical knowledge, the kind that addresses and changes situations. It is not the case that only speculative thinking is common. I can share someone else's mind even in regard to what I should do, even in regard to my assessments and deliberations.

What we could call the phenomenon of nakedness, in its various forms, follows from the fact that a client or patient subordinates himself or herself to the prudence of the professional. The client has to remove the cover used for both protection and privacy in his or her normal exchanges with others. The most vivid instance of such nakedness occurs in regard to medicine; patients must not only tell the physician about their experiences and activities, but may also have to remove their clothing, that most elementary of shelters. This is done so that the physician can carry out an assessment and an intervention on the patient's behalf. A client has to lay open to his lawyer everything that happened and everything that he did concerning the issue he has brought to the lawyer, and another client must tell her architect everything about how she wants to live in the building the professional will design for her. If in any such cases the client were to retain part of his or her cover or shelter in the relevant area, the appeal to the professional's prudence would be in vain; the very item that is kept concealed might be the key to the situation.

Some special obligations befall professionals because their prudence is being called upon to help steer clients' lives. The exercise of professional judgment and skill must, first of all, be for the client's good. This obligation does not stem from any personal benevolence or private virtue on the part of the professional, but from the very nature of the relationship between professional and client. The client addresses *this* individual not because of any personal characteristics as such, not as a friend to whom he or she has come for advice, but as the embodiment and agent of a certain kind of formal knowledge. It is only to activate this knowledge on his or her own behalf that the client has come to the professional. Second, clients need to shed their privacy only to the extent required by the exercise of the professional's judgment and skill. The physician does not need to be told about the patient's savings, and the real estate lawyer does not need to be told about the client's deafness. Third, the confidentiality required of the professional stems from the fact that things were told or shown to him or her only so that the expertise he or she embodies could be brought to bear on the life of the client. The professional's mind in this respect becomes like an expansion of the client's own mind and the information the professional acquires remains the client's own, unless and until the client wishes to disclose it. Ultimately, the one thinking and acting, the one taking the initiative, is the client. The client has come to the professional, has initiated and established the relationship, and keeps it in being.

The obligation of professionals to put their knowledge and skill at the service of the client is vividly perceived in instances in which this obligation is broken. Suppose a client discovers that his lawyer is using information the client provides and even perhaps soliciting information from him, for the lawyer's own financial benefit; or suppose a patient discovers that her physician is making decisions regarding her case in view of some institutional or personal purposes or gain that the doctor has. In such cases the prudence of the professional steers the client's life for the benefit of the professional, and yet the client has come to the professional to have his or her own good pursued.

It is instructive to distinguish the way we turn to a friend for help in deliberation and share in the friend's prudence from the way we turn to a professional. A friend is not specialized; my friend knows my whole way of being. I ask him for help in making a decision that affects me in my entirety; he helps me deliberate whether the course of action will be for my good as such, not just for my good health or for my legal standing. In contrast, I turn to a professional for help within a certain domain, the domain in which he or she is the expert. Furthermore, the "knowledge" I draw on when I turn to a friend is not a formal kind of knowledge. It is the friend's understanding of my general strengths, weaknesses, possibilities, and achievements, his understanding of my character, history, and expectations. It is a knowledge he has about me which is analogous to my own knowledge of myself. We, my friend and I, deliberate together about how the proposed action will affect the whole of my life, and although the final decision will have to be my own, the deliberation that leads up to it can be done in common. In contrast, the knowledge I appeal to in the professional is not primarily a knowledge about me in my entirety, but the knowledge of a domain in which I need expert assistance; it is a knowledge about general rules and principles, joined with the ability to apply them to particular cases. It would be out of place for me to ask the professional as such to deliberate with me in the way a friend would.

We have been describing the relationship between professional and client from the point of view of the client; the client's life becomes directed, in part, by the prudence of the professional. We could reverse our perspective and describe the same relationship from the viewpoint of the professional. From this standpoint the professional is understood to be capable of exercising independent judgment; this ability is based on his or her knowledge, training, and experience. In listing some of the features of the professional, Philip Elliot, in *The Sociology of the Professions*, mentions "broad, theoretical knowledge used in non-routine situations to reach unprogrammed decisions. . . ."[21] The "unprogrammed decisions" of a professional are usually made in respect to other persons, in respect to clients. They are almost always decisions that steer the lives of others. The autonomy of the professional is not an isolated independence, nor is it one that deals with mere things.

Once a client has engaged a professional, the professional does not like to have his or her recommendations disregarded. As Everett C. Hughes wrote, "The professional in some cases refuses to act unless the client—individual or corporate—agrees to follow the advice given."[22] By its nature, prudential deliberation is done in view of action, and if a professional is to share her deliberation with someone else, she wants to do so with the same certainty of action she would have if she were deliberating for herself alone. Most of us, surely, at one time or another, have had the embarrassing experience of admitting, say, to our physician, that we did not do what he or she told us to do: to lose weight, to take medicine, to get an X-ray. When this happens, the physician is not amused. He is not just worried about what will happen but offended by our neglect. He exercised his prudence, he deliberated on our behalf, and our failure to follow through was something like a personal affront. We did not just neglect advice, we slighted the physician's prudence.

The claim that a client subordinates his or her prudence to that of the professional may seem not to hold in the case of a profession such as engineering, in which the expert deals with materials and not with persons. However, it is quite clearly true of the paradigmatic professions, the four that originally were called "professions" in English: divinity, medicine, law, and "the gentlemanly occupation of the military."[23] It is true of many forms of social work, it is true of the professions of architects, teachers, financial advisors, and the like. The feature of dealing rather directly with the decisions to be made by other people is an important element in the definition of the professional.

The relationship between professional and client is a fiduciary relationship. The client trusts the professional and entrusts himself or herself—not just his or her possessions—to the professional. The professional is presented as trustworthy not primarily in the way a friend is found to be faithful, by having proved himself or herself in many situations, but by having been certified as a professional. There is an elegant anonymity to professional trustworthiness; if I get sick away from home and must go to the emergency room of a hospital, I can in principle trust doctors and nurses I have never met before. I enter into a fiduciary relationship with them because they are presented as members of the medical *profession*, persons who are certified by the profession and who can, *prima facie*, be taken as willing to abide by its norms. I do not have exactly the same kind of trust if my car breaks down somewhere away from home; I am delivered over rather to the personal honesty, trustworthiness, and competence of the local mechanic. It is as though I had to find a temporary friend rather than being able to appeal to a professional.

The difference between a profession and an art, therefore, lies in the fiduciary relationship that is built into the profession but not into the art. The fiduciary relationship is based on the fact that in the paradigmatic professions, and in the paradigmatic practitioners of those professions, the client partially blends his or her prudence with that of the professional. Even members of a profession who do not treat clients directly can participate in this fiduciary relationship, because what they do—their medical research, their legal administration—receives its sense ultimately from its application to the lives of clients. Such persons do not merely promote an intellectual discipline; they develop a discipline that will bear on someone's prudence.

In this respect the profession of divinity, one of the four original "professions," is an interesting case. We would be hard put to determine what the "art" of the clergy might be, and we would find it somewhat odd for clergy to form guilds. The profession of divinity seems to be the critical test for distinguishing between the arts and the professions. The clergy do have a certain specialized, theological knowledge, and do deal with a special domain of the "client's" life: with the client's relationship to God. But the relationship to God is "partial" in an unusual way, and it clearly engages the prudence of the client. The believer comes to the cleric for help in determining how to live. In the clerical profession we seem to find the fiduciary relationship *par excellence*, and it may well be that the profession of divinity established a kind of field of force that emphasized analogous relationships in the other professions.

III. The Natural and the Conventional in Professions

The professional relationship between practitioner and client can be morally interpreted in both a utilitarian and a deontological way. The profession is geared toward providing a service, and one can evaluate policies and performances in regard to how effectively and how extensively the service is furnished. But the one who benefits from the service is an autonomous human being, a person, and must be treated as such. This demand brings about deontological obligations for the professional, who must avoid paternalism in his or her involvement with the client. The professional's knowledge and judgment are offered to expand the prudence of the client, but they must not replace it. John Stuart Mill reminds professionals that they must aim at increasing the well-being of others, while Immanuel Kant reminds them that they must respect the client as a person. As Kultgen says, "Determination not to harm and if possible to help others to achieve such benefits as health, justice, desirable structures and artifacts, education, and solace is the utilitarian dimension of the professional's dedication to service. The deontological dimension is respect for autonomy."[24]

The utilitarian and the deontological perspectives bring out different moral aspects of the professional relationship, but even when taken together they do not exhaust the moral dimension. Indeed, they tend to make the relationship appear almost entirely conventional. They underemphasize the dimensions of the relationship that are by nature. The professions as such tend to lay stress on convention and human art. As institutions, they have come about through the development of technology and bureaucratic social structures; even the knowledge associated with them has arisen in the context of technology and complex, capitalist social orders.[25] The knowledge of lawyers, accountants, and social workers, for example, is largely concerned with rules and regulations that cultures and individuals have devised, and it might easily seem that even medicine, with its dependence on technology, is primarily a matter of human contrivance, a matter of what we can make and what we can do. The professions then might appear to be purely human institutions sharply distinguished from the natural world; islands of human ingenuity dealing with human persons, exalting human techniques and human choice, regulated only by utility in service and respect for persons.

But the utilitarian and deontological emphases must be

complemented by a recognition of those aspects of the professional relationship that are by nature. We can distinguish two ways in which "what is by nature" is at work in the professions: (1) there are natural relationships and natural processes that precede the professions and provide a focus for them; and because of this focus, (2) the professions themselves can be seen to have a nature and a proper end.

(1) Professional practice, although empowered by formal knowledge, is ultimately based on relationships that are established naturally, relationships that do not arise through human decisions but come to be as part of the natural human condition. The formal knowledge that empowers the professional is itself ultimately knowledge about such natural relationships, no matter how amply human convention and contrivance may have articulated the relationships. The profession of medicine, for example, ultimately depends on the fact that human beings become sick and become well again, but sometimes need the assistance of others who can adjust and improve the healing process. The whole of medical science and technology is about healing, and the process of healing has its own definition and nature. The natural process occurs before there is a profession of medicine. The physician and the patient are defined in relation to the healing process, to something established by nature. The teaching profession depends on the fact that we can and must learn things, and that such learning can be assisted by others, who have become identified as members of a profession; but all the conventions, technology, and knowledge that empower the teaching professionals would immediately turn to worthless dust if the natural process of learning were to disappear. The scale and complexity of formal knowledge and technology may give us the impression that the human world is made up entirely of our interventions and of ourselves as interveners, but the heady self-confidence to which our technological achievements may tempt us must bow down before the natural order that comes first and remains always as the form and substance of our activity. Formal knowledge may empower the professional, but the professional is authorized by nature.

Indeed, the natural order in a professional relationship is what allows the relationship to be more than a merely contractual exchange, a purely conventional agreement in which the client comes asking for something and the professional is expected to deliver what is wanted. Both the client and the professional are subject to the nature of the relationship, and for this reason the professional has a certain authority over the client. A client *ought* to take proper care of his health; he is subject by nature to this obligation. Therefore the doctor can tell him what he *ought* to do according to the nature of things. The doctor is not limited to being able to say, "Well, you want to be healthy and you have come to me for help, so I recommend that you do this and that." Such a remark would be appropriate for, say, an automobile salesman or a clothier, someone who is merely assisting someone else in a purely contractual exchange. The governing principle in such cases is the desire or the will of the customer, not the nature of the client; but a professional is not a supplier, and a client is not a customer. Also, the formal knowledge of the professional is not mere information that can be useful to the client in satisfying his or her desires, but knowledge about the client in his or her own nature, in what he or she is. The knowledge of the professional can therefore help a client to understand herself better and thus be able to live more authentically according to what she truly is. A patient who lives temperately according to the medical knowledge of her physician is living more appropriately according to her nature as a human being, and so is a student who, through the knowledge and skill of his teachers, learns to think more precisely and more truthfully. The utilitarian and the deontological aspects of the professional relationship must be complemented by the goods and obligations in the relationship that are by nature.

The knowledge of the professional is concerned with the natural relationship between professional and client, and the skill of the professional is concerned with that natural dimension as well. The skill is exercised in imitation of nature: the physician promotes healing, the teacher promotes learning, the judge redresses wrongs, the social worker promotes familial cohesion and independence. The phrase "art imitates nature"[26] does not mean that art makes a copy of the things that nature brings about; rather, it means that human skill makes things develop the way nature would make them develop, if it were not impeded in a particular case by sluggish circumstances or excessive complexity. When we exercise our skill, we let it be guided by the way things would occur according to their own nature. We imitate and assist the natural process, we do not subdue the natural process or replace it with a process of our own making. Professionals do not create what they achieve; they add their skill to a process that is already there, a process they try to bring to a more perfect completion. We imitate, we do not subdue nature, we do not wrestle nature to the ground.

The relationship between nature and human intervention (whether as art or as convention) is not as clear-cut as we might suppose. It is not the case that we have, on the one hand, nature pure and simple, say in some primitive people, and on the other hand, sheer human making and convention. Rather, in human affairs, nature and art, and nature and convention, always permeate each other. The natural manifests itself to us in and through the conventional and the skillfully transformed. The nature of a river is more fully disclosed when the river is bridged; the nature of wood is exhibited more vividly when wood is worked into a piece of furniture; the nature of familial relationships is more fully expressed when they are confirmed by good laws. Because nature and skill, and nature and convention, usually come to us as blended together and not as detached, it takes insight to ferret out the natural dimension in the human things that surround us; it takes insight to know what is at the base and the core of medicine, military affairs, legal transactions, and the like. It is easy to get so caught up in the arbitrary aspects of such things that we overlook the fact that something humanly substantial is going on in them. It is easy, for example, to claim that the law is just what we lay down as being law, and to overlook the fact that whether we want it to be so or not, an issue of justice is always germinating in and through the law that we lay down. It takes insight to see what is the naturally just thing in a particular legal controversy.

Sometimes we have to bring the natural core to mind because the conventional has taken a course and a form that threatens its own natural basis: welfare programs may destroy families and human character, medicine may get caught up in procedures that impede health instead of promoting it, education may become so bureaucratized that young people are prevented from learning. When we criticize a way of doing something, and specifically when we criticize an established profession, we do so on the basis of a distinction we have drawn between the natural and the established. We claim to be able to see that the natural and the conventional, or the natural and the skilled, do not cohere. It is the generation of this distinction that presents both nature and convention or artifice and skill to us; it is not the case that we first have nature fully given as a standard against which we measure our conventions and plan our arts. But it is not only in such negative cases, in which criticism is needed, that we see the distinction between nature and human intervention. In happier instances, in a more positive way, if we are insightful enough, we can rejoice at how well what we are doing seems to blend and fit with what naturally needs to be done in the activity we perform.

(2) A profession is based upon a natural process that it tries to imitate and bring to as perfect a condition as it can. Through this focus, the profession itself, as an institution and as an activity, has its own nature and its own end: the formal knowledge and the skill involved

in the profession are employed to bring this end about. The end of medicine is to restore and maintain health, the end of architecture is to construct buildings in which people can live and work, the end of teaching is the education of students. Such ends are built into the professions and they exist independently of the purposes the individual professionals may have in mind when they exercise their professions. A doctor may pursue her practice with the intention of becoming rich and famous, but medicine remains what it is whether or not her purposes cohere with its end.

The professional is obligated not only to his or her client but also to his or her profession. Professionals must act to preserve the profession. Their purposes, as Francis Slade says, must be congruent with the ends of their professions.[27] In discussing medicine and the difference between healing and destroying life, Slade says,

> Killing those upon whom they attend is forbidden to physicians by the Hippocratic Oath, not because it is morally wrong to murder people—the wrongness of murder is something that applies to all men and it is forbidden by whatever laws they acknowledge themselves to be subject to—but because to use the art of medicine to kill people destroys the art. The Oath, then, is for the sake of the art. The Hippocratic Oath does not forbid murder by medicine to physicians on account of the patients, but on account of the art of medicine.[28]

Thus, euthanasia is wrong not only because it injures another person, but also because it threatens the profession of medicine:

> . . .[I]f physicians acquired a reputation for killing rather than for curing, no one would wish to consult them. Since everyone would do everything possible to avoid them, there would soon be no physicians, for without patients the art cannot be practiced, and so could not be learned.[29]

Unprofessional conduct, therefore, such as violating confidentiality or financially exploiting the client, not only harms the client but damages the profession as well. Professions have ethical codes and they police themselves not only in order to protect vulnerable clients but to preserve themselves.

IV. The Religious Dimension of Professions

There is a religious overtone to the English word "profession." Freidson, drawing on the history of the term provided in the *Oxford Classical Dictionary*, observed that the oldest meaning of the word, dating from before the sixteenth century, was that of "a declaration, avowal, or expression of intention or purpose."[30] He says that this usage was "originally connected with taking consecrated vows and stemming [sic] from the clerical foundation of the medieval university." The term implied "religious and moral motives to dedicate oneself to a good end."[31] (We might note that the word "profession" is derived from the Latin *profiteor, profiteri*, the basic meaning of which is "to state openly, declare, avow."[32] The root is *fateor, fateri*, which means, in this context, "to admit, to assert, to state." This sense of a public declaration is an interesting correlative to the words "calling" and "vocation," which are sometimes used to name one's decision to enter a profession. In response to being called, one goes on to declare publicly. To profess is also to confess.)

Concerning the religious overtones of the word "profession," Philip Elliot notes that before the Reformation, the close affiliation of the universities with the church gave an ecclesiastical and hence religious tone to most professions.[33] But he also observes that modern professions arose with the development of secular branches of learning which were often "separate from the religious orthodoxy."[34] Such an origin would suggest less of a religious and theological dimension in the modern profession.

Is the etymological overtone the only religious sense left to the professions? Has the secular knowledge the professions are now based upon removed any religious and theological dimension from them? There are some aspects of the professions that can easily be given a religious meaning: dedication to the service of others can be seen as a form of charity, and respect for others, for one's clients, can be infused with respect for them as created in the image of God. Thus the utilitarian and deontological aspects of the professions seem easily able to accept a religious interpretation. However, the natural relationships that underlie professional relationships ought also to be given religious significance. They ought to be reverenced as parts of the world that are there before our intervention. To an Aristotelian, such things that are by nature would appear simply as part of the way the world is; but to one who believes in biblical revelation, they would appear as nature created by God. They would express a religious opportunity and obligation: it is a duty of the professional to preserve this natural foundation, to criticize institutional distortions of it, and to promote the human cultivation of it.

One might think that the religious aspect of the professions consists in the motivation that religion can provide for the virtuous performance of professional activities. A person would be given greater reason to furnish good service to others and to respect them. Motivation is certainly part of what religion contributes, but it is not everything. Religion provides not only motivation but also understanding; perhaps one could say that it provides motivation through understanding. Because we understand ourselves and others as created and redeemed by God, we are motivated to act with charity toward others, and because we see the world as created, we have a religious reverence for the nature of things. For example, the Christian religious understanding of the family, of human life, and of human sexuality will motivate a social worker or a health care professional to act in certain specific ways and to formulate certain policies in regard to families and young people.

In closing, I would like to mention a particular challenge to theology in the modern professions. In the past, Christian theology was able to find a religious sense in the knowledge that people acquired about the world and about themselves. Origen and St. Augustine gave a theological interpretation to the world of Plato, the Neoplatonists, and the Stoics, and St. Albert, St. Thomas Aquinas, and other Scholastics were able to do the same for Aristotle's world. The analogous challenge now is to provide a religious interpretation of the formal knowledge that distinguishes the professions. In what way can formal knowledge be seen as a reflection of the reason and wisdom of God? To clarify the religious dimension of professional knowledge is an important task, because the development of this knowledge will very likely continue apace in the future, and will continue to be one of the major cultural factors in human life. There is something metallic and mechanical about formal knowledge; like mathematics, it tends to eschew questions about the good (about what are now commonly called "values"). It is culturally important to determine whether such knowledge must indeed avoid questions of the good, why it must do so, and how questions of the good are to be formulated and how related to formal knowledge. To do all this is a philosophical and cultural challenge, but it is also a theological one. It is the task of showing how not only professionals as persons, but also the formal knowledge that empowers them, can be seen as reflections of God's wisdom.

Notes

1. Aristotle, *Metaphysics*, trans. W.D. Ross, in *The Basic Works of Aristotle*, ed. R. McKeon (New York: Random House, 1941), I.1.

2. B. Barber, "Some Problems in the Sociology of Professions," *Daedalus* 92 (1963):672.

3. G. Harries-Jenkins, "Professionals in Organizations," in *Professions and Professionalization,* ed. J.A. Jackson (Cambridge: Cambridge University Press, 1970), 58-59.

4. J. Kultgen, *Ethics and Professionalism* (Philadelphia: University of Pennsylvania Press, 1988).

5. Ibid., 347.

6. Ibid., 360.

7. Ibid.

8. Ibid, 361.

9. Ibid., 369.

10. John Paul II, *Laborem exercens (On Human Work)* (Washington, D.C.: U.S. Catholic Conference, 1981).

11. Ibid., 1.

12. E. Freidson, *Professional Powers: A Study of the Institutionalization of Formal Knowledge* (Chicago: University of Chicago Press, 1986).

13. Ibid., xiv.

14. Ibid., xii.

15. Ibid., 3.

16. Ibid., 16.

17. Ibid., 3.

18. Ibid.

19. Ibid., 9.

20. Aristotle, *Nicomachean Ethics,* trans. W. D. Ross, in *The Basic Works of Aristotle,* ed. R. McKeon (New York: Random House, 1941), 1140a 26-29.

21. P. Elliot, *The Sociology of the Professions* (New York: Herder and Herder, 1972), 96.

22. C.E. Hughes, "Professions," *Daedalus* 92 (1963):655.

23. Freidson, *Professional Powers,* 22.

24. Kultgen, *Ethics and Professionalism,* 352.

25. Freidson, *Professional Powers,* 3-4.

26. Aristotle, *On the Cosmos,* trans. D.J. Furley. Loeb Classical Library (Cambridge, Mass.: Harvard University Press, 1955), 369b 11.

27. F. Slade, "Ends and Purposes," unpublished text (February 1984), 1.

28. Ibid., 1-2.

29. Ibid., 1.

30. Freidson, *Professional Powers,* 21.

31. Ibid.

32. *Oxford Latin Dictionary,* ed. P.G.W. Glare (Oxford: Clarendon Press, 1982), 1476.

33. Elliot, *Sociology of the Professions,* 16-19.

34. Ibid., 20.

Discussion

Dr. Zaner: I wonder how you conceive the relationship between the two senses of nature; that is, take for example the body's natural healing and then the healer, the ancient healer or modern physician's development of a certain nature, telos, or end pertaining to this. How do you conceive those two?

Fr. Sokolowski: It is hard for me to understand how anyone could deny that through a medical intervention one is restoring something or letting the body be what it ought to be. You see, when you say art imitates nature—this is one of the points I tried to bring out—it doesn't mean that you make a copy of nature. It means you let nature work in ways it would normally work, except under the circumstances it can't do that. So you have to come in and let it restore itself. Now, even transplants or artificial organs really are letting the body function ultimately.

Dr. Gorovitz: Let me ask just one question to try to get at this notion of the thing that is there by nature that the profession builds on. For medicine it is healing. I don't understand what it is for law.

Fr. Sokolowski: Justice, I would say.

Dr. Gorovitz: Surely justice isn't there in the same way that healing is there by nature.

Fr. Sokolowski: I wonder if it isn't. There are some sorts of human relationships that are as real, even though they are not bodily, but they are there prior to our improving on them. The reason someone is called a lawyer is because of something that germinates in the more central cases of law, the paradigmatic cases. It seems to me that one looks at best cases to define a thing. You don't determine what a golfer is by looking at me. You look at Nicklaus or somebody to see what golf is, and in the same way you look at the good cases to see what medicine or law is.

Dr. Brock: I'd like to express some skepticism about a couple of points. The first is the distinction between the professional to whom one submits oneself as opposed to the auto mechanic to whom one submits something one has. I guess I am not sure that this distinction works across very many professions. In fact, the better distinction is probably that one submits different kinds of concerns and/or concerns of different importance to one versus the other.

The other question concerns the issue that was just talked about, about having obligations by nature. In section III, part 1, you say that the "client *ought* to take proper care of his health; he is subject by nature to this obligation." You go on to say that the authority of the professional derives from this.

I am not sure I understand what it is or how it is that obligations arise by nature. If you really pressed this issue of authority, then professionals would seem to have authority to go out and get people who haven't solicited their services at all to try to get them to be healthy.

Fr. Sokolowski: In regard to the first question, I agree that this distinction doesn't cut across all the professions, but I think that in these areas some imprecision is unavoidable. I am not using that to get out of the problem, but I think that the level of precision here is appropriate to the thing being discussed, and in this case the paradigmatic professions are the ones you deal with.

The very notion of profession is a problem, whether there is any such thing, and Kultgen, as I said, tried to say that there isn't. But I think that in the most crucial cases, as I said earlier, you look to the paradigm cases to define the thing, that there is an element of this subordination of yourself to the professional. I shouldn't even say subordination, but fusion of minds, where it is you and not just things that are involved. I tried to spell it out fully and maybe more controversially by saying that even in the case of an architect you are sort of subordinating your style of life to the architect. It is more than just going to an artisan.

Now, I grant that those intermediate cases are problematic, but that is true of any kind of sociological category, and I think one would look to the dominant cases of law and medicine and teaching, and so on.

In regard to the second question I would like to say that I think the sense that a patient has an obligation to take care of his health is reflected in public health measures such as vaccination.

Prof. Kimura: Do you think the professional has the authority to praise or blame the values of the patient—to tell the client what to do?

Fr. Sokolowski: To the extent that the client wants to remain with that professional, then I think that the professional does have that authority.

Prof. Kimura: This is an accepted standard of the medical profession in Japan. The medical profession will say very clearly to the patient: you shouldn't smoke, or something like that; but I have the impression that here and in Europe there is more of a respect for patient autonomy.

Fr. Sokolowski: The professional can't force you to do something, but I think there is more at work there than a mere recommendation, and I am trying to pick out what that more is. I am not saying that the man has a kind of authority that a military commander would have over one of the troops, but there is a sense in which, in this relationship, one ought to do something if it is central and important, and so on. There is a certain authority there; it is imprecise but I think it is there, and I am trying to pick it up and highlight it. This authority is a function of the fact that you are involved in something that is there by nature—again, in that limited way, with a lot of nuances, but it is something you can't completely wash out of the picture.

Dr. Meilaender: When you try to talk about what it means to be a professional, when you look at it from the side of the patient or client or person who comes to the professional, your main move, I think, is in terms of the sort of subordination of my prudence to the prudence of the professional, and you look at it from the point of view of the professional. Your central move is in terms of the kind of knowledge that is involved.

Why don't you make more of what for you becomes just a kind of etymological note when you take up religious significance, that in a fiduciary relationship the client's subordinating prudence suggests a kind of faith and the availability of the one who professes something suggests a faithfulness.

Might this suggest that a claim to being a professional involved a certain kind of availability?

Fr. Sokolowski: Right. I didn't say that, but I certainly wouldn't deny it. In professing, you are making it publicly known that you are there to handle this domain from then on. You can hang up a shingle and declare yourself as available for the people who need this.

Dr. Buchanan: For people who need it and who can pay. That is an important qualification.

Fr. Sokolowski: Yes, all right. But then, how one pays is another thing, too. I think you have to have a certain survivability in order to really help other people. That is very important. I don't think that that is demeaning at all or wrong as part of the picture.

Dr. Freidson: I think Dr. Buchanan and others have already stated really what my concern is, that by and large there is a difficulty in your terms. You take medicine as paradigmatic. That is extremely convenient for your argument, particularly if you eliminate engineers. You might want to rule them out as professionals entirely, and of course, this is part of this game that is so confusing in dealing with the issue of professionalism.

But I think in one way or another it is extremely important to bring in even lawyers, who are perhaps less problematic than accountants, architects, or some of the others, but take the professor also as being a professional. I think if you attempt to cast a wider comparative net, there will be a much greater challenge to your approach, and I think in dealing with that challenge it would probably illuminate some things about medicine that don't come out from just thinking about the doctor and the patient in and of itself as the paradigmatic profession.

But the difficulties of using something other than medicine have already been mentioned, and I don't want to take any more time. But I think they should be recognized.

Richard M. Zaner

The Phenomenon of Trust and the Patient-Physician Relationship

I. The Fiduciary Relation and the Professional

The concept of the fiduciary denotes a relation that is commonly assumed to be central to professional ethics. Often, however, discussions of the relation emphasize the professional in abstraction from those served (clients, patients, students, etc.). Presumably, those who are served are conceived as quite secondary, if not actually extraneous, to the fiduciary relation. Indeed, for many authors, the assumption of the primacy of the professional is followed by another: the fiduciary relation is typically understood as a form of paternalism for which beneficence is the governing principle. For instance, in his study of *The Foundations of Bioethics*, H.T. Engelhardt, Jr. takes those assumptions for granted. The fiduciary appears simply as an adjectival qualifier: "fiduciary paternalism," that is, the "professional judgment to determine what forms of therapeutic intervention would maximize the patient's best interest."[1]

James Childress seems similarly persuaded. The fiduciary, "another basic value in the medical sphere,"[2] expresses the expectation that the professional's actions will show respect for the person, and thus is understood as beneficent paternalism. The main question for him is thus "whether trust in health care professionals to act as paternalists, that is, as beneficent decision-makers on our behalf, is warranted."[3]

This view is even clearer in Ruth Faden and Tom Beauchamp's study of informed consent. Contending that traditional codes of ethics

45

in medicine focused on the physician's duties or virtues, they argue that "a paternalistic or authoritarian ethics easily flowed from this." The emergence of a "language of rights," however, "abruptly turned the focus in a different direction,"[4] that is, away from a fiduciary relation and toward informed consent—that is, to discourse focused more on autonomy, entitlement, and rights than on beneficence. In any event, to think about the fiduciary is, for them, to think about paternalism, and this concerns the professional first of all.

It may be that the initial emphasis on the professional, and de-emphasis on those served, is key to the tendency to treat the fiduciary relation as a matter of paternalism. The danger in this approach is that it risks conceiving professional ethics as unilateral, whereas, as I wish to suggest, it is to the contrary, reciprocal: clients are quite as significant to the relation as are the professionals. In somewhat different terms, client or patient *trust* is crucial to the understanding of professional *trustworthiness*.

II. Trust and the Trustworthy

With some qualification, Professor Sokolowski's analysis in this volume seems to make the same assumptions; it risks muting the place of trust. That the professional and client relation is fiduciary means for him that the client subordinates some limited part of himself or herself, his or her prudence, to the professional. The main question thus concerns professional trustworthiness, which can most often "in principle" be assumed from the fact of his/her having been certified as a professional. Thus, there is

> an elegant anonymity to professional trustworthiness; if I get sick away from home and must go to the emergency room of a hospital, I can in principle trust doctors and nurses I have never met before . . . because they are presented as members of the medical *profession*, persons who are certified by the profession and who can, *prima facie*, be taken as willing to abide by its norms.[5]

The "fiduciary" concerns the professional first of all, specifically his or her "trustworthiness," which can "in principle" be trusted[6] precisely because of the "elegant anonymity" of socially approved certification. It thus seems clear that client trust is a function of professional trustworthiness; it is, in a way, the guarantee for the former. Still, the client remains the "ultimate agent" since "the professional assumes responsibility for only a limited part of the client's life."[7]

It might be noted here that Childress may seem an exception: at one point he argues that "if it is effective, paternalism presupposes trust. . . ."[8] It is not precisely clear just how "presuppose" is intended, however, and much depends on that. Nor, as I've suggested, is it at all obvious that the fiduciary relation is necessarily paternalistic. In any event, the more cogent analysis needs to focus on the *relation* itself of client trust and professional trustworthiness. In the following analysis, however, I wish to probe what has too often been taken for granted or muted: the place of the client in the relation, that is, the phenomenon of trust itself.

III. Trust from the Client's Perspective

My reason for emphasizing the typical approach is to bring out what is taken for granted: the fiduciary relation from the perspective of the patient or client, that is, the phenomenon of trust rather than trustworthiness. It is just this, I think, that Edmund Pellegrino and David Thomasma have in mind when, after showing that medicine is an inherently moral discipline, they insist that an "ethics of trust" is its essential feature.[9] With its focus on the vulnerable, sick person, the classical axiom of medicine since Hippocratic times—"To help or at least to do no harm"[10]—makes trust on the part of the patient the central requirement of the fiduciary relationship.

Elsewhere, Pellegrino argues that the physician "takes upon himself" the responsibility of taking care of the sick, injured, or debilitated, "not as a negotiated task but as an imperative built into the very nature of clinical medicine."[11] This imperative derives from the essential vulnerability of the patient, who places himself (or is placed by others) "in the 'hands' of the physician in a total response of trust." Matters are more complicated, however, and what seems granted at one point is then apparently qualified. Since the physician probes and even violates the patient's body "in closer proximity and more intimately than is usually permitted even to those the patient loves," trust is itself taken as grounded on the trustworthiness of the physician. In Pellegrino and Thomasma's terms, "the axiom of care for the vulnerable individual is the ground for an ethics of trust . . . between doctor and patient."[12] The crucial phenomenon, therefore, is the vulnerable person's act of placing himself "in the hands" of the professional: this act receives its proper emphasis only when seen as based in the "axiom of care," i.e. physician trustworthiness.

I want to return to this later. For now, it is important to note that, to enter into a professional relationship with a physician or any other professional providing some form of expert help to others, is to enter a domain that is already textured by multiple forms of trust on the part of the vulnerable individual.

Here, a distinction of some importance seems called for. In a sense, it is true enough to say that one can trust doctors, lawyers, teachers, and the like who are total strangers, thanks to the "elegant anonymity" of professional trustworthiness. The sheer fact of having been socially "certified" as professionals means that clients will typically take it for granted that professionals are "willing to abide" by the norms of the profession.

It is important to note the crucial ellipsis here, however: "I can in principle trust" can only mean that the professional's trustworthiness is typically taken for granted. Here, trust refers strictly to what is taken for granted as part of the typified knowledge each of us has just so far as we are members of the same culture. Probing into specific clinical encounters, however, invariably confronts us with a quite different sense of trust. For with illness, injury, handicap, or any other compromising condition prompting a visit with a physician, for instance, the patient presents not only specific sorts of bodily distress but also personal suffering and anxiety. An essential component of that personal dimension is that, to one degree or another, the person can no longer, by the very fact of illness, take for granted much of what he or she had hitherto been taking for granted—just that is compromised by the illness or injury.

To experience illness or another form of need sufficient to bring one to a professional is to find that one does not know or cannot do for oneself, and can no longer take it for granted. In fact, one of the most common themes of the fiduciary relation is that the professional's typically taken for granted (and "elegantly anonymous") trustworthiness is itself an issue or question for the client or patient. A key part of what the illness experience means to the patient or client is whether trust, even though in many ways unavoidable, is actually warranted. While it may be that this theme tends to become a more explicit question with more grievous need, that is not always the case. Even when the need for help seems or is in fact less serious, many people still express that theme, albeit often in more subtle and even muted ways.

Being in need of help, furthermore, invariably includes vulnerability and thus various types of uncertainty, which texture every individual encounter between patient/client and professional.

From the client's or patient's perspective, thus, the professional's trustworthiness is closely tied up with various forms of unavoidable trust, the very fact of which can only enhance the tensions already ingredient to need, including no longer being able to take for granted one's typical ways of relating to other people, and so on. We should consider this point more carefully, as it has real significance for the fiduciary relation.

IV. Unavoidable "Trust"

Suppose we continue to consider the situation of a sick person. As illness variously impairs the ongoing, integral connection of body and self, so too it alters the ordinary relationships with others and the surrounding world of people, things, and events. As those relationships are more or less disrupted, the patient finds himself/herself involved in various kinds of unavoidable trust.

One patient stated with considerable dismay: "you have to trust these people, the physicians, like you do God. You're all in their hands . . . I trusted [that surgeon] not to let an inexperienced [resident] mess up my life."[13] Patients must trust not only physicians, but a host of other people as well, such as nurses, lab technicians, researchers, administrative personnel, manufacturers. They also have no choice but to trust a great many things: the material used to repair body parts, bandages, drugs, surgical equipment, and the like. They also have to trust numerous procedures: sterilization, the administration of anesthetics, surgical techniques, referrals, the preparation of drugs, and so on.

Having no choice but to trust in all these ways, communication clearly takes on acute significance. A man with lung cancer emphasized: "When the doctor told me I had this tumor, frankly, it alarmed me, but he did it in such a way that it left me with a feeling of confidence."[14] A diabetic underscored the point: "if you can't communicate and you can't understand your disease, then you don't have confidence in the medical help you are getting."[15]

V. Unavoidable Trust and Uncertainty

Illness provokes a need to know and to understand: What's gone wrong? Is it serious? What does it mean for me and my family, now and in the future? Is it curable or only treatable? If so, by what means, at what risk, and at what cost? What should be done?

Each of the three main phases of clinical judgment[16]—determining what is wrong, what can be done about it, and what ought to be done about it—involves more or less uncertainty and ambiguity, and thus fallibility on the part of the professional.[17] As Robert Hardy discovered in his interviews of numerous patients and their families, they are concerned not only to know and understand but equally to know that those who take care *of* them also care *for* them. For the patient, there can be a serious question whether trust is truly warranted. The sick person concretely experiences his/her body as a source of uncertainty: for instance, what is causing pain, how long it will last, what it signifies now and for the future. Patients have a profound and understandable desire to know with as much certainty as possible what can and should be done, and whether those who take care of them also care for them—that is, whether they can trust those who have and communicate that knowledge and concern.

It is true that where there are some specific and effective treatments for some diseases (for example, penicillin for pneumococcal pneumonia), trust is often unproblematic or muted and the typical and typified presumption about the professional's conduct remains for the most part unchallenged. Clinical judgments are often not so clear, however, especially with regard to the major diseases of our times—heart disease, cancer, stroke, etc.—which often can only be managed, not cured. Clinical judgments are even less clear as it is increasingly imperative to reckon with and take into account the person's experience of and meanings given to the illness.

As such issues multiply and grow in uncertainty, so do the chances of compromise to the patient's unavoidable trust. For patients seeking to know what is wrong, what can and should be done about it, and whether they are really cared for, it is hardly appropriate merely to cite statistical probability patterns for classes of diseases and/or persons. Although thought of as ways to evoke trust, they often backfire. For the patient, uncertainty and ambiguity more often have the sense of being at a loss, being adrift and unable to take one's bearings and to know what to hold by—which is to discover that trust is itself the critical issue. To know what one can count on is to know what can be trusted, and if the one fails, so is the other compromised. The experience of illness, notable for its sense of peril and urgency, thus makes prominent the need for candid, sensitive conversations that can evoke genuine trust so that decisions, at times critical and irreversible, can be made even when their basis is only relatively incomplete, uncertain, or ambiguous.

VI. Unavoidable Trust and Strangers

For a patient, to enter the world of medicine is to enter forbidding and at times alien environs, even when the doctors and nurses are familiar to the patient and family. Most often, however, the patient is nowadays surrounded by strangers: other patients, families, visitors, hospital personnel, etc.; and by strangeness: things, equipment, schedules, procedures, etc.

Sociologically and even architecturally, hospitals and clinics seem designed more to enhance than to ameliorate these types of strangeness. Stripped of familiar things (clothes, possessions, surroundings) and told they must wait while clothed in anonymous garb providing ready access to body parts and places otherwise forbidden to others, patients are then asked to discuss the most intimate details of personal and bodily life with whoever may by chance be assigned to them. Their illness narratives[18] quickly become converted into "cases" openly discussed by doctors, nurses, and others, with confidentiality and privacy very often little more than words on a document. They are poked and prodded, swabbed and stuck, palpated and felt, in intimate and even humiliating ways, all in the service of being taken care of, in whose necessity and efficacy they must simply and unavoidably trust. To be a patient one must be patient indeed; to trust, however, surely requires more than mere patience.

Illness itself is alienating, rupturing the person's usual ways of feeling, acting, moving, and integrating body and self.[19] Indeed, a crucial dimension of trust—trust in one's own body—is existentially breached, the person's bodily experiences taking on a kind of inner strangeness—new and peculiar feelings in one's body, for example, that are often at best difficult to convey. Illness disrupts the usual routines of daily life, including the ways in which the person typically relates to other people. Even if the person is gently encouraged to talk about these sensitive feelings and relations, patients must trust that the professionals are correct in insisting that the discourse is important, and that they will not only hear but listen; not only understand but be understanding.

When communication is among strangers, the experience can be even more confounding. This, as much as anything else, compromises patient trust. Even when one knows in typical ways that these professionals may "in principle" be taken as willing to abide by such norms as confidentiality, patients and families quickly realize that such norms are open to suspicion in our complex, bureaucratic institutions of health care, in which one's most intimate secrets are readily accessible to all sorts of people one rarely bargained for on admission.

In a society in which relationships among strangers predominate, communication tends to be designed more for temporary ease of social passage and commerce than for intimate disclosures. For the hospitalized patient, matters can become acute, especially regarding trust: talking and listening are often only exercises in remoteness with only the outer shell—the words merely—of intimacy, and thus can be more sham than real. With that, the "elegant anonymity" of professional trustworthiness often flies out the nearest exit. Yet it is precisely the sick person and family who need to know what's wrong and must unavoidably trust that those who take care of the patient genuinely care for him or her; a major index of this care is candid, continuous, and sensitive discourse about findings that will, one hopes, be kept confidential.

As Alfred Schutz has vividly shown, commonsense life consists of a relatively well-organized set of typifications (of people, things, events, etc.). So long as things remain relatively unruffled, for the most part we simply take it for granted that our typical and typifying ways of thinking and acting are for the most part assumed without question as correct for all practical purposes. That is, we take it for granted (a) that "life and especially social life will continue to be the same as it has been so far," (b) that we may continue to rely on what has been handed down to us (by parents, teachers, tradition, etc.), (c) that in the ordinary course of affairs it is sufficient merely to know *about* the general style or type of events we usually encounter, and (d) that neither our typical ways of acting, interpreting, and expressing ourselves nor these underlying assumptions "are our private affair, but that they are likewise accepted and applied by our fellow-men."[20]

The point is obvious: if any of these assumptions fails or becomes questionable, commonsense ways of thinking and acting also become unsettled: a "crisis" occurs; what hitherto "worked" works no longer. It is precisely this which textures the encounter with the stranger. The stranger is "essentially the man who has to place in question nearly everything that seems to be unquestionable to the members of the approached group" or individual members of the group.[21] He has not participated in their cultural life and history and thus, "seen from the point of view of the approached group, he is a man without a history."[22] In the case of illness, thus, the act of "history taking" is far more than of mere medical interest. The patient may know that the approached group (the medical profession) has its ways and routines, but these are not an integral part of his or her own biography; hence, what is taken for granted by the one cannot be taken for granted by the other.

By the same token, from the point of view of those "at home," while the stranger is perhaps seen as having a culture and a history, perhaps even a personality, these are precisely what is not known in any detail (or known only typically); hence, those at home cannot take for granted regarding the stranger what they otherwise typically take for granted regarding one another.

When what brings the newcomer (patient) to approach those at home (medical professionals) is something critical like illness, moreover, things can be exceedingly difficult. What is otherwise typically regarded as obvious or settled now comes into question; the familiar and the routine, including even common language, are now no longer so. It is thus evident that the meanings of trust and being trustworthy are significantly different from situations where people are less strange to one another.

Peter Lenrow rightly insists, I think, that in the best of times all that may be hoped for among strangers are situations of merely temporary trust.[23] Even that, however, must be labored for, since there is little basis for trust among strangers; and lack of trust can only mean that an essential part of the helping relationship is missing or threatened. To be a patient is thus often to find oneself in a deeply ironic predicament: actions of touching, feeling, talking, and probing, which typically promise or attest to personal intimacies, now go on between strangers, and thus have a very different significance in the relationship between professional and patient.

VII. Trust and the Professional's Power

It has been noted that there are compelling difficulties that both patient and doctor experience while trying to communicate and to preserve even minimal conditions for trust within the complex, bureaucratic institutions of health care. This survey, however, is still only a glimpse at the fundamental asymmetry of power in favor of the professional that characterizes the relationship with patients.

Understandable and at the same time unavoidable, the asymmetry itself disadvantages patients. The mother of a partially sighted girl, for instance, noted how "overpowering" physicians can be: "They've got the edge on you,"[24] and a surgical patient plaintively wondered: "You're all in their hands, and if they don't care for you, who's going to?"[25] Pellegrino seems right on target: patients are "condemned to a relationship of inequality with the professed healer, for the healer professes to possess precisely what the patient lacks—the knowledge and the power to heal."[26]

This inequality is nevertheless constitutive of the helping relationship. Doctors have special knowledge and skills (won through education and training) in the ways of the body. They have access to resources (people, technologies, medications, institutions, funding) and are socially and legally legitimated and protected (licensure statutes, professional acceptance) to act on behalf of sick people. Indeed, it is thanks to the socialization, cultural distribution, and common acceptance of the asymmetry by the members of the society, that one can at all say that "I can in principle trust" health professionals, that through being certified one can take it for granted that they can be trusted to abide by its norms, and thereby be experienced as trustworthy.

Strongly enhanced by formal institutionalization, social legitimation, and legal authorization, this inequality of power is intensified by the sick person's illness and vulnerability. The patient is a supplicant whose appeal is precisely an endorsement of the very phenomenon that constitutes the inequality: the ability to know, treat, heal, restore. All of which is rendered more difficult when the participants are strangers to one another and cannot automatically assume that they share values, attitudes, desires, aims, etc., in such a way that it is warranted for the patient to believe in, to trust, the professional's trustworthiness.

VIII. Responsiveness to Trust

To be a professional is to profess the ability to help, and that is fundamentally to embody a promise to those in need of help. While all the usual responsibilities of making and keeping promises hold here, there are crucial differences for the fiduciary relation between professed helper and person in need of help. The professional promises to be the finest he or she is capable of being in the sense of knowledge and technical competence. He or she also promises not only to take care of, but to care for the patient and family—to be candid, sensitive, attentive, and never to abandon them.

While the asymmetry of power in favor of the professional presents the constant temptation to take advantage of the vulnerable patient—perhaps, indeed, precisely because that temptation must be understood in moral terms—that very asymmetry imposes quite special obligations and responsibilities on the professional. Not only must the power be used competently and concernfully, but it must never be misused or abused. The professional's abilities and knowledge are placed strictly at the service of patients and their families.[27] These special responsibilities arise to a significant extent from the existential situation, the vulnerability of the patient and family generated both by illness and asymmetry.

The eminent medical historian, Ludwig Edelstein, has observed that even in ancient medicine, the powers at the disposal of the healer and the intimacy of contacts with patients provoked an essential question the professed healer had to confront: "What about the patient who is putting himself and 'his all' into the hands of the physician?" The issue is all the more acute because the sick or injured person is un-initiated in the art, does not know what is wrong with him or what to do about it, and does not even know how to assess whether the pro-fessed healer is capable of healing—at least not until that healing is achieved. But how can the patient be sure, Edelstein insists, that trust in the doctor (his knowledge, skills, ultimately the person himself) is warranted?[28] Paradoxically, trust seems warranted only after the fact, even while it is required beforehand.

IX. Trust and the Professional's Duty

By providing some texture to the fiduciary relation, noting in par-ticular how the patient or client is unavoidably situated within vari-ous forms of vulnerability, I hope to have highlighted that the phe-nomenon of patient or client trust is crucial to the fiduciary relation.

My point may be put another way. The patient or client is the one who initiates the relationship with the professional, even if the person is brought to the latter (temporarily or permanently) unconscious or incompetent. Without the universal fact of illness, there is no call for physicians. The patient or client experiences some form of real or ima-gined lack or failure in knowledge and ability to do for him/herself, and turns to the professional for help. Integral to that need or lack is a breach in the person's otherwise taken for granted knowledge and ability, which frequently carries with it one or another degree of dis-ruption in the person's usual ways of relating to others.

Precisely because of these various disruptions or failures in the taken for granted, the first and continuing task for the professional is given: responsibly attending to each individual's specific concerns, ex-periences, self-interpretations, and lacks. The concept of responsibility is thus essential to the profession, and in the complex sense inherent to it: to *be responsive to* each individual within his or her unique cir-cumstances and condition, to *be responsible for* whatever is then said or done on behalf of that individual, and to *be responsible to and for* the profession itself.

The professional as such takes on the critical task of enabling the individual patient or client to be restored in respect of the needs that brought him or her to the professional in the first place. The profes-sional has the responsibility of helping the person, ultimately seeking to enable him/her to be restored to himself or herself (to the extent possible in each instance).

In this respect, there is a crucial methodological injunction for the professional that harbors significant moral content: as far as possible, *take nothing for granted*, patient or client trust most of all. The professional has the moral imperative of recognizing that the typically taken for granted trustworthiness attaching to professional status by the mere fact of social certification is itself the first and most pressing issue of any fiduciary relationship.

This, it seems to me, holds true regardless of whether the fiduciary relation, as Faden and Beauchamp argue, must now be conceived in terms of "valid entitlement" and "rights." They contend that things have changed in recent decades, and that "the new kid on the block in medical ethics" is entitlement. Although "usually reserved for law . . . it literally invites replacement of the beneficence model with the autonomy model."[29] Thus, whatever may have been its origins in simpler times, informed consent is a matter of rights and entitlement, and this is the core of the fiduciary relation.

One should not for a moment concede that point, however, for even if trust and trustworthiness are shifted into informed consent language, all the themes and issues of the first only reappear with the latter, perhaps with even greater urgency. The point is clear enough regarding confidentiality. But so is it with informed consent, most especially when this is an ongoing process between persons asymmetrically related. In order for a person to be appropriately "informed," much less uncoerced and free in giving consent, trust remains the *sine qua non* for the professional's disclosure of pertinent information, as well as for the actions proposed and carried out. Professional trustworthiness is still a critical issue in constant need of warranting trust in every individual encounter, whether or not informed consent is brought in as a way to provide formal guarantees (or the threat of subsequent legal recourse).

X. The Phenomenon of Trust

The attempt to shift the discourse away from beneficence to entitlement and autonomy does not in the least undermine the phenomenon of trust. Moreover, it seems clear that trust cannot be simply predicated on professional trustworthiness. That only obscures the fact that trust is then only part of the typified and taken for granted recipes for knowing and acting in the everyday social world—precisely what cannot be taken for granted, at least in many of the encounters in question. My suggestion has been that whenever one probes into any specific individual's encounter with a professional, the latter's trustworthiness is often the initial and continuing issue characteristic of every fiduciary

relation. Professional trustworthiness may be more accurately characterized as the essential promise that trust is warranted and always an
issue to be made good on in the course of the encounter.

Trustworthiness is an issue and a promise precisely insofar as it is
essentially a response to someone's appeal: the one, professing the
ability to help, responds to the other, standing in need of and asking
for help. Central to an ethics for the professions, thus, is the idea of
specific responsibility: responsiveness to and responsibility for, defined within each context. To articulate this vital moral idea, the phenomenon of trust is essential. To get at this phenomenon, and the ethics connected with it, thus requires that we probe into the
phenomenon of appeal at the heart of the fiduciary relationship. As
Gabriel Marcel showed throughout his life and many writings, however, this notion turns out to be quite complex, its faithful analysis
most intricate. Here, I cannot hope to do more than suggest what
seem to be some of its salient points.

Although the situation of the one in need of help doubtless varies
depending upon the kind of need at issue, it seems clear that existential vulnerability, to whatever degree it may be, is a common theme.
The patient or client, student or penitent believer, experiences some
need to be helped, and to that extent exposes himself/herself as being
unable to do whatever it may be. In this, therefore, as Sokolowski
rightly notes, "when I approach a professional, I subject something
more than a possession of mine to the professional's expertise; in a
distinctive way, I subject myself and my future to his or her assessments and to his or her judgment."[30] Handing over the "steering of
my life," to whatever extent, "I let him take over not just one of my
things, but my choices and activities themselves," something for
which my own knowledge and resources have proven inadequate.
The other side of this "handing over," if you will, is that I am myself
at stake; I am disadvantaged, am at risk, in a most concrete way within the relationship itself, for my vital wherewithal and abilities are insufficient to see me through and I appeal to another professing the
ability to help. An essential component of the person's vulnerability,
thus, is this exposure of self, this being unequipped to carry through,
and this inequality before the professional.

That vulnerability, I suggest, is experienced by the person as a
compelling need for the other's responsiveness, and has a quite concrete format: that appeal for help is a call to the other, the professional,
to affiliate with me, literally to *feel with* and understand me from within my vulnerable state. Consider again the example of illness, now
from the perspective of the physician who is called on to be responsive

to the patient. Not only must he or she be able to stand back, analyze, classify, measure, and reason, but also, Pellegrino emphasizes, to

> feel something of the experience of illness felt by this patient. He must literally suffer something of the patient's pain along with him, for this is what compassion literally means. Often the physician heals himself while healing the patient; oftentimes he cannot heal until he has healed himself. . . ."[31]

We must be cautious about this "compassion" as "literally" suffering "something of the patient's pain," for there is something at once more subtle and more precarious here.

Sick people frequently, although not always expressly, want the doctor to see things from their point of view: "put yourself in my shoes," as we say. The patient is surely asking the doctor to do something the patient regards as quite vital; but what is it? It seems clear that the patient is not asking the doctor to think about his or her predicament as if it were in fact the physician's own ("What would you do if you were me?") It is not a matter of a sort of imaginative identification (asking the doctor somehow to become the patient and actually feel the very pain felt by the patient). Nor is the patient asking the doctor to consider what he would do if he were faced with the same problem, through a sort of imaginative transposal ("Suppose you faced this dilemma . . .?"). To "put yourself in my shoes," rather, is to attempt to see things as the patient experiences them while yet remaining oneself. To be compassionate is not to obliterate the always crucial distinction between doctor and patient.

Not to belabor the obvious, the patient is urgently asking the doctor to understand the needful situation from the patient's own point of view. For this, Kleinman insists, the doctor has "to place himself in the lived experience of the patient's illness," to understand the situation "as the patient understands, perceives, and feels it."[32]

On the face of it, to "put yourself in my shoes" may seem extravagant, if not absurd. Still, in a sense we do this all the time. Thanks to socially derived and typified everyday knowledge, each of us typically knows something of what it's like, for instance, to be a firefighter or lawyer, even though we are neither; to drive a semi or a tractor, even though we do not drive; to use a wrench or operate a crane, even though we have done neither; to suffer acute pain or be faced with an urgent dilemma, even though we currently experience neither.

As Alfred Schutz has pointed out, our everyday knowledge of

the life-world is incredibly rich and detailed, even while it is also un-
evenly distributed into different regions (each of us knows some
things better than others). Despite the inadequacies, inconsistencies,
and inconstancies of commonsense knowledge and understanding, it
is for the most part quite sufficient in the context of daily concerns—
we get along for "all practical purposes," as we say. For the most
part, when we are asked to "put yourself in my shoes," we typically
do not go beyond such taken for granted, typified forms of
understanding.

At times, though, something more than this typified knowledge
and understanding is demanded. The doctor may be urgently asked to
understand the patient's dilemma as it is actually faced and experienced: to "feel with" the patient from within his or her own perspective and set of moral beliefs, values, etc. In these terms, "put yourself
in my shoes" involves several critical steps: helping the patient to articulate and understand what that moral framework actually includes,
what values the patient has and how they are ordered; identifying
which issues seem most pressing, given the patient's concerns, circumstances, and basic ordering of values and commitments; considering the several alternatives with an eye on the compatibility of those
concerns, etc., with possible outcomes.

To experience things as the patient experiences them, in other
words, requires helping the patient understand and talk about just
what this patient believes, desires, aims for, values, and the like. Not
only are we in our daily lives rarely called on to engage in this kind of
reflection and self-inspection, but it is a quite difficult act to undertake
and sustain. At the same time, for the professional to provide that
kind of help, disciplined self-knowledge by the professional is clearly
required—that is, frequently practiced, disciplined reflection intended
to delineate the professional's own feelings, moral beliefs, social
framework, etc., along with a rigorously disciplined suspension of it,
in order to understand what things are like for the other person. This
can be understood as a kind of ongoing practical distantiation that undergirds the act of compassion or affiliative feeling.[33] This difficult act,
I believe, turns out to be crucial for establishing a basis for patient
trust; hence, it seems to me integral to the patient's appeal for the professional's responsiveness.

If these suggestions are on the right track, it is important to emphasize a significant implication. While calling for an "ethics of
trust," Pellegrino and Thomasma end up suggesting that "the axiom
of care for the vulnerable individual is the ground for an ethics of
trust . . . between doctor and patient."[34] What I have suggested is that

this axiom of care is closely tied in with the pathos of trust: the vulnerable individual appealing for responsiveness within an unavoidably asymmetrical relationship. The inner demand of this relation is not only that the professional must never take advantage of the multiply disadvantaged person in need of help; it is also that the professional must, by virtue of the commitment to enter and remain a professional, specifically "put himself in the shoes" of each client or patient—a complex reflective act that the professional must at once experientially exhibit with each client or patient, and enable each client or patient to do for himself or herself. It is this complex set of acts that is, I believe, at the basis of professional ethics: in a word, trust and care are mutually, dialectically interrelated in the ethics of professional life.

Finally, seen in this way the fiduciary relation is most appropriately understood, not as a form of paternalism, but rather on the model of dialogue. Precisely because of the complex forms of uncertainty that texture, for example, every clinical event, no matter how apparently trivial, communication between physician and patient has critical significance. The key question concerns how that communication should be conceived: whether as a discourse with formalized rules and legal guarantees, or rather as an ongoing experiential discourse of appeal and response, trust and care. Just here, it seems to me, Pellegrino captures the critical issue: the "moral imperative" for the physician is to be responsive to the way the patient wishes to spend his life. Given that, how should the conversations between a doctor and a patient be understood? What is the force of this "moral imperative"?

A person needing help asks, appeals to, a doctor for help; the doctor then begins to respond, first by asking questions to which the patient in turn responds, followed by further questions and responses, etc., all designed to delineate what's wrong, what can be done about it, and then what should be done. But the person's appeal and responses to the doctor are not trivial; they arise from and constantly refer to the distress, the dis-ease, experienced by the person. In one way or another, they are critical for the person. The more grievous the illness (as perceived by the patient), the more urgent is the appeal. Hence, for the doctor to be responsive, he or she must seek in every appropriate way to understand the patient's own ways of experiencing the illness, and probe every clue available for what the illness means to the patient. In these terms, Cassell is right to emphasize that "all medical care flows through the relationship between physician and patient," and because of that, "the spoken language is the most important tool in medicine."[35] However, as Joel Reiser suggests, there is more to it: "medical encounters begin with dialogue" in the course of which the patient's experience of illness gets transformed into "subjective portraits"[36] or narratives.

Merely asking for help does not of itself guarantee a response. In most settings, the one appealed to, the doctor, may well refuse to respond for a variety of reasons (which themselves are subject to assessment, of course). Still, if the doctor does respond, a form of interpersonal relating, a dialogue, begins and has its own intrinsic demands and aims. To respond to the patient means both that the doctor believes (professes) the ability to help, and that whatever that response may be, it is inherently open to the patient's further queries—for it is the patient who urgently needs to know and asks for help. Not only does the doctor profess the ability to help, but it is essential to the course of dialogue that both physician and patient engage each other as truthfully and amply as possible, and for as long as the relationship continues.[37]

To be sure, as with any conversation, the dialogue may break down, for any number of reasons (each of which is subject to evaluation). In clinical encounters furthermore, dialogues with patients are intrinsically periodic as well as limited: at various points in the course of diagnosing and treating illness, for instance, the doctor shifts from the person to the embodying organism, in a sense embarking on another kind of dialogue, with the patient's body, to ascertain the nature of the disease.[38] At some point, too, the doctor's work is over and the patient leaves (permanently or temporarily). Even when such shifts of attention are necessary during the course of the dialogical relationship, however, being responsive to the patient means that the doctor should never lose sight of the specific circumstances of the person being diagnosed and treated, nor of the patient's specific narrative expressing the experience and meaning of illness.

The doctor-patient relationship, thus, is essentially a special form of what Schutz calls *Du-Einstellung*: being oriented to another. He points out that this can be either *unilateral* (as when the other person ignores me) or *reciprocal* (the other is oriented toward me, recognizes that I am a person, too).[39] In the healing relationship, however, the orientation to the other is inevitably more intimate, intense, and unequal; but since the very point of the relation is to work toward transcending that inequality, and since the moral imperative at its heart is to be responsive to a full person in need of help, it seems to me far more accurate to understand it as a form of *mutual* relationship; specifically, a relationship of trust and care, which I take to be the essence of dialogue.

Notes

1. H.T. Engelhardt, Jr., *The Foundations of Bioethics* (New York: Oxford University Press, 1986), 281. Although he seems willing to accept "explicit fiduciary paternalism" as having some legitimacy in some circumstances, his view of most forms of "implicit fiduciary paternalism" is unmistakable. The argument that there is an implicit presumption of beneficent decision-making by professionals is rather problematic, and the argument that paternalistic interventions are implicitly agreed upon as a sort of insurance against unwise or dangerous actions by patients is "difficult if not impossible to defend if one takes the freedom of individuals seriously" (283), which he assuredly does.

2. James F. Childress, "Who Shall Live When Not All Can Live?" *Soundings* 53 (1970):339-55; reprinted in *Ethics in Medicine: Historical Perspectives and Contemporary Concerns*, ed. S.J. Reiser, A.J. Dyck, and W.J. Curran (Cambridge, Mass.: MIT Press, 1977), 624.

3. James F. Childress, *Who Should Decide? Paternalism in Health Care* (New York: Oxford University Press, 1982), 47. Childress has other things to say about trust which I will mention later.

4. R.L. Faden and T.L. Beauchamp, with Nancy King, *A History and Theory of Informed Consent* (New York: Oxford University Press, 1986), 94.

5. R. Sokolowski, "The Fiduciary Relationship and the Nature of Professions," in this volume, 23-43.

6. Ibid., 31.

7. Ibid., 27.

8. Childress, *Who Should Decide*, 47.

9. E.D. Pellegrino and D.C. Thomasma, *A Philosophical Basis of Medical Practice: Toward a Philosophy and Ethic of the Healing Professions* (New York: Oxford University Press, 1981), 67.

10. Hippocrates, *Epidemics I*, trans. W.H.S. Jones, Loeb Classical Library (Cambridge, Mass.: Harvard University Press, 1923), 165.

11. E.D. Pellegrino, "The Healing Relationship: The Architectonics of Clinical Medicine," in *The Clinical Encounter*, ed. E.E. Shelp (Dordrecht: D. Reidel, 1983), 164.

12. Pellegrino and Thomasma, *A Philosophical Basis*, 185.

13. R.C. Hardy, *Sick: How People Feel about Being Sick and What They Think about Those Who Care for Them* (Chicago: Teach 'em, Inc., 1978), 40.

14. Ibid., 9.

15. Ibid., 236.

16. E.D. Pellegrino, "The Anatomy of Clinical Judgments: Some Notes on Right Reason and Right Action," in *Clinical Judgment: A Critical Appraisal*, ed. H.T. Engelhardt, S.F. Spicker, and B. Towers (Dordrecht: D. Reidel, 1979), 169-94.

17. S. Gorovitz and A. MacIntyre, "Toward a Theory of Medical Fallibility," *Journal of Medicine and Philosophy* 1 (1976):51-71.

18. A. Kleinman, *The Illness Narratives* (New York: Basic Books, 1988).

19. Sally Gadow points out that as "the felt capacity to act and the vulnerability to being acted upon," the lived body is precisely the "primary being-in-the-world that is ruptured by illness or injury." See Gadow, "Body and Self: A Dialectic," in *The Humanity of the Ill: Phenomenological Perspectives*, ed. V. Kestenbaum (Knoxville: University of Tennessee Press, 1981), 88.

20. A. Schutz, "The Stranger: An Essay in Social Psychology," in *Collected Papers of Alfred Schutz*, ed. I.M. Natanson (The Hague: Martinus Nijhoff, 1964), 96.

21. Ibid.

22. Ibid., 97.

23. P.B. Lenrow, "The Work of Helping Strangers," in *Things That Matter: Influences on Helping Relationships*, ed. H. Rubenstein and H.M. Bloch (New York: Macmillan, 1982), 42-57.

24. Hardy, *Sick*, 92.

25. Ibid., 40.

26. E.D. Pellegrino, "Being Ill and Being Healed," in *The Humanity of the Ill*, ed. V. Kestenbaum, 1981, 161.

27. Pellegrino and Thomasma, *A Philosophical Basis*, 210.

28. L. Edelstein, *Ancient Medicine: Selected Papers of L. Edelstein*, ed. O. Temkin and C.L. Temkin (Baltimore: Johns Hopkins University Press, 1967), 329.

29. Faden and Beauchamp, *A History and Theory*, 94-95.

30. Sokolowski, "The Fiduciary Relationship," 27.

31. Pellegrino, "The Healing Relationship," 165.

32. Kleinman, *Illness Narratives*, 232.

33. See my *Ethics and the Clinical Encounter* (Englewood Cliffs, N.J.: Prentice-Hall, 1988), 315-19.

34. Pellegrino and Thomasma, *A Philosophical Basis*, 185.

35. E.J. Cassell, *Talking with Patients*, vol. 1 (Cambridge, Mass.: MIT Press, 1985), 1.

36. Ibid., ix.

37. The cases of not telling the truth, fictitious illness, Munchausen's syndrome, and hypochondriasis, therefore, understandably present the doctor with acute problems, as does a doctor's reluctance or refusal to tell the truth create acute problems for the patient. For the nature of the healing relationship and its dialogue begins with the presumption of truthfulness. To fail in this—to fake symptoms, or not to inform the patient—is to violate the moral imperatives of the relationship.

38. Pellegrino and Thomasma, *A Philosophical Basis*, 113.

39. A. Schutz and T. Luckmann, *The Structures of the Life-World*, vol. 1, trans. H.T. Engelhardt, Jr. and R.M. Zaner (Evanston, Ill.: Northwestern University Press, 1973), 72-88.

Discussion

Dr. Buchanan: I liked in particular the fact that you recognized that trust in one sense has to be assumed and, in another sense, has to be earned in encounters between physician and patient.

I am a little worried, though, about what seems to be a kind of slipping back and forth between a kind of ideal, a kind of normative paradigm for what a physician-patient relationship should be like or what one should be if one is a medical professional, on the one hand, and the reality of medical practice on the other.

I would like to focus particularly on your claim about the importance of the physician stepping into the patient's shoes and in some sense being able to empathize with the lived experiences of suffering and doubt that brought the patient to the physician's office in the first place.

But what I am concerned about is that if you look at the actual institutional setting of a great deal of medical care in this country and other so-called developed countries, you will see that it is very difficult for physicians in general to be in a position to enter into the psyche or the feelings of the patient.

Take your paradigm of dialogue. I agree that is the way things should be. That is the way we would like them to be. I would like for there to be this progressive give and take, this opening up of channels of communication and trust.

But if you look at what actually goes on, particularly in tertiary care settings, the physician encounters a patient who is not himself or herself because the patient has been put into this bizarre environment under conditions of illness which, as you say, disrupt the ordinary modes of behavior. The physician has very little time, as a rule, to deal with the patient.

My question is, to put it sort of irreverently, once you paint this beautiful ideal we have to ask ourselves is this the right ideal for our real world or is holding onto this ideal in circumstances where it is not likely to be implemented without massive structural changes in medical care just likely to be something that is going to reinforce an illusion and in fact cause people to trust physicians when they shouldn't. There are a lot of statements in the literature on fiduciary relationships about the beneficial effects of trust, but there is little about the harmful effects of misplaced trust.

I just wonder whether after painting the ideal we have to think very hard about whether we can implement it; if we can't, whether there may be dangers in maintaining that ideal instead of thinking harder about how to approximate it under difficult circumstances.

Dr. Zaner: As you may have seen, this has been very much with me. If you look at the architectural design of hospitals or tertiary care centers, they are not designed to promote the kind of thing you talk about.

It may be that the best we can hope for are situations of temporary trust. I have not probed that idea very thoroughly as yet, but I am attracted to trying to do so to see how far one can take it in these contexts.

My interest has not been to propose that medicine be looked at in this way, but to try to articulate what I have found doctors and patients themselves talking about, and it is this kind of model they talk about. I wanted then to draw out the implications of that more deeply, further than anything they have done, to see where it might lead.

I am not sure what the implications are for what you raise about the dangers of trust. I think you are right.

Dr. Brock: I have a question just about the claim that trust precedes trustworthiness and so is completely based on trustworthiness. I guess I am not clear on the argument there.

It sems to me that as a historical matter the two grow up together. We think of a relationship which isn't defined by norms the way medicine is, and one tests them. What can I be expected to do? One learns and then builds trust.

I think that all that one could say is that the desire and the need for trust may precede trustworthiness, but it is not clear to me why trust itself does.

If my car breaks down in a small town and there is one mechanic in it, I would like to be able to trust him, I want to be able to trust him, but I don't, and that is just because I don't have any expectation of trustworthiness from him.

Dr. Zaner: I think I exaggerated the point in the paper in my anxiety to focus attention on the client or patient's point of view. I got tempted in the opposite direction, if you like. With respect to healing and such, I think it is true what Dr. Pellegrino pointed out in several papers, that there is first and foremost the fact that people get sick and get injured, and only in view of that do we have attention slowly growing, specific professional attention to that. The first step then does seem to be a need for that trust, the appeal to that trust.

Dr. Gorovitz: I just wanted to press a little bit on this notion of putting yourself in his shoes. You say each of us typically knows what it is like to be a postman or lawyer, driving a semi-tractor, and so on.

That seems to me implausible at best. I think if one looks at the literature of physicians who have themselves become patients, they often very powerfully recount how it is as if the scales fell from their eyes and for the first time they came to understand the enterprise that they have been in perhaps for decades.

Dr. Zaner: The point there, the context in which that occurs, is that of the development of trust, the typified everyday knowledge of everyday life. I can understand pretty much what it is like to be a seller of cigarettes or a seller of aspirin as opposed to a taker thereof or a purchaser thereof. That is part of my taken for granted everyday knowledge in the society, and that is all I was referring to. In one sense, to put yourself in another's shoes could mean no more than this kind of everydayness, typified, taken for granted knowledge of everyday life.

Fr. Sokolowski: Let me ask you a question people have asked me on my paper: how can this be applied to engineering? Especially the case of an engineer who is working for a big company, not somebody who is dealing with customers who come in?

Dr. Zaner: That is fair, and I will take your answer. I am not sure. What we have here may well be something about the development of increasingly complex societies, fields of expertise of increasingly divided distribution and division of knowledge, and also the social prestige attaching to the idea of professionalism itself. Given all of this, some activities may not appropriately be termed professions, even though many groups certainly want that status.

I am inclined in some respects for some of these analyses to stay out of the language of professions and use, for example, MacIntyre's notion.of social practice, where there are certain coherently organized bodies of practices with their own forms of knowledge and ways of doing things, and so on. The question would then become whether engineering isn't a social practice rather than a profession.

Fr. Sokolowski: If you eliminate the whole element of personal rapport in order to keep the definition of a profession clean so that it could apply to engineering, it seems to me that you would lose something from the notion of a profession. But there is also a problem if you want to keep the personal dimension because this does not apply in the case of the engineer who works for a large company.

Dr. Zaner: I am not entirely sure how to handle the issue, frankly.

I think you can identify, as MacIntyre suggested, certain goods internal to certain kinds of practices. In so doing, one could not coherently understand the notion of a social practice without referring to those other persons who in some way or other are served by or benefit from that practice.

EDMUND D. PELLEGRINO

Trust and Distrust in Professional Ethics

Ademantus. "I wonder men dare trust themselves with men."
—*Timon of Athens*, 1.2.43

I. Introduction

Trust is ineradicable in human relationships. Without it, we could not live in society or attain even the rudiments of a fulfilling life. Without trust, we could not anticipate the future and we would therefore be paralyzed into inaction. Yet to trust and entrust is to become vulnerable and dependent on the good will and motivations of those we trust. Trust, ineradicable as it is, is also always problematic.

Trust is most problematic when we are in states of special dependence—in illness, old age, or infancy, or when we are in need of healing, justice, spiritual help, or learning. This is the situation in our relationships with the professions whom circumstances force us to trust. We are forced to trust professionals, if we wish access to their knowledge and skill. We need the help of doctors, lawyers, ministers, or teachers to surmount or cope with our most pressing human needs. We must depend on their fidelity to trust and their desire to protect, rather than to exploit, our vulnerability.

This ineradicability of trust has been a generative force in professional ethics for a long time. To be sure, there have always been professionals who violated trust but they were the moral renegades and pariahs. Not until recently has the central place of trust in professional ethics been seriously doubted or attacked, not only as an illusion, but

69

even as a radical impossibility.[1] Indeed, what amounts to an ethics of distrust has been gathering force. It would place higher restraints on professionals or eliminate the need for trust entirely. To this end, alternatives to trust in the ethics of the professions are proposed— reducing professional relationships to contracts or appointing ombudsmen or other intermediaries to monitor the advice and actions of professionals.

Without depreciating the reality of the factors that generate the distrust, arguments for an ethic of distrust are flawed empirically, phenomenologically, and conceptually. Translated into professional ethics, the ethics of distrust is perilous, self-defeating, and ultimately impossible in practice. It is sounder to acknowledge the ineradicability of trust and to restructure the ethics of our professions even more solidly on this foundation. This restructuring in no way necessitates the subjugation of patient choice to the professional's value system or a blunting of the salubrious move toward an ethics of patient autonomy and participation.

To advance the ethics of trust against the ethics of distrust we shall first examine the phenomenon of trust, both in general and in the professional context. Then we shall examine the rise of the ethics of distrust and its inherent fallacies, and finally, the inescapable obligations that the ineradicability of trust imposes on professionals and on patients as well.

II. The Phenomenology of Trust
A. Trust as a General Phenomenon in All Human Relationships

Despite its ubiquity in human affairs, trust has been examined only tangentially by philosophers. It has yet to receive extended and formal philosophical analysis. Recent writers have entered upon such an inquiry from different points of view and with different conceptual formulations.

Bernard Barber, a sociologist, identifies trust with the expectation that social actors will observe three conditions: (1) they will act within a persistent moral order, (2) they will perform their technical roles competently, and (3) roles that require a special concern for others, such as the fiduciary role, will be faithfully fulfilled.[2] So far as professions go, Barber sees three distinctive characteristics that have a special bearing on trust: (a) their possession of powerful knowledge, (b) the autonomy necessary to their practice, and (c) their fiduciary obligation to individuals and society.[3] Barber's analysis is largely descriptive, and it treats the moral foundations of trust only indirectly.

Luhmann, another sociologist, provides a much more sophisticated and detailed account of trust and distrust. His account offers valuable insights into the ineradicability of trust and its functions in complex societies. Luhmann's hypothesis is that trust is associated with "reduction of complexity" and more specifically with that complexity which enters the world as a consequence of the freedom of other human beings.[4] By trusting, we remove the burden and impediment of complexity. "Trust then is the generalized expectation that another will handle his freedom, his disturbing potential for diverse action in keeping with his personality, or rather in keeping with the personality which he has presented and made socially visible. He who stands by what he has consciously or unconsciously allowed to be known about himself is worthy of trust."[5]

While trust aims to reduce complexity, it also unavoidably involves contingency. Some attempt to avoid contingency by distrust—by withdrawing confidence in the expectation that the person trusted will not abuse that confidence. But, at the same time, distrust reduces the range of possible human relationships and thus the fulfillment one can attain in life. Obviously, all but the most reclusive humans can, or would want to, rule their lives by trust rather than distrust.

Luhmann seeks a possible way out of the risks inherent in trust by transferring trust from person-to-person relationships to "system trust." Confidence is placed in institutional and social structures to reduce complexity by the restraints they impose on individuals who function within them. This seems a highly problematic solution, given that the relationships between individuals and institutions are neither less notably complex nor more notably reliable than person-to-person relationships.

Annette Baier has undertaken the ambitious task of a formal inquiry into the nature of trust, a subject that has been neglected in philosophical discourse. As she points out, except for Hume's focus on promise and contract, and trust in God emphasized by theologians, most writers have given only tangential attention to this subject.

Baier defines trust as "reliance on others' competence and willingness to look after, rather than harm, the things one cares about which are entrusted to their care."[6] She defines different kinds of trust relationships; the differences between promise, contracts, and trust, and the conditions that make trust "morally decent." She emphasizes the vulnerability involved in trusting another person, the indispensability and dangers of discretionary power given the one trusted, and the necessity of confidence that the trusting person's vulnerability will not be exploited, even if the one trusted has motives for doing so. Baier's inquiry illustrates the complexity of trust and the need for a better understanding of the philosophical foundations for morally valid trust relationships. Her account notes some of the special qualities of the professional relationship. Although she does not examine these in detail, she provides insights into the general phenomena that are relevant to any consideration of the special features of relationships with professionals.

Most construals of trust involve several elements, the strength and combinations of which vary with the nature of the relationship between the person trusted and the person trusting. One element is confidence that expectations of fidelity to what is entrusted will be fulfilled. Second, is the sense that the person trusted has explicitly or implicitly made a promise to act well with respect to the interests of the person trusted. Third, is the belief that discretionary latitude of certain proportions is necessary if trust is to be fulfilled, and that the one trusted will use it well, neither assuming too much nor too little. Fourth, is the congruence of understanding on these first three elements between the one trusting and the one trusted. Finally, underlying all of these aspects is an act of faith in the benevolence and good character of the one trusted. Each of these five elements takes on a special meaning in the special context of relationships with professionals.

B. Trust in Relationships with Professionals

Like other human relationships, our relationships with professionals ineradicably involve trust. Here, trust has special moral dimensions which are the foundation for professional ethics, what Barber has called "fiduciary relationships."[7] Trust in the helping professions—medicine, law, ministry, and teaching—has many features in common. Each relationship deserves examination in its own right, but only one will be examined here. The medical relationship will serve to illustrate the way trust shapes the ethical relationships between patients and physicians, and by analogy the relationships between lawyers and clients, ministers and parishioners, and teachers and students.

People seek out physicians when some adverse sign or symptom threatens their conception of their health sufficiently to impel them to seek expert advice. As soon as persons decide they need help, they become "patients"—they "bear" a burden of anxiety, pain, or suffering. To seek professional help is to trust that physicians possess the capacity to help and heal. From the very first moment, the patient makes an act of trust: first, in the existence and utility of medical knowledge itself, and then in its possession by the one who is being consulted. Trust at this initial level is more like what Baier calls "reliance," the kind of trust we place in airline pilots, firemen, or policemen—a trust inspired less by the person than the common recognition of a defined social role.[8] It is an expression of general confidence somewhat akin to Luhmann's "system trust."

We do not usually interview the pilot who is to take us over the ocean or worry about his motives or self-interest. Presumably, he wishes to make as safe a crossing as we. The pilot's competence is vital and his discretionary powers in flight are well-nigh absolute. But his involvement with us as persons is remote. Our trust in him is situated in trust in the system more than the individual.

If we take medical relationships as our paradigm case, we recognize a certain amount of trust in the system of education, credentialing, and the processes of licensure. But the intimacy, specificity, and personal nature of relationships with physicians compel us to be more concerned with personal qualities—with personality, but most of all with character.[9] Except in emergencies, at the earliest stages of a medical relationship, we are freer than we are in the choice of our pilot. We can consult other physicians, former patients, and credentials, as well as do research on the advice we receive. Here, the system can serve to establish or reinforce trust.

But before we engage this presumably competent physician, we are interested in much more. We expect to open the most private domains of our bodies, minds, social and family relationships to her probing gaze. Our vices, foibles, and weaknesses will be exposed to a stranger. Even our living and dying will engage her attention and invite her counsel. This is not at all like our trust in the pilot. The "system" cannot provide the reassurances we may want. Ultimately, we must place our trust in the person of the physician. We want someone who knows about us and treats us nonjudgmentally and is still concerned with our welfare. We will want someone who will use the discretionary latitude our care requires with circumspection—neither intruding nor presuming too much nor undertaking too little. We must be able to trust her to do what she is trusted to do, i.e., to serve the healing purposes for which we have given our trust in the first place.

We must trust also that our vulnerability will not be exploited for power, profit, prestige, or pleasure. The physician or lawyer's superior knowledge and skill foreordains inequality in the relationship. Even if we are physicians or lawyers ourselves, our capacity for objectivity is compromised when we are ill or named in a lawsuit. We know we can be deceived or led to the choice the lawyer or physician wants by the way he or she selects the facts about what can be done to help us. We can, to be sure, elicit other opinions, read for ourselves about our illnesses, or speak to other patients. But, ultimately, we must decide not only what we should do, but who will do it. What we want and what the doctor prescribes may be in conflict. We have to choose between our own judgment and that of someone we trust to have knowledge and a commitment to our well-being.

No professional can function properly without discretionary latitude. The more discretionary latitude we permit our professionals, the more vulnerable we become. Yet to limit that latitude is to limit the capacity for good as much as it may limit the capacity for harm. When all is said and done, we cannot anticipate every contingency even in a disease we understand well. Chronically ill patients often understand their illnesses better than physicians. Yet they can also be distressingly misinformed. At some point even our intimate knowledge of our needs must be translated into action. That action will be taken by another person, the physician, or lawyer, or minister on whom we are forced to depend if our goals are to be realized.

We can consult different authorities about our medical, legal, or spiritual problems. We may evaluate their logic, the evidence they adduce, or their compatibility with our personal values. Yet when there are differences among experts we must choose among them. And when we do, we really are choosing the professional we think we can trust to carry out our wishes and respect our values in carrying them out. Even then, every iota of our evaluation of our own situation may not be perfectly congruent with that of our physician, lawyer or minister.

We cannot subject every suggestion, recommendation, or counsel to the same intensive process of investigation for logical credibility. Even the most skeptical and distrusting patient would be exhausted by such an effort. At some point we must trust in our mutual understandings of what is in the sick person's interests. One might argue that only "serious" decisions need to be thoroughly examined. But what constitutes a serious decision? To decide this question, the patient needs information, again from a source that can be trusted. We can consult other experts or textbooks of medicine. But, once again, how does one choose among conflicting opinions? How does the patient deal with the fact that textbooks and articles are quickly out of date? A competent clinician will usually be more closely attuned to the rapidity of changes in the state of the art.

Let us suppose that a physician has been chosen because his opinion and recommendation after our investigations seem more credible than his colleague's. We still have the question of skill in carrying out the recommendations. How does one check on skill? Some patients seek out a surgeon's morbidity and mortality statistics or the opinions of her peers. Here we must trust the surgeon's honesty in reporting or the objectivity of her peers. We would find out that all surgeons have a certain irreducible mortality and morbidity. We must trust that the one we have chosen will have the skill requisite for a beneficial outcome.

Even the most distrustful and skeptical patient must at some point confront the fact that the physician is the final pathway through which all things medical must funnel. It is the physician who writes the orders, performs the procedure, and interprets the recommendations of other health professionals. The physician is a de facto "gatekeeper" who we trust to be the patient's advocate, and not simply an instrument of social, institutional, or fiscal policies.[10] Depending on his character and fidelity of trust, he may treat the patient as a statistical entity or he may be the patient's last protection against the "system." These contingencies are all exacerbated by the fact that trust in professional relationships is forced; it is trust generated by our need for help. When we need a doctor, lawyer, or minister, we have no choice but to trust someone, though we might prefer to trust none.

Living wills are a good example of attempts to supplant trust by contractual agreement. They seek to make the wishes of patients explicit to family and physician, particularly regarding terminal care. Morally and legally they have the same force as a competent patient's decision. They can settle or avoid disputes about what is in the patient's best interests. They also forewarn the physician, who may choose not to enter the relationship if he or she disagrees with the patient's values.

But living wills cannot specify every detail and every contingency. They are open to interpretation, particularly the physician's or family's understanding of what the patient meant by "ordinary" or "extraordinary" measures or doing "everything possible."

If living wills are written too tightly, they limit the physician's discretionary latitude in ways the patient might not really want. If written too broadly, they leave too much room for dispute and presumption. Living wills must be implemented through human agency. Those who write them must trust that those who eventually carry out their wishes act out of good will. In short, living wills cannot supplant trust because their execution depends on it.

Replacing trust relationships by contracts for care is equally dependent upon trust. Contracts can diminish the risk of frustration of the patient's will, but again they are based on trust that the things agreed to will, in fact, be performed. Contracts cannot envision all contingencies. They must allow discretionary latitude to the professional or they are self-defeating.

Moreover, the whole concept of a contract between someone who is ill, in need of justice, or worried about salvation, and the professional who can help meet those needs, is illusory.[11] Contracts are negotiated between equals or near equals. This is simply not the case in relationships with doctors, lawyers, or ministers. Contractors must also trust that there is understanding of mutual interest beyond the phraseology of the contract. The same words only too often carry different meanings. The frequency with which breach of contract is alleged is ample testimony that there is implicit trust even in the most explicitly worded agreement.

It is clear from the empirical and from the conceptual points of view that trust cannot be eliminated from human relationships, least of all relationships with professionals. Given this fact, an ethic based on mistrust and suspicion must, by the nature of human relationships, ultimately fail. To be sure, living wills, contracts if one wants them, durable powers of attorney, or appointment of a patient advocate or health care manager can diminish some of the vulnerability of trust relationships. In the end, however, all of these arrangements displace trust from the physician or professional and locate it elsewhere—but trust remains.

Given the empirical inevitability of trust in professional relationships, what is needed are not attempts to eradicate it, but rather a reconstruction of professional ethics grounded in its ineradicability. Such an ethic of trust must be based in the "internal morality" of each profession[12]—those ethical obligations that arise in the nature of each profession, the kind of human activity each profession encompasses.

The features of our trust relationships with professionals are, taken singly, not unique. What is specific to them is the peculiar constellation of urgency, intimacy, unavoidability, unpredictability, and extraordinary vulnerability within which trust must be given. It is this context that makes trusting professionals so problematic, so fragile, and so easily ruptured. A number of factors in contemporary society and medical practice have conspired to threaten and destroy this fragile fabric and create a growing mistrust of trust that is damaging to patients as well as to professionals.

III. The Ethos and Ethics of Distrust
A. The Milieu of Medical Practice

Distrust of professionals, especially doctors, is not a new phenomenon. Venal, greedy, incompetent, dishonest, and insensitive professionals have never been a rarity. They have been the satirists' favorites for a long time.[13] Their acid comments had their origins in real experiences of the sick. In part, they arose from the gross misbehavior of professionals themselves and in part from the hostility of the sick to fate which forces them to seek out physicians and then to pay for something they do not want in the first place. Because of our resentment at our loss of freedom, and at the powerlessness that serious illness imposes on all of us, the physician, good or bad, has always been a lightning rod for the frustrations of the sick.

In the last two or three decades, these perennial sources of distrust have been reinforced and expanded by a wide variety of events within and outside medicine—the malpractice crisis; the commercialization of medical care by advertising and entrepreneurism; the excessive income and free-spending life-style of some physicians; the bottom-line, marketplace, "pay-before-we-treat" policies of hospitals and some doctors; the depersonalization of large group prepayment practices; physicians' growing preferences for nine-to-five jobs and time off; the retreat from general to specialty practice; the early retirements—the list is long and growing daily.

As a result, patients, as the opinion polls show, increasingly think doctors are less available and less interested in them and more interested in money than they used to be. In self-defense, patients feel they must take charge of their own care, do their own research about their symptoms and their doctors, and even order their own tests to become as informed as the doctor to be sure of getting good care. The doctor is, in this view, merely one resource among many.

The eroding effect of these attitudes on the trust relationship is clear. Wariness replaces trust. Physicians and patients approach each other as potential enemies rather than friends. Patients perceive doctors as less interested in them than in their money, more interested in time off than service, and more the exploiters than stewards of medical knowledge. For many, the whole enterprise of medicine has increasingly called forth the principle of "caveat emptor" rather than the principles of fidelity to trust, beneficence, and effacement of self-interest.

These erosive tendencies within medicine have been reinforced by powerful forces within the social fabric of our times. Participatory democracy, better public education, the attention of the media, a mistrust of authority and experts in general—all have weakened the trust relationship. On the positive side, they encourage greater independence in patient decisions and thus help to neutralize the traditional paternalism of the professions. This is a salubrious move to more adult, open, and honest relationships. Indeed, now the problem is often the absolutization of autonomy which must be tempered by the interests of third parties, and the moral right of physicians to refuse to do what they consider to be unethical. The line between healthy protection of patients' autonomy and dangerous depreciation of medical expertise is becoming more difficult to define.

B. The Ethos and Ethics of Distrust

The most serious outcome of the erosion of trust is the emergence of an ethics of distrust, i.e., the formal, and ultimately most destructive, attack is on the very concept and possibility of trust relationships with professionals. Perhaps most serious of all, an ethics of distrust compromises the chance of achieving the purposes of professional relationships. Can a sick person be healed—made "whole" again—when she is suspicious of the motives and methods of her healer? A sick person must be empowered to heal herself. Is this possible when the person empowering is suspected of fostering her own self-interest? Can a client feel that her just cause is safe in the hands of a venal lawyer? Can a parishioner be saved or reconciled with God if she cannot see the minister as a reliable avenue of access to spiritual healing? Not only is trust totally ineradicable from professional relationships but the cultivation of trust is indispensable to the telos of each profession.

An ethos of distrust asserts the radical impossibility of trust in professional relationships.[14] Using medicine as an example, the ethics of distrust asserts that physicians cannot know all of a patient's values, that medicine deals only with a subset of things important to human fulfillment, and that physicians by the very nature of their profession necessarily place medical values over all other values. Moreover, since physicians are human they have personal values which they cannot suppress. Physicians, therefore, select and weigh the facts to be presented on the basis of their own rather than the patient's perceptions of what is good. Even so-called medical facts are tinged with value desiderata to such a degree that there are no value-free facts. Finally, we cannot trust in some standard of virtues inherent in professional practices which will protect the patient against the doctor's value system. The virtues of a profession are not intrinsic to that profession but derivative from a wide variety of ethical and philosophical systems. There is nothing in the nature of medicine, law, or ministry per se that entails honesty, compassion, fidelity to trust, or suppression of self-interest; the so-called internal morality of the professions is a fiction. On this view, an ethos of distrust assumes the formal character of an ethics of distrust.

An ethics of distrust entails that professionals and those who seek their help assume primarily a self-protective stance. Patients must seek strict contractual relationships with their doctors. Specific instructions as to care must be spelled out by patients and must be observed to the letter by physicians. In addition, for further protection, some insist on the interjection of a presumably objective third party who will be the patient's advocate in place of the physician and who will monitor the physician's compliance with the terms of the contract.

There are empirical and conceptual difficulties in such an ethics of distrust. The empirical ineradicability of trust has already been discussed (see II.B above). Mechanisms proposed to bypass this ineradicability are illusory. If, for example, we prefer an ombudsman or health care manager to help us make decisions, we merely displace our trust from physicians to some other person. This person is still able to interject his or her own values into clinical decisions. The "manager" is susceptible to being co-opted by the physician, the family, societal expectations, or by self-interest. Doubtlessly, in some cases, patients would be better served by an ombudsman than by the professional. But this is by no means assured in the majority of cases. It introduces a serious and dangerous impediment to the discretionary latitude essential in professional decisions and action. The possibilities of confusion and conflict of opinion are multiplied. The patient will still have to trust one of the parties in any dispute between professionals and lay advocates. What is "best" is a decision with both technical and moral components.

The ethos and ethics of distrust confers a legalistic quality on relationships with professionals—one which leads to ethical minimalism. Professionals will tend to limit themselves to the precise letter of agreement. They will feel free of the expectation that they are advocates, counsellors, and protectors of the patient's welfare. The professional's necessity to efface self-interest will be blunted since legalistic and contractual relationships call upon the participants to protect their own self-interest, not that of the other party—except to the extent the contract requires. The impetus to do the "extra" that requires some compromise of self-interest is blunted if not destroyed entirely. These attitudes are already evident in professional relationships. They will be legitimated and reinforced by an ethos based in mistrust.

In addition to its empirical impossibility, there are conceptual and logical difficulties in a radical ethos of distrust. The fact that some physicians have violated their trust relationship does not vitiate the concept of trust. Other physicians do, in fact, respect it. Moreover, the fact that trust cannot be guaranteed or may be respected only in part cannot eradicate its reality in human and professional relationships.

It is also true that all of a patient's good is not subsumed in his or her medical good. I have argued elsewhere indeed that medical good is only one of the components of the complex notion of patient good, and that the key concept is beneficence in trust.[15] The doctor has an obligation to help define the patient's medical good, that is, the good that the recommended treatment can achieve. In this the physician is, or should be, the expert. But if the physician is to "heal" in any true sense, he or she must place the medical good in the context of the patient's assessment of his total good. In this the patient is the expert. The whole concept of patient autonomy is vitiated if it is assumed that trust entails granting to the physician determination of the other levels of good beyond medical good. The other levels of patient's good include the patient's own assessment of what is good given his or her values, age, sex, occupation, aspirations, and the myriad things each of us as individuals may think more important than medical good or which would modify the degree and kind of medical treatment we would choose.

The logic of the argument against trust fails because its target is a gratuitous concept of global trust. This is not what the concept of trust in professionals need entail. We trust professionals in realms over which they have expertise. We trust them not to use that expertise to exploit our vulnerability for their own interests. We trust them for accurate information and we trust them to empower and enable us to place their recommendations into the full context of our own hierarchy of values. We also trust them to carry out the procedures in which they are skilled and which we cannot perform for ourselves.

But, it will be argued, even in the presentation of the medical facts and indications, trust is an incoherent concept because facts and values are never separable; the physician's personal and professional values cannot help but color the way he presents his data. This is not the place to deal with such a fundamental epistemological problem as the fact/value dichotomy. However, it is worth considering some examples in which it seems clear that in some sense fact and value are separable.

If a child falls out of a tree, fact and value decisions have to be made by parents and physician. Whether or not the skull is fractured, the spleen is ruptured, or shock is present, are all "fact" questions. Physical examination and x-rays will establish kind and degree of fracture and provide a basis for what mechanically needs to be done to set it right. The choice of mechanical procedures is based on empirical facts related to risk, effectiveness in healing, restoring function, and the like. Personal values cannot change the physical signs or x-ray images.

Values enter the process when the factual data are used as a basis for choice between alternative treatments. Assuming the child cannot make her own decision for reasons of incompetence, parents will weigh the alternative choices presented to them—treatment or no treatment, types of fracture reduction, or anesthesia, functional result expected, length of rehabilitation, pain, and dozens of other facts which go into an assessment of what is "good" for this child.

At this point the process becomes a dialogue and dialectic between fact and value. In this dialogue the doctor cannot be expected to "know" what is "best" for the totality of the child's well-being but he is expert in what is medically wrong, what can be done, what can be expected, and what alternatives are available if healing or cure are to occur. To "trust" the doctor does not mean we expect him to know everything important to the child and her parents. Rather, they must trust him to enable and empower them to make their own choice based on the most reliable facts.

The physician, of course, can shape the decision by the way he presents the factual data. He may give a higher value to health and medical care than the patient because of his professional commitment. He might also interject his own values, or prejudices about life, politics, religion, etc. into the dialogue openly or covertly. The fact that this might happen does not mean that it must happen or that it is totally impossible to dissociate personal and professional values from medical indications. The fact is that some, indeed many physicians are sensitive to their power to shape decisions covertly or overtly. While trust cannot be absolute or cover every aspect of the relationship with professionals, professionals can and do dissociate their personal and professional values, to varying degrees, from their recommendations.

That this dissociation is not perfect is not surprising, given that professional relationships are, and will remain, relationships between humans. The absence of perfection does not make the concept invalid. It only underscores the need for a clarification of the content and extent of trust in professional relationships. A refurbished ethic of trust will accept the fact that trust cannot be absolute, that it can be and is violated, but that nonetheless its ineradicability makes fidelity to trust a central obligation in all professional relationships.

IV. The Ethics of Trust Restructured

Trust in professionals can no longer be absolute or open ended, much as physicians and even some patients might wish it to be. Public education about medicine and medical ethics, the prominence of patient autonomy as a central principle of professional ethics, the potential conflict between the physician's and patient's best interests—all necessitate a more restricted and realistic view. Nevertheless, the ineradicability of trust mandates that it remain a central element in any coherent ethic of the professions.

Since trust is a permanent feature of human relating, fidelity to trust is an indispensable virtue of the good professional—lawyer, doctor, minister, or teacher. Without this virtue, the relationship with a professional cannot attain its end. It becomes a lie and a means of exploitation of vulnerability rather than a means of helping and healing. If there is any meaning to professional ethics, it must revolve around the obligation of fidelity to trust.

But what is to be entrusted to the professional? Clearly, from what has been said, patients should not entrust to the physician the responsibility for determining the totality of their good. Only the patient or the morally valid surrogate can know this. Physicians must not assume they are entrusted with such a broad mandate. Some patients may feel overwhelmed by having to make a choice. Some may not trust anyone but the physician. They might then ask the physician what he or she thinks "best." Patients should be encouraged and enabled to make their own decisions. But if the patient empowers her to make the decision, the physician cannot refuse to help. That would constitute moral abandonment. Under these circumstances, the physician must make every effort to learn as much as he or she can about the many dimensions of what constitute the patient's best interests. Then, under these unusual circumstances, the physician must be particularly self-critical. She should attempt to place the medical good within the larger context of the patient's total good, his value system, way of life, life history, spiritual and temporal commitments, etc., as precisely as possible. The temptation to overstep the authority even when the patient provides the mandate must be resisted.

In an ethic of trust the physician is impelled to develop a relationship with the patient from the very outset which includes developing familiarity with who, and what, the patient is and how he or she wants to meet the serious challenges of illness, disability, and death. It is essential that the physician help the patient to anticipate certain critical decisions such as withholding or withdrawing life-sustaining treatments, cardiopulmonary resuscitation, request for assisted death, abortion, and the like. The physician must prepare the patient for these eventualities before they become urgent or the patient loses competence. Patients should be able to rely on the physician for the proper timing, sensitivity, and degree of detail appropriate in each case. These cannot be written into a contract. They must be entrusted to the physician or some physician substitute.

In an ethics of trust, the physician is obliged to present clinical data as free as possible of personal or professional bias. Fidelity to trust precludes manipulation, coercion, or deception in obtaining consent. It requires assisting patients to perform the calculus of effectiveness, benefit, and burden as carefully as the situation permits. What is known must be distinguished from what is uncertain, or simply, unknown. The indispensability of keeping information up to date is obvious. Consultation with or reference to those with more experience or skill or with closer congruence with the patient's values is required. When patient and physician values are sharply at variance, the physician should decline to enter the relationship or withdraw from it graciously, with candor, and without recrimination.

A realistic ethic of trust does not absolutize the professional's fiduciary role. Nor does it ignore the realities that may compromise trust—for example, the potential intrusion of the physician's personal and professional values, the complexity of the notion of the patient's best interests, the difficulty of disassociating fact and value.

Nor does an ethic of trust ignore the sad facts of incompetence, quackery, fraud, inadequate self-regulation, and peer review of the addicted and alcoholic professional. To recognize the ineradicability of trust is not therefore to argue against regulation of the professional by licensure, educational and certification procedures, quality controls, periodic relicensure, and liability laws. Professionals are ordinary humans called by the nature of the activities in which they engage to extraordinary degrees of obligation and trust. Living wills, durable power of attorney, and inquiries into competence are all legitimate measures those who seek professional help are entitled to invoke. A certain degree of distrust based on experience of the caprices of human behavior is unavoidable.

But these reasonable constraints on trust do not justify an ethic of distrust which takes fidelity to trust relationships to be invalid and impossible. That trust may be violated in varying degrees does not entail the inevitability of its violation. Moreover, even if all the current measures which place restraint on trust were implemented, an inerasable residuum of trust would remain. It is with the acknowledgment of this residuum, its enhancement and strengthening, that an ethic of trust is most concerned. A restructured ethic of trust therefore recognizes simultaneously the origins of distrust and the ineradicability of trust.

On balance, an ethic of trust is more realistic, conceptually sounder, and phenomenologically more consistent than an ethic of distrust. To highlight trust in professional relationships, to make it explicit and more precise, is to provide the very protection an ethic of distrust seeks but cannot reach. Older notions of absolute trust are inadequate and were always so. What is needed is a redefinition of trust relationships consistent with the contemporary context of autonomy, participatory democracy, and the moral pluralism of the interacting parties in professional relationships.

Clearly, an ethic of trust must go beyond principle and duty-based ethics to an ethics of virtue and character. This is consistent with the current revival of interest in virtue theories. In general and professional ethics it also calls for a reconciliation between autonomy and beneficence along lines we have detailed elsewhere as "beneficence-in-trust."[16] More attention to character formation and professionalization are essential since virtue is best taught by practice in the presence of teachers who themselves are models of virtuous behavior.[17,18]

It goes without saying that trust must be earned and merited by performance and fidelity to its implications. Professionals cannot expect to be trusted simply because they are professionals. The ineradicability of trust is a source of obligations, not of privilege. Professionals who resent the queries and the skepticism of their patients or clients are insensitive to the changed climate of professional relationships. They fail to sense the predicament of vulnerability in which those who seek their help must find themselves.

Essential to an ethics of trust is the professional's realization that if there is distrust, the problem may not rest entirely with the patient or client. Trust is easily destroyed sometimes over minor failures—forgetting to provide results of a test, failing to perform some needed service, or sidestepping some important question. Trust must be engendered and built up gradually by fidelity to promise from the very first moments of a professional relationship. It is as fragile a phenomenon as it is an ineradicable dimension of a helping and healing relationship.

Difficult as these requirements may be, the effort to meet them is worthwhile. The alternative is an ethic based on the presumption of distrust which can only degenerate into a minimalistic and legalistic ethic which is no ethic at all but merely a relationship of mutual self-defense. Professionals no longer under any obligation of fidelity will feel free to pursue self-interest. Patients or clients will harbor the illusion that they can protect themselves from all harm by regulation and personal management of every potential risk. Such a scenario will not only destroy any concept of professional responsibility but will be far more perilous than a strengthened and restructured ethic of trust.

Notes

1. R.M. Veatch, "Is Trust of Professionals a Coherent Concept?" (this volume).

2. Bernard Barber, *The Logic and Limits of Trust* (New Brunswick, N.J.: Rutgers University Press, 1983), 9.

3. Ibid., 135.

4. Niklas Luhmann, *Trust and Power*, T. Burns and P. Gianfranco, eds. (Ann Arbor: Books on Demand, 1979), 30.

5. Ibid., 39.

6. Annette Baier, "Trust and Anti-Trust," *Ethics* 96 (January 1986):259.

7. Barber, 14-16.

8. Baier, 245.

9. E.D. Pellegrino, "Character, Virtue and Self-Interest in the Ethics of the Professions," *The Journal of Contemporary Health Law and Policy* 5 (Spring 1989):53-73.

10. E.D. Pellegrino, "Rationing Health Care: The Ethics of Medical Gatekeeping," *The Journal of Contemporary Health Law and Policy* 2 (1986):23-45.

11. William F. May, *The Physician's Covenant* (Philadelphia: Westminster Press, 1983).

12. E.D. Pellegrino, "The Healing Relationship: The Architectonics of Clinical Medicine," in E.E. Shelp, ed., *The Clinical Encounter* (Dordrecht: D. Reidel, 1983), 153-78.

13. Mary B. Mahowald, "The Physician," in R.W. Clarke and R.O. Lawry, eds., *The Power of the Professions* (Lanham, Md.: University Press of America, 1988), 119-31.

14. See the papers by Buchanan, Brock, and Veatch in this volume.

15. E.D. Pellegrino and D.C. Thomasma, *For the Patient's Good* (New York: Oxford University Press, 1988).

16. Ibid.

17. Charles S. Bosk, *Forgive and Remember, Managing Medical Failure* (Chicago: University of Chicago Press, 1979).

18. George Agich, "Professionalism and Ethics of Health Care," *The Journal of Medicine and Philosophy* 5 (1980): 187-99.

Discussion

Dr. Buchanan: If we are trying to improve professional-client relationships, it is a real live question of strategy as to whether we are likely to better the situation by painting an extremely lofty ideal and then drumming into people's heads to follow it. There will be some like you who will follow it, quite naturally, but there will be many who won't. Would we do better to concentrate not so much on a lofty idea but to start trying to make structural changes that will, as it were, give ethics a boost by giving it the right kinds of economic incentives?

In the past, prior to the advent of corporatized medicine and all the changes that you have pointed out, altruism was relatively cheap for physicians because there was a wonderful congruence between self-interest and the Hippocratic Oath because of the fee-for-service system where most people were privately insured. Altruism for physicians was relatively cheap. It was easy to do because you got paid to do the things that your conscience sort of told you to do.

Now, there is a kind of radical separation or divergence of these things. Altruism is not so cheap to physicians any more. The question is how do you respond to that—by making physicians willing to be altruistic even if it costs them a lot more, exhorting them, or by trying to get a new set of incentives that will give ethics a boost, if you will?

Dr. Pellegrino: First of all, I don't think the two approaches are mutually exclusive, and I don't think that focusing on one necessarily takes your focus off the other. I argue for both, as a matter of fact.

Dr. Veatch: You do agree with that, Dr. Buchanan?

Dr. Buchanan: Yes. I think you have to do moral exhortation, but I don't think that it has to be elevated to this unrealistic level. I think you also have to change the incentive structure. So I am not saying that there should be no place for morals. I said ethics needs help, not that ethics should be replaced. But I think we would disagree as to what the ideal is and how high it should be set, and I think that there is a danger in setting the ideal too high. I think it is counterproductive.

Dr. Pellegrino: I think that the ideal I have defined, at least as I take it, grows out of the nature of medicine. I don't think it is unrealistic. I think it is an ideal which is there, built into the nature of this process.

I think if we say that this is what ought to be, we know people are going to fall short, that is for sure, but when you fall short from this ideal you end up a lot higher than if you fall from the merely feasible.

Everybody is arguing for the merely feasible right now, and everybody is saying, well, like Machiavelli, it isn't possible to be moral when everybody else is being immoral. I don't think that is an exhortation that argues one out of the nature of the activity.

Dr. Buchanan: I think if the target is set too high it invites cynicism. They may not try and fall short. They may not even try in that direction at all.

Dr. Pellegrino: I will take that as a possibility, but let me just respond in this sense. In my looking at it, I tried to look at it philosophically, and philosophically one tries, at least in some traditions, to define what a thing is. I am an essentialist, and I gather you are not. That is a difference in our basic philosophical presuppositions.

Let me take a series of questions and then give my responses.

Fr. Langan: I would submit that this exchange that just occurred needs to be in some way disaggregated with a number of different problems, one having to do with the question about the demands of the profession on the professional in terms of time and keeping some space for the development of professionalism.

As a person with a fairly broad range of interests, and so on, and at the same time, say, in a field like medicine, being committed to ideals of personal care and professional competence, keeping abreast of the literature, and so on, there are lots of stresses and demands built into that sort of commitment. That commitment is, I think, one part of establishing trustworthiness.

There is another set of concerns about economic incentives, and I doubt that those are totally divorceable from the third set of concerns about sacrifice and danger. For instance, it seems to me very unwise to think of imposing disastrous economic costs on physicians and somehow saying this is an appropriate ideal. But I do think that one has to be willing to say that in certain situations physicians may be required to risk their lives in accordance with their professional moral responsibilities.

Now, I realize I have shut off a lot of controversial things, but the general discussion of ideals and practice I think has to recognize that there are a number of different areas of conflict and also that we may need, in terms of long-term moral development, to keep both a sense of ideals which we will never be able to attain—I believe we are on the subject of the relevance of an impossible or an impractical ideal—and ideals that are a lot closer to attainment.

Dr. Zaner: Just a brief point, also, on the issue of lofty ideals and the point that altruism has become very expensive. The question occurs to me: according to what, in relation to what, in contrast with what, with respect to what ordering of values has altruism become expensive?

It may well be that altruism gets expensive because we have shifted, perhaps improperly shifted, the whole ordering of values, the scale of values. It is expensive in relationship to what? Buying an MRI? For what purposes? It seems to me that such a claim needs to address the underlying issue of some accepted order of values far more clearly and directly.

I think the kinds of things that I have urged here are not only realistically possible; they have to be possible. Otherwise, much of the practice of health care in our time is simply irrelevant. People do it. The question is how do they do it and under what circumstances.

One has to shift and change by way of values, and so on. Other people are like what you have urged. They do less than what their teachers told them that medicine is all about, but then that means they have shifted fundamental values and what they understand their jobs to be, and it is a question of whether that needs to be criticized on its own.

Dr. Meilaender: I want to quickly make a connection with a couple of other professions. On this general issue I am probably more with Pellegrino than Buchanan, but what started me thinking was the commodification language. Though I don't have any desire to make a case for it, the question is how one should criticize it. You don't want to criticize it by telling people how special they have to regard a good. They may regard a good as more or less special.

My examples are from a couple of professions I do know something about. In teaching, students come to a course for a variety of reasons, and I have learned to take them in that way. Some just show up. They seem to want three hours credit. That is okay with me. I don't tell them they must have more. Some want a little more. They will pursue it in different ways. They want some advice about where to go, and so forth. I try to do my best to give it. A few really want the kind of intense experience and exploration of the material. To the best that I can, I make myself available to do that for them.

I don't try to tell any of them how special they must or must not regard it. There are some things I won't let any of them do in this interchange between us.

I think there is a kind of integrity to what we are up to—and this is the Pellegrino side of me, you see—that shapes what we are doing, and therefore there are some things beyond the pale.

Analogously, I have on occasion worn for short periods of time ministerial hats, and I know from other contexts that clergy often tend in their frustrations to feel that all their parishioners must be sort of constantly involved in the life of the parish when in fact people come there—there are some people who come for worship and not a lot else. There are others who for whatever set of reasons need a deeper involvement. There are others who need not only that deeper involvement, but a lot of contact with the minister.

It seems to me we don't tell them kind of exactly how special this good must be in their life, though once again there are certain ways we wouldn't let them distort it. It does have its own integrity.

To say that seems to me to hold on to Pellegrino's point without telling them how special this good must be. It seems to me that is a useful way to think about it.

Dr. Pellegrino: Fr. Langan, I will take your point as to the different kinds of roles in the model we are talking about. Here again I suspect I will be accused of being idealistic, but there is an order involved when you are involved in a helping profession.

I would apply analogously the things I have said to law, to teaching, and to the ministry. We will leave the military out of it because I think the others are all helping professions, and they are all based in this notion of vulnerability and seeking, and so on.

Now, I think Dr. Meilaender has made a good point here. No one here would suppose that we are expected to be perfect or superperfect but it is one thing to recognize the essential notion, as I do, as an existential fact, that we are all going to get there and we do it in different ways. So here as you unravel those, it is going to depend on the particularities of that person's life circumstances, but there will be an ordering principle at times. There are some things you cannot do and still remain committed to what the profession is.

II.
What Does Trust Require?

ALLEN BUCHANAN

The Physician's Knowledge and the Patient's Best Interest

I. The Interdependence of Knowledge and Duty

What knowledge is it reasonable to expect the physician to have in the physician-patient relationship? What is the physician obligated to know or to try to know? One way to approach these questions is to begin with the orthodox assumption that the physician is the patient's fiduciary. As a fiduciary, the physician is obligated to act in the patient's best interest, and hence, is obligated to know or to make reasonable efforts to know, what is in the patient's best interest. I shall argue, however, that this way of approaching the issue is mistaken. We cannot start with an independent conception of the physician's duty and then ask, in the light of that conception, what it is reasonable for us to expect the physician to know and what she is obligated either to know or to try to know. To proceed in this way is mistaken for the simple reason that what the physician's duty *is* depends on what it is reasonable to expect the physician to know. If it is not reasonable to expect the physician to know something, then she cannot have a duty to do that which she would need such knowledge to do.

Another difficulty with the orthodox assumption is that the familiar slogan that the physician is to act in the patient's best interest is both ambiguous and, at least on the most straightforward interpretation, in conflict with what may be the most fundamental principle of modern bioethics: that a competent patient is to be allowed to accept or refuse treatment or care according to his own preferences, even when doing so may not be in his best interest.[1] For even if it is true that *in general* a competent person is the best judge of his or her own good and *in general* is effectively motivated to pursue it, there is no guarantee that respecting patient autonomy and acting in the patient's best interest will always be compatible. Thus, on the most straightforward interpretation, the slogan that it is constitutive of the physician's role to act in the patient's best interest either falsely assumes that this will always be compatible with respecting the competent patient's autonomy or acknowledges the possibility of such a conflict but implies that the duty to act in the patient's best interest overrides the duty to respect the competent patient's autonomy when the two conflict.

Because I am convinced that respect for the competent patient's autonomy is a value not to be compromised—especially not to accommodate a conception of the physician's role-constituting duty (which, in effect, endows the physician with authority resembling that which a parent has over children)—I will not here rehearse the familiar arguments to support this fundamental principle.[2] I will only summarize by saying that self-determination, both as something valued in itself and as having great instrumental value in contributing to the individual's well-being, is sufficiently important that our understanding of the role of the physician should be adjusted to accommodate it rather than vice versa.

Once this assumption is granted, it is something of a puzzle to understand how it can still be the case that the physician's duty is to act in the patient's best interest. Although respecting patient autonomy will in general serve the patient's best interest (given the assumption that a competent individual is generally most knowledgeable about and motivated to pursue her own good), a fundamental commitment to patient autonomy seems to leave little or no room for the patient's best interest as an independent, much less role-constituting principle of duty for physicians. We seem to be faced with the following disturbing dilemma: either respecting the patient's autonomy and acting in his or her best interest converge, in which case there is no need for a distinct principle of duty stating that the physician is to act in the patient's best interest, or they diverge, and the duty to respect patient autonomy should take precedence. In the latter case, the duty to act in the patient's best interest should not be acted on. A principle that is always either redundant or overridden is a poor candidate for capturing the essence of the physician's role.

Shortly, I shall argue that this dilemma rests on an inadequate conception of the different functions a physician can and ought to serve while still respecting the patient's autonomy. But for now I wish only to note that there is a way of interpreting the principle that the physician is to act in the patient's best interest—what I shall call the purely negative interpretation—that makes it both compatible with acknowledging the preeminence of respect for patient autonomy (and yet nonredundant) and of considerable practical importance. According to the purely negative interpretation, the slogan that the physician is to act in the patient's best interest is to be understood as an admonition to the physician not to allow the interests of others—including the physician's own—to compromise his or her commitment to the patient. The best-interest principle serves to focus the physician's attention on the patient as the center of his or her concern, ruling out other possibly conflicting interests as irrelevant or as having, at best, secondary importance.[3] The principle of respect for patient autonomy then specifies the proper content of the commitment to the patient by stating that it is the patient as a self-determining being, an agent capable of choice, who is the focus of the physician's commitment.

II. Best Interest and Autonomy

Assume for a moment that the physician's duty is not, strictly speaking, to act in the patient's best interest but rather to respect patient autonomy while avoiding serving anyone else's interests in ways that would work to the patient's detriment. Under these circumstances, how is the physician to act and what is it necessary for him or her to know? It might be thought that this negative interpretation of the best-interest principle along with the principle of respect for patient autonomy reduces the role of the physician to that of a technician who prepares and explains a menu of medical options for the patient, and then competently implements whatever option the patient selects. This understanding of the physician's role, however, is defective, and its incompleteness shows that the purely negative interpretation of the principle that the physician is to act in the patient's best interest is too narrow. There are four additional positive functions which a physician can fulfill and which are of such importance that they must be addressed in developing an adequate characterization of the physician's duties as physician. Moreover, each function can be put (though somewhat roughly) under the heading of "acting in the patient's best interest," yet without denying the preeminence of the duty to respect patient autonomy.

First, even with a patient who is, in general, competent to accept or refuse options the physician articulates, there will sometimes be situations in which the physician will be faced with decisions upon which it will be impossible or too time-consuming to consult the patient. For example, a decision to administer a drug may need to be made immediately, while the patient is sleeping. Frequently, the patient's explicit choices on other matters may provide an adequate guide for such a decision. But sometimes, prior choices will not fully decide the issue and, in these cases, it will be appropriate and indeed necessary for the physician to select an option that serves the patient's best interest. Second, the physician will need to be guided by the patient's best interest in preparing the menu of medical options among which the competent patient is allowed to choose. Given the patient's particular needs and interest, it may not even be appropriate to list some technically feasible options that might be live options for other patients. Third, many patients quite appropriately believe that they should be able to rely on their physicians, not just to list options but to exercise judgment in making a recommendation. Unless he is instructed otherwise by the patient, the physician should, of course, make a recommendation based on what he takes to be in the best interest of the patient. Fourth, a patient may delegate decision-making authority to her physician and again, in the absence of explicit instruction to the contrary, the physician, as proxy, should choose according to the patient's best interest.

Each of these four functions is important to the role of physicians traditionally conceived. Each requires the exercise of responsible judgment as to what is in the patient's best interest, and each is compatible with respect for patient autonomy. So we now have a more complete conception of the role of the physician than that afforded by the notion that he or she is merely a technician who prepares a menu of options, allows the patient to select among them, and then implements the patient's choice competently while avoiding any influence from conflicting interests. In each of the four functions listed, the physician must be guided by a positive conception of the patient's best interest—not merely by the admonition *not* to be unduly influenced by the interests of others. In addition, the physician can carry out these positive functions without compromising the principle of patient autonomy.

Suppose I am correct in assuming that, upon reflection, most would affirm that being a good physician requires a readiness to undertake each of these four functions. Being a technician who presents the patient with a menu of options and faithfully and competently implements the patient's choice does not suffice. Yet until we have examined the question of what sort of information the physician can reasonably be expected to have, the claim that the physician's duty encompasses all of these functions will be rather uninformative. Further, if it should turn out that, under the conditions of medical practice that actually exist today, physicians will often not be in a position to have the information needed to make reliable positive judgments about the patient's best interest, then we may even be forced to revise our conception of the good physician and to retreat toward the narrower conception of the physician as a technician who simply offers a menu of options and faithfully implements the patient's choice. Whether our ideal of what a physician should be can serve as a practical standard for assessing the behavior of physicians in our world will depend upon whether, and, if so, in what sense, we can reasonably expect physicians to make reliable judgments about what is in the patient's best interest. It will be necessary to interpret the ideal—if not to modify or reject it—in the light of the epistemic constraints under which the physician finds himself or herself.

The first source of skepticism about the physician's ability reliably to judge a patient's best interest stems from the recognition—belated as it has been among paternalistic physicians—that the patient's good is at least in part determined by what he or she values. Once a purely objective conception of a person's good is abandoned and it is conceded that different persons have different conceptions of the good, it becomes clear that the physician's technical expertise is not a sufficient basis for making reliable judgments concerning the patient's best interest. Whether or not it is in a patient's interest to undergo a treatment that will have certain side effects will depend not just upon the physiological character of the side effects, but upon the extent to which they hinder or render impossible that particular individual's pursuit of her own distinctive conception of the good. Indeed, although good health is valued by almost everyone, its importance relative to other goods will vary widely, depending upon the individual's conception of the good life. And for some, an extension of life will mean little or nothing if life extended is bereft of certain activities that are central to their conception of the good life. Hence, even if a physician's technical knowledge is flawless, this is no guarantee that he will know what is in his patient's best interest. To know what is in the patient's best interest, the physician must understand the patient's values, aspirations, and priorities. To render a best interest judgment, the patient's values must be applied to the medical facts, so that the options may be evaluated in the light of them.

III. Medical Best Interest

In the not so distant past, paternalistic physicians who saw their duty as that of acting in the patient's best interest—even if this meant a denial of patient autonomy—failed to recognize or in some cases willfully denied the fact that in order to judge what is in a person's best interest, more than medical knowledge is needed.[4] Now that this charade has been exposed, and the complexity of the best-interest judgment is understood, it may be tempting to retreat to the principle that physicians are to restrict their best-interest judgments to the "medical best interest" of the patient, leaving it to the patient or to some other proxy such as a family member (if the patient is incompetent) to integrate the medical judgment into a wider best-interest judgment overall.

Presumably, what is meant by "medical interests" is best understood by way of contrast: we can distinguish a patient's financial interests and his interest in the well-being of those he loves from his medical interests, understood roughly as those factors which will impede or enhance his various important physiological functions. The idea is that we can avoid saddling the physician with the overambitious task of making a judgment about the patient's overall best interest as a person by restricting his or her judgments to the patient's best medical interests—those which *do* lie within the scope of the physician's special expertise. The task of integrating the physician's judgment of the patient's medical interest would then have to be undertaken by someone better acquainted with the patient's values—either the patient herself, if she is competent, or a suitable proxy, such as a trusted family member, if the patient is incompetent.

There are two reasons why the attempt to limit the knowledge the physician needs in order to fulfill his or her role to the patient's best medical interest does not suffice to dispel skeptical reservations as to whether the physician can be expected to have the relevant knowledge. First, even if we can separate out the patient's medical interests from his or her overall interests, determining the patient's *best* medical interest may be difficult or impossible, even for the most technically knowledgeable physician.

In a patient afflicted by two or more diseases, a course of treatment that serves some of her medical interests (i.e., enhances or restores certain physiological functions) may not be optimal from the standpoint of some of her other medical interests (it may impede or at least not optimally facilitate some of her other physiological functions). Of course, in some cases the functions in question will be hierarchically interdependent so that there will be a rational way to resolve conflicts regarding them (for example, if the patient will surely die without a transplant, it will be in the medical best interest of the patient to undertake a heart transplant even if the postoperative medication will reduce kidney function). However, there are some cases in which the outcomes of the various options are so uncertain that it will not be possible to determine a unique option that is in the patient's medical best interest even if we can successfully segregate those interests from his or her interests as a valuing person. Here, as elsewhere, the physician cannot be expected to know what cannot be known. At most, the physician can be expected to make a reasonable conjecture but to make it clear to the patient or proxy that the bounds of knowledge have been traversed. It follows that the physician has a meta-obligation, therefore, to try to ascertain and to disclose to those who depend upon his or her judgment the limits of his or her knowledge.

There is, however, a second and perhaps more important reason why invoking the notion that the physician can only be expected to know what is relevant to the patient's best medical interest does not settle conclusively the limits of what we can reasonably expect the physician to know. In spite of the fact that physicians' technical training does not itself equip them to make overall best-interest judgments concerning the good of the patient, patients have often in the past relied and still continue to rely on their physicians to provide counsel, to make recommendations, and in some cases to serve as a proxy. Under present conditions, some patients will have no option but to rely upon the physician's judgment as to what he or she believes is best for them as persons, not merely as hierarchical systems of physiological functions. Given this, it is reasonable to expect physicians to endeavor to fulfill this broader role as best they can so long as no better alternatives exist. They must do so, however, in a candid way in which their function as counselors is not disguised under the cloak of technical medical expertise. A physician who, through his own choice, makes the role of counselor an important constituent of his professional identity thereby places himself under an especially challenging and indeed onerous obligation: to make special efforts to build trust and open channels of intimate communication with the patient in order to gather the kind of information about the patient's value history that is essential for making this sort of inclusive best-interest judgment. Thus, what it is reasonable to expect a physician to know about the patient's interest will vary, depending upon two factors: (1) the extent to which the physician is or is not the person who is best placed to fulfill this important counseling function and (2) whether the physician has chosen to include a more or less ambitious counseling function in his or her professional activity.

In some cases the current organization of medical practice not only makes the physician ill-placed to gain the sort of information required for the counseling function but also fails to provide alternative counselors for those who wish them. Worse still, physicians who are not in a position to gather the information required for the counseling function nonetheless make presumptuous and ill-grounded judgments about the patient's best interest as a person and use these judgments to determine the course of the patient's care. They do so under the cloak of their prerogatives as persons having technical medical expertise. I have in mind here especially the tendency of some tertiary care physicians to venture best-interest judgments (sometimes in a coercive way) about patients who are virtual strangers to them and whom they have only known under conditions that are unlikely to reveal much about the person's stable values and normally functioning personality. The proposal that the physician can only be expected to know the patient's best medical interest, then, provides no easy resolution of the problem of grasping the interdependence of what the physician should do and what he or she is obligated to know.

The results of our reflections on the distinction between the patient's medical good and her best interests can now be summarized. To the extent that it can be given any determinate meaning, the phrase "medical best interest" must refer to that which is most conducive to the well-functioning of the patient considered as a hierarchical system of biological subsystems. However, given the uncertainty of medical prognosis in some cases and the fact that a treatment may be beneficial to some functions but not to others, even the best-trained and most knowledgeable physician simply may not know the patient's best interest even in this narrow sense. More importantly, even if the patient's best medical interest can be known, this will not necessarily coincide with his or her self-understood best interest overall. Yet patients often expect their physicians to offer judgments about their overall best interest, not just their medical best interest narrowly defined. Either by choice or for lack of alternatives, physicians often serve in capacities that require them to venture best-interest judgments that include, but are not limited to, medical best-interest judgments. Knowing the patient's best medical interests (difficult though this may be) will not suffice.

IV. Alternative Principal-Agent Relationships: Their Implications for the Role of the Physician and What the Physician Should Know

I have emphasized that in medicine as we know it, the physician plays several distinct roles: technical expert, counselor, and sometimes proxy. We should not make the mistake of assuming either that this constellation of roles is a fixed feature of professional identity or that it represents the most efficient or morally desirable division of labor. As I intimated earlier, the emergence of tertiary care facilities and the proliferation of specialties, subspecialties, and other related institutional developments in the more technologically advanced countries have made it more difficult for some physicians to gain the sort of knowledge about their patients as whole persons that is needed if they are to serve as more than narrow technical experts.

We are already seeing the beginnings of a new social division of labor that may both respond to this problem and at the same time exacerbate it. Here I will concentrate on only two new developments: the increasing use of the case-management approach and the development of new forms of surrogate decision making for incompetent patients, in particular, the durable power of attorney for health care. I focus on these two examples for the sake of concreteness, but I wish to emphasize that they are only examples of changes in the division of labor which may come to transform the physician-patient relationship and what it is reasonable to expect physicians to know.

In the case-management approach, one individual (usually, but not always, a nurse) is designated as the person responsible for coordinating and tracking the various stages and strands of a patient's treatments across specialties and over time. At present, case managers may often be thought of by physicians as subordinates who facilitate the physician's performance of his or her traditional functions, especially those involving the making of recommendations about the patient's best interest and the exercise of decision-making authority which some patients explicitly delegate to the physician. But there is a different way in which the role of case manager might come to be understood. If the case manager does the job well, he or she may be the person who is best equipped—better than the physician— to discharge roles that extend beyond the presentation of technical menus and the explanation of the physiological consequences of implementing one option rather than another. If patients come to recognize this, they may come to rely upon the case manager more than the physician to venture overall best-interest judgments—if the medical power structure allows them to do so. If this development occurs, it will not signal a universal narrowing of the physician's role. At most, it will mean that others are more frequently performing some of the functions that have, in the past, been thought to be integral to the professional identity of physicians. These functions are performed in those settings where a high degree of specialization has made it very difficult, if not impossible, for the physician to do so effectively.

A durable power of attorney for health care is a legal instrument by which a competent person may appoint another person (or a committee) to make health care decisions after he or she becomes incompetent. I have argued at length elsewhere that the growing use of such surrogates can be seen as a rational response to certain widely perceived *agency risks* in the physician-patient relationship.[5] By appointing a surrogate, the patient creates a secondary principal-agent relationship as a protection against the contingency that the primary principal-agent relationship—the patient-physician relationship—fails to protect his or her interest or carry out his or her wishes.

A physician may fail to serve the incompetent patient's best interest for either or both of two different reasons: he may allow interests other than those of the patient to influence his judgment about patient care; or he may simply not know what is in the patient's best interest even if he is thoroughly committed to pursuing it. If it becomes very common practice for people to appoint surrogate decision makers for health care, at least for those decisions that are made in the highly specialized tertiary care setting, then it may be appropriate to modify both our conception of the role of the physician who operates in such institutions and our expectations of the sorts of knowledge he or she should possess to perform that role well.

To summarize: a growing uneasiness about whether physicians in some practice settings possess the knowledge to perform the ambitious roles of proxy and counselor may lead to shifting these functions to others, and, once this shift occurs, a new and more limited conception of the role of the physician may emerge. In principle, the readjustment could proceed in the opposite direction: we might hold fast to the ambitious, multifunctional conception of the physician's role and attempt to ensure that physicians have the knowledge that they will need to fulfill this role, even if doing so requires radical changes in the training of physicians and a restructuring of the settings in which they practice. In my opinion, this response to the growing gap between the traditional conception of the physician's role and the knowledge it is reasonable to expect physicians to have is less likely to occur. Reversals of the tendency toward increased specialization seem rare, especially in areas in which technology is expanding and diversifying.

V. The Social Division of Labor and the Existence of Professions

The existence of professions, including the medical profession, is one instance of the social division of labor. While human nature and the natural environment place some constraints on the set of feasible divisions of labor, we must take care not to assume that the division of labor we find in our society at present is either the "natural" or the uniquely rational arrangement, or that it will continue to be optimal in the future even if it is so now. The existence of the medical profession exemplifies a social division of labor in the trivial sense that the members of the profession have a distinctive occupational function which is not, for the most part, performed by others. But this, of course, does not distinguish physicians from others who have a special occupation, such as plumbers, whom we do not ordinarily think of as professionals in the same sense as physicians. There are at least two additional features which distinguish professions from mere occupational groups: (1) professions are to some extent and in some respects supposed to be self-regulating and (2) professions are granted a certain degree of autonomy or freedom from interference by government and other social agencies to which other groups are usually subject. It also seems to be a distinguishing mark of professions that the behavior of the members of such groups is to be guided by group norms, which sometimes, but not always, take the form of explicit oaths or written codes. Moreover, the individual professional's internalization of these norms is supposed to be an important element in the group's self-regulation, even if the application of tangible sanctions by the group or its officials to recalcitrant members is also sometimes necessary.

The relationship between these two distinctive features of professions can be understood (with a great deal of simplification) as a kind of exchange or bargain between the members of the group or its leadership and society at large (or government as the putative representative or agent of society). Society grants the group in question a degree of autonomy (along, usually, with certain marks of status) in exchange for the group or its officials performing certain socially valuable functions, not the least of which is the regulation of the behavior of the group's members. Two things are worth noting here. First, the assumption is that there is a need to regulate the behavior of the group's members and a need of such importance and of such a character that distinctive arrangements, in the form of a special social division of labor, are warranted. Second, it is assumed that the most efficient and ethically sound way to achieve control of the members of the profession involves, in large part, special group norms to be made effective by a combination of peer-group pressure, individual internalization, and official group sanctions. Indeed, a feature of professions that goes beyond mere freedom from some forms of social control to which other groups are subject and that plays an important role in enabling the group to form and transmit norms in a way that facilitates their internalization by individuals in the group, is that professions are granted powers to control the education and training of members and have considerable power over admission to and expulsion from the group. Professions also typically enjoy a degree of autonomy, not simply in being allowed to inculcate and enforce norms, but in developing or at least in specifying the content of the norms as well.

To summarize: The existence of a profession, as opposed to a mere occupational group, can be seen (at least in part) as a social response, taking the form of a particular division of labor, to a perceived need to exert control over the behavior of the members of an occupational group. This social response is based on the assumption that exclusive reliance on direct modes of social control through agencies outside the group would be suboptimal either from the standpoint of ethics or of efficiency or both. In the case of the medical profession, it is not difficult to see why it would be thought necessary to provide special forms of control over the behavior of members of the group: the often-remarked asymmetry of knowledge between physician and patient, as well as the anxiety and diminution of competence which sometimes accompany illness, make the patient especially vulnerable. Once we understand the existence of a profession in this way, we are led to a very straightforward question: is this arrangement a good bargain for society? Does this particular social division of labor achieve an appropriate level of control at an acceptable cost (where "cost" is construed broadly to include ethical considerations as well as efficiency in the narrow sense)?[6]

Two questions have emerged from the foregoing analysis which are pertinent to answering this larger question. First, would the goals of health care be better served by a narrower conception of the physician's role (and a correspondingly constrained conception of what the physician should be expected to know) than that which is currently included in our conception of what it is to be a medical professional? Should we encourage new social divisions of labor, such as the case-management approach and the durable power of attorney for health care, which assign to others functions that, traditionally, have been thought to be distinctive of physicians and that have probably been important in justifying the special status of physicians as professionals? Second, do the internal norms of the medical profession actually facilitate the kind of social control which provides the chief rationale for recognizing such a group as a medical profession, given that this recognition carries with it certain privileges and freedom from other modes of social control for the group and its members? The risk, of course, is that the members of a profession will develop their own distinctive interests and that these will shape the group's distinctive norms in ways that interfere with the group's ability to be self-regulating in a manner that protects patients or clients adequately. For example, it is often alleged that the norms of the American medical profession (whether this is reflected in official codes of ethics or not) place a higher value on the prolongation of life through invasive artificial means than do many members of the population they are supposed to serve. If this is the case, then the profession's control over the behavior of its members, to the extent that this control is effected through education, indoctrination, and role modeling which internalizes these norms, will not provide, from the perspective of society at large, adequate protection for patients.

It is important to note that we are not faced with the simple, all-or-nothing choice of whether to have a medical profession or not. The distinguishing marks of professions—group autonomy and self-regulation through group norms—are phenomena that admit of degrees. It seems likely that under most conditions the proper social division of labor will rely upon some combination of external social controls and group norms. The question is one of proportion.

VI. Conclusions

The chief conclusions of our inquiry can be stated, with some simplification, as follows: (1) What a physician's role-constituting duty is and what it is reasonable to expect a physician to know are interdependent. We cannot first settle on a conception of what the duty of the physician qua physician is and then say that he or she ought to know whatever is necessary for performing that duty, because the scope and nature of the physician's duties are constrained by what it is reasonable to expect him or her to know. (2) The traditional conception of the physician's role, even when interpreted in such a way as to make it compatible with showing due respect to the autonomy of the competent patient, includes several functions that go beyond that of being a technician who selects and presents a menu of medical options. These other functions require the physician to offer to the patient (or to the incompetent patient's surrogate) judgments as to what is in the patient's best interest. (3) Consequently, even if the notion of the patient's best medical interest can be clearly specified, the proposal that the physician need only know what is in the patient's best medical interest is in conflict with the traditional conception of the physician's role. (4) At least in some practice settings, growing specialization is creating a widening gap between the traditional conception of the physician's role and the expectations of physician knowledge that correspond to it, on the one hand, and what it is reasonable to expect the physician to know on the other. (5) Several emerging institutional arrangements, including the growing use of the case-management approach and the widening reliance on proxy advance directive, can be seen as attempts to develop a new division of labor that recognizes the constraints that modern specialized medicine places on physician knowledge. This new division of labor also seems tacitly to endorse a more limited role for physicians. (6) If we are indeed in a period of transition in which new experiments in the division of labor in health care will continue to develop, then the question "What ought physicians qua physicians to know?"—like the question "What is a physician?"—has at present no determinate answer or at least none that can be discovered by philosophical or ethical analysis. Here, at least, the Marxist slogan that theory is no substitute for social practice has the ring of truth. (7) An exploration of the question "What ought the professional to know?" pushes us back, ultimately, to the much more radical question, "What is the rationale for recognizing a group as a profession?"

Notes

1. For a comprehensive treatment of the topic of informed consent, see R. Faden and T.L. Beauchamp with Nancy King, *History and Theory of Informed Consent* (New York: Oxford University Press, 1986).

2. For a brief and accessible presentation of the main arguments in favor of self-determination for the competent patient, see President's Commission for the Study of Ethical Problems in Medicine and Biomedical and Behavioral Research, *Making Health Care Decisions*, vol. 1 (Washington, D.C.: U.S. Government Printing Office, 1982), 42-51. For a critique of arguments that purport to justify physician's not observing the requirement of informed consent, see A. Buchanan, "Medical Paternalism," in *Paternalism*, ed. R.E. Sartorius (Minneapolis: University of Minnesota Press, 1983), 61-81.

3. The need for an explicit admonition to direct primary attention to the patient and to disregard or subordinate the interests of others has always been recognized in codes of medical ethics. In the current U.S. health care system, the need is, if anything, more urgent than in the past due to the rapid evolution of new forms of medical practice and reimbursement schemes in which the physician is subject to a complex array of incentives, and enmeshed in a number of different contractual relationships within an increasingly corporatized medicine. For an excellent discussion of codes of ethics, see R.M. Veatch, "Medical Ethics: An Introduction" in *Medical Ethics*, ed. R.M. Veatch (Boston: Jones and Bartlett, 1989), 1-26.

4. Buchanan, "Medical Paternalism."

5. A. Buchanan, "Medical Decisionmaking and Principle/Agent Theory," *Bioethics* 2 (1988):317-33.

6. An examination of relationships between ethical and efficiency evaluations is found in A. Buchanan, *Ethics, Efficiency, and the Market* (Totowa, N.J.: Rowman and Allanheld, 1985), chap. 1.

Discussion

Dr. Sass: I was intrigued by Dr. Buchanan's first point, the first part of the paper, on the interdependence of knowledge and duty. Normally, we think of particular professions as having specific knowledge, with medical knowledge being distinct from legal knowledge or engineering knowledge. But, if we look more precisely, a particular profession has various forms of knowledge. And one member of a particular profession may not be an expert in all areas; for example, a corporate lawyer may not be an expert in tort law. The same can be said for anesthesia and surgery in medicine and so on. What then is the specific relationship of duty and responsibility within professional interrelationships?

For example, how is the transfer of technical information accompanied by the transfer of values?

Dr. Buchanan: If you take seriously my proposal that what the professional's duty is and what the professional should be expected to know are interdependent, and you realize that there are many subspecialties within a particular profession, like the medical profession, then there may be different duties and different requirements of knowledge, depending upon the specialty.

Yet, these people are supposed to be working together and somehow, out of their interaction, within their own separate spheres of expertise and knowledge requirements, there is supposed to be a way of acting responsibly for the whole patient.

I think the case management approach has been one attempt to respond to this difficulty by assigning someone a kind of overall responsibility for integrating the activities of each of the players according to their own specialties and making sure that nothing falls between the cracks. There is some kind of overall duty of providing good continuous care to the patient, which might not be achieved if all were simply performing their own specific duties according to their own specialties and expertise.

I think that is an important issue. Most of us who have worked as consultants in medical ethics at the clinical level have probably

encountered cases where we have seen different professionals working together in specialties on a particular case. But their work was too
fragmented. Each had a conception of his own expertise and corresponding duties, but there was nothing linking it all together in an effective way, and there were communication problems among the specialists. There were things that would fall between the cracks.

I think the case management approach is a definite type of response to that, but that is only one example of a kind of division of labor or kind of temporary approach to these issues. And if the team approach is to be ethically responsible, there has to be an appropriate
division of ethical labor, that is, of specification of duties that correspond to the different technical activities and expertise of the players
on the team.

Dr. Sass: The divisions of duty and responsibility have to be reconciled. Someone has to be made the chairman or the chief in communication with the patient, in getting a product developed, or doing a
legal case.

Dr. Buchanan: I think we have a kind of hangover of the exceptional physician role that goes back to an earlier period, where the
whole medical approach was not a team approach. We have to adjust
our whole idea of physicians' duties and responsibilities to fit this
new team approach.

Dr. Pellegrino: I would like to raise another issue: the distinction
between the notions of guild and profession, as far as medicine is concerned. One interpretation of the Hippocratic Oath is that it is a combination of a guild statement, seen in the preamble, and then a professional statement, going back to the original meaning of the word: a
declaration.

The first part emphasizes the medical fraternity. In those days the
fraternity of physicians was a secret organization whose function was
to protect the art, that is to say, the knowledge of the art, so that it
could be transmitted among those who were admitted to the
brotherhood.

The first part, the preamble of the Hippocratic Oath, has not been
commented on very much, but it has some interesting implications. It
implies the notion of the guild whose function is to protect the craft
and its quality and to do so by admitting into it only those persons
worthy of admission, those who really had a relationship of son to father with their teachers.

The second part of the oath is an act of profession, a declaration of the imposition on oneself of certain obligations. The connection between the two parts historically is not easy to establish. They may not have been part of the same document in the first place.

I would say the important part of the profession is its attention to the one served rather than the protection of the craft.

Dr. Buchanan: But these things are related; the reason to protect the craft is because of its effect on people.

Dr. Pellegrino: Historically, that is not the case. You see, most of the early Greek physicians were not professionals in the sense we are talking about today. They clearly were craftsmen. And they were craftsmen who had as their ethos, being able to have a good reputation, being able to be kindly. Philanthropy was not the love of mankind. Philanthropia was sufficient kindness to the patient to enable you to maintain a practice. It was quite self-serving. The Greek physician was not the noble creature that comes out of the Pythagorean philosophy of the second part of the oath.

So, in terms of the profession/guild division, physicians first were a guild. They became a profession when Thomas Latimer established the Royal College of Physicians, which added to the craft concept of the guild this notion of a set of responsibilities.

I also want to say something about case management. Whoever or whatever should be the case manager, the role is absolutely essential. Many of us think today that that is what we are trying to maintain or resuscitate. I think that there is no question you need a synthesizer. You need a *primus inter pares*.

The more you have team care, the more you have the need for someone who can be the patient's advocate on that team because one of the functions that is very badly needed is that of the critic of the specialists. There is a great tendency to believe that because someone is a medical specialist his or her recommendation, which might be medically correct, is the right and good decision for the patient. I think therefore, that "generalist" might be a better term than case manager.

Dr. Brock: Dr. Sass asked whether we consider a group like the AMA a special interest group or a special responsibility group. It seems to me that the answer to that question has to be both.

If you take a thought experiment on whether we want to make this group self-regulating, or whether we want to construct various institutional mechanisms and designs to regulate it, the answer, again, seems to be obvious. Namely, that we would want to use both components of both of these alternatives. The only implication I would stress is that it is a mistake to object to proposals to do one or the other. Clearly, we want both of those things.

Dr. Buchanan: I agree. I really think it is a matter of degree as to how much self-regulation is appropriate and how much autonomy is appropriate for the group.

I want to emphasize something that is actually implied in a paper that Dr. Brock wrote some time ago: the question of the extent to which we should rely upon internal norms for self-regulation and to what extent we should rely upon institutional arrangements to complement those internal norms. These are not questions that can be answered by trotting out some alleged list of basic rights of physicians, or of any other profession.

It is not the question of basic rights of that group at all. There is no such thing as a basic liberty of the medical profession to practice in a fee-for-service system, for example. And if there is any argument for a legal right to do that, the argument is quite complex and has to proceed from many considerations of both social utility and justice, as well as considerations about what risk one wants to take in giving certain powers to government versus giving groups internal control.

Dr. Freidson: I would like to elaborate a little bit on what Dr. Pellegrino said. If I recall correctly, guilds were frequently called mysteries and their knowledge, in fact, was proprietary. Members were to divulge it to nobody; it was owned by the guild, as it were. That is analogous to what is happening here in the United States, and perhaps even more so in Japan, where the chemists or the scientists in industry produce knowledge that is owned as a trade secret by industry. Then they patent it, and it becomes proprietary.

This is directly contrary to at least the ideal of the modern profession in which knowledge is supposed to be for everyone, and it is not a mystery except insofar as one has to go to school to learn it. But anyone, in theory, can go to school and learn it. It is not privately owned for the benefit of the profession itself.

From an ethical point of view, at least as I, a sociologist, think of ethics, which is not the way a philosopher thinks of ethics, this is a significant distinction.

Dr. Gorovitz: A small comment on Dr. Pellegrino's remark about the need for someone to be a case manager or a patient advocate, a critic of the specialists. My only concern is that those are quite distinct functions and what patient advocates do sometimes serves as a counterbalance against the case manager. I am not sure that one can ever successfully combine all of these roles in a single individual because they are quite different and are sometimes explicitly separated.

Dr. Pellegrino: But they are not mutually exclusive.

Dr. Buchanan: They can be in particular cases.

Dr. Pellegrino: They can be, but they need not be. I have no problem with a patient advocate whose responsibility is to be there when this process fails, when the patient feels ill-treated, badly treated. I believe that is an important role. That role should be independent of the physician's, clearly. But, on the other hand, when I use the term "advocate," I am proposing someone who will stand against, if you will, all of the array of specialists and others who are saying do this, do that, and do the other thing and say, Well, now, you asked me to be your personal representative.

The patient is free to enter that agreement or leave it. But, in teaching, my greatest problem is dealing with the house staff officer's willingness to accept anything a specialist says.

Dr. Buchanan: I would prefer a sort of political analogy here, checks and balances. I am not sure there is one person being given all these responsibilities. Sometimes, the hospital ethics committee will do it and sometimes the patient advocate will. Sometimes, the patient advocate and the hospital ethics committee will do it working together. Sometimes, a person is technically designated as the case manager. Sometimes, the primary physician acts to fend off the specialists in their zeal to do whatever they think is appropriate.

In most cases, it will not be important that there be an ultimate arbiter, a sovereign, to use the analogy, who can be a tie-breaker in the last court of appeal.

In principle, there needs to be some way of resolving potential conflicts, but that is not to say that that person with the ultimate power should be actively involved in those cases. Instead, there should be a kind of consensus that emerges from the interplay on a number of different forces. I like the checks and balances idea better than a single person trying to combine all of these features.

Dr. Pellegrino: How about saying the patient is the ultimate arbiter? But by this, I do not mean that the patient reaches a decision in isolation.

DAN W. BROCK

Facts and Values in the Physician-Patient Relationship

I. Introduction

Probably no other profession has given as much attention as has medicine to the relation of facts and values in professional relations. Thus, in order to focus my inquiry, I will confine my attention here to facts and values in the physician-patient relationship, with the hope that what I have to say will have at least some interest and relevance for other professions. A common ideal in medical ethics for the physician-patient relationship involves shared treatment decision making, with a division of labor between physician and patient.[1] Most simply put, the physician's role is to use his or her training, knowledge, and experience to provide the facts to the patient about the patient's diagnosis and prognoses if alternative treatments, or the alternative of no treatment, are pursued. The patient's role in this division of labor is to provide the values, his or her own conception of the good, with which to evaluate these alternatives and to select the one that is best for himself or herself. As a rough guide to practice, this is a reasonable conception that is likely, most of the time, to produce sound treatment decisions. Nevertheless, as an ideal, it is too simplistic and subject to several challenges that I will explore here.

Some challenges are to the account of the *physician's* role. This facts/values division of labor seems to assume that the physician can and should provide the facts about treatment alternatives in a value-neutral form, but some have questioned whether the sciences themselves on which medicine is based are or can be value free. More-over, the concepts of health and disease, and of the normal and patho-logical, in terms of which the fundamental aims of medicine are com-monly defined are held by many to be value laden. But even if it is possible for physicians to provide only value-neutral facts in the pro-cess of shared decision making with the patient, should their role be restricted in this way?

Other challenges that I will present in the paper are to the role giv-en the *patient* in this facts/values division of labor as provider of the values for the evaluation of the different treatment alternatives. One defense of this role for patients is based on the claim that physicians are not in a position reliably to know what is in a patient's best inter-ests. This issue is explored by Allen Buchanan in another paper in this volume. I believe at least as influential, even if often not explicitly stat-ed, in the assignment of the role of values-provider only to the patient is an extreme subjectivism about values according to which a patient's own ultimate values that define his or her own conception of the good are thought to be incorrigible. In the standard case in which treatment is pursued for the patient's benefit, this extreme subjectivism about values is thought to support the patient's values guiding treatment de-cision making and treatment. I shall explore this incorrigibility claim for the patient's ultimate values as defining the patient's good and will argue that on each of the main philosophical conceptions of the good for persons it is indefensible and should not be the basis for shared treatment decision making.

Underlying this view of the physician-patient division of labor are assumptions and beliefs about the nature and relation of facts and val-ues, and science and ethics, that are , in significant part, the legacy of a logical positivism that has long since been rejected by most philoso-phers. It is time that these unstable foundations for our normative ideal of the physician-patient relation were finally removed and re-placed with more defensible underpinnings.

II. Two Models of the Physician-Patient Relationship

Positivists insisted on a relatively sharp distinction between descrip-tive or empirical claims and science, on the one hand, and evaluative claims and ethics, on the other.[2] Descriptive statements and the claims of science were to be true or false according to whether they in fact cor-rectly described and explained the world. By remaining properly de-scriptive or empirical, science could, at least in principle, be entirely value neutral or value free. In its more extreme versions, positivism held that ethical judgments lacked cognitive content, but were instead expressions of emotions or attitudes, and as such could be neither true nor false, correct nor mistaken. Because no evaluative statements were held to be logically entailed by any descriptive or empirical statements, moral reasoning was thought to be properly understood not as reasoning but as attempts at nonrational persuasion.[3] Many drew from this an extreme subjectivism in ethics along the lines of what I have called above the incorrigibility thesis—there is no meaningful sense in which an individual's ultimate values defining his or her own conception of the good life could be mistaken, false, or unfounded.

These positivist views, and in particular this extreme subjectivism about values, are in need, at the very least, of substantial qualification and revision. They did, however, contribute to one extremely important and beneficial historical change in medicine, and specifically in ideals of the physician-patient relation. It is a commonplace of the history of medicine in this century that until roughly the last two decades the physician-patient relationship could be characterized as authoritarian or paternalistic. Moreover, this was the generally accepted normative ideal for that relationship, not just a reality that failed to measure up to the ideal. Physicians, because of their medical training, knowledge, and experience, were seen as the experts on what treatment would be best for a particular patient. Medical treatment decision making, in this account, was thus appropriately left in the hands of physicians who would use their expertise to determine what treatment was medically indicated for their patients. Patients had no significant role in decision making about their treatment. Instead, their role was largely passive—to follow "doctor's orders"—and so patients needed only the information necessary to ensure their compliance with treatment, but not to enable them to participate in treatment decisions. The positivists' insistence on the distinctions between facts and values, and science and ethics, contributed to the eventual erosion of the physician's claim to a virtual monopoly on treatment decision-making expertise and authority. Positivism thus contributed significantly to a substantial reduction in unjustified paternalistic action by physicians on behalf of patients.[4]

A few critics of the paternalist model of physician-patient relations would turn it on its head and give patients sole decision-making authority, with the physician's role now to carry out the patient's (or surrogate's, in the case of incompetent patients) orders for treatment. One author labeled this account "physician as body mechanic," with the physician the one to whom we bring ourselves in for whatever repairs we desire.[5] Robert Veatch some years ago labeled this the engineer model of the physician's role—the physician is the technical expert who knows what can be done to or for the patient and who is trained to carry out the various procedures.[6] The physician's job is to provide just what the patient orders in this revision of "doctor's orders."

This ideal of physician-patient relations has few defenders, though the positivist legacy provides it with more support that is often thought. Two main considerations have been paramount in the rejection of this consumer sovereignty model. First, it fails to take account of the reality of sick patients who are often fearful and anxious, suffering the physical and psychological effects of their illness, and deeply desirous of putting their treatment in the hands of health care professionals they can trust.[7] Many patients' ordinary decision-making capacities are substantially diminished by serious illness. And even when a patient's usual decision-making capacities remain intact, the enormous expansion of medical science, knowledge, training, technology, and treatment capacity would seem to leave the average patient ill-equipped to make decisions about his or her own health care. Second, this consumer sovereignty model fails to acknowledge physicians as independent agents with professional and moral commitments that limit the extent to which they should simply respond to and serve patients' wishes or desires.

As noted earlier, the account of ideal physician-patient relations that has, in fact, largely replaced the paternalistic or authoritarian model is often characterized as "shared decision making." In this account, both physicians and patients have essential roles in ideal treatment decision making. Physicians are to use their knowledge, training, and expertise to provide their patients with a diagnosis and a prognosis if no treatment is undertaken, together with information about alternative treatments that might improve prognosis, including the risks and benefits and attendant uncertainties of treatment alternatives. Patients articulate their own aims, preferences, and values in order to evaluate which alternative is best for them. Uninformed patient choices or consents will lead to decisions that fail to serve patient interests—thus, the need for physician participation. Decisions guided by physician values will fail to reflect patients' own conceptions of their good and thus fail to respect patients' self-determination interest in making important decisions about their lives for themselves—thus, the need for patient participation.

While shared decision making is an ultimately sound ideal, a simple physician-patient division of labor between facts and values cannot be plausibly maintained. One difficulty is that it appears ultimately still to leave physicians' actions fully under the direction of patients.

No more than the consumer sovereignty model does it recognize physicians as independent agents, with moral and professional commitments that can appropriately limit their actions in the service of a patient's aims and values. A second difficulty is the assumption that, in principle, facts and values can always be distinguished, and in practice can be sufficiently distinguished to permit the physician-patient division of labor.

A third difficulty with the facts/values division of labor is that it assumes that the patient's own ultimate values or account of the good is correct and so must be accepted and respected by the physician, whatever its content. One reason for that acceptance is thought to lie in what I have called the extreme subjectivity of values—if a patient's conception of his or her own good cannot be false or mistaken, and cannot be logically incompatible with any facts, then there is no basis for rejection of it as incorrect, false, or unfounded. (Nor is there any basis for accepting it as correct, true, or well founded, a point commonly overlooked by extreme subjectivists.) Of course, it will be acknowledged that patients can be, and often are, mistaken about factual matters concerning their good in a number of ways. They can be mistaken about what will or will not, in fact, lead to some valued state of affairs, for example, what treatment will produce a desired or valued outcome. They can be mistaken about how they may adjust to a particular treatment outcome over time, and how they may come to find satisfaction in new activities and pursuits. But what patients cannot be mistaken about, in this account, are the ultimate values that define their conception of the good or their life plan. These values are thought to be isolated from corrigibility by the extreme subjectivity of values.

III. The Incorrigibility Thesis and the Patient as Values-Provider
A. Incorrigibility vs. Self-Determination

Now some will quite rightly argue that a different reason underlies physicians' acceptance of patients' own values or conceptions of their good in shared treatment decision making. In fact, the most common explicit reason offered for accepting patient choices about treatment, as reflected in the doctrine of informed consent both within the law and medical ethics, is that doing so respects patients' self-determination or autonomy. Self-determination is not just important when patients are choosing wisely, but it also protects at least some bad or defective choices. The right to self-determination includes at least some right to make mistakes in choosing our own life path, and so it can be the importance of patients' self-determination, not the incorrigibility of their values and conceptions of their own good, that undergirds the facts/values division of labor and respecting patients' choices in shared treatment decision making. This appeal to self-determination is correct in the sense that persons commonly do value making important decisions about their lives for themselves, even in some circumstances in which they may grant that others might be able to decide for them better than they themselves can, even as judged by their own values. Making such decisions for ourselves is a way in which, for better or worse, we take responsibility and control over our lives.

The importance of self-determination requires that physicians nearly always respect the voluntary and informed treatment choices of competent patients. But it is of fundamental importance to distinguish two issues: one, whether competent patients can be mistaken in their conception of their own good and in the ultimate values that define that conception, and two, whether others, including physicians, should paternalistically interfere with or set aside a patient's treatment choices if and when they are mistaken. The importance of self-determination bears only on the latter issue, not the former. And even if personal self-determination should nearly always bar paternalistic interference, it is important for the ideal of shared decision making whether the extreme subjectivity of values, with its implication of the incorrigibility of patients' ultimate values, is correct. If it is, then the physician's role in shared decision making would seem to be restricted to providing the facts necessary to determining which treatment, if any, will best serve the patient's values. With respect to the patient's values themselves, the physician's role would seem at most to be to seek to discern what the patient's values are (thus, the talk in some quarters that replaces moral reasoning with "values clarification") so as to help ensure that treatment choices serve those values.

This still seems closer to the consumer sovereignty model than to a model of shared decision making that acknowledges the physician as an independent moral and professional agent. At least as important is the failure to differentiate the issue of the corrigibility of a person's own conception of his or her good from the issue of whether the importance of self-determination largely bars paternalistic interference by physicians. When these two issues are not kept distinct, but are instead conflated, the quite reasonable rejection by physicians of patients' incorrigibility about their good can mistakenly lead them to infer that paternalistic interference with their patients' competent decisions about treatment is thereby warranted.

B. Incorrigibility Based on Metaethical Subjectivism

The champions of individual self-determination, then, are at least correct that it provides an alternative basis for a presumption for ultimate deference to patients' choices in shared treatment decision making. But we need to examine more directly and critically the claim that a person's ultimate values and conception of the good are incorrigible. I believe this claim should not be accepted, however natural and even obvious it might seem to many. Two versions of this extreme subjectivity of values need to be distinguished and discussed separately— what I will call meta-ethical subjectivity and normative subjectivity. Until recently, with the revival of interest among philosophers in moral realism, much meta-ethical concern focused on the problem of the justification of moral judgments.[8] If epistemological intuitionism in ethics of the sort associated with Moore, Prichard, and Ross had proved defensible, then the problem of justification would have been "solved" by our faculty of ethical intuition together with the truth of the ethical propositions that it guaranteed. For a variety of reasons, well known at least to philosophers, intuitionism and the ethical truth it was supposed to certify have been widely rejected. The alternative of ethical naturalism, too, came under a variety of widespread criticisms in the 1950s and 1960s because it seemed to leave out the evaluative content of ethical discourse and because appeal to naturalistic definitions seemed too slim a reed on which to rest the entire enterprise of justification in ethics.[9] Both ethical intuitionism and naturalism are cognitivist accounts of ethical judgments according to which those judgments as well as ethical concepts have truth values that are usually explicated in terms of correspondence theories of meaning and truth.

The current conventional philosophical view of justification in ethics acknowledges that ethical judgments do express attitudes, as the positivists had it, but also that they have substantial cognitive content and are backed by reasons which make them capable of support and admitting of reasoned argument. In this view, justification is usually developed along coherentist lines with one or another version of John Rawls's "reflective equilibrium" at the heart of the account.[10] A moral judgment is justified if it survives a critical screening process for reaching wide reflective equilibrium among all of a person's moral judgments. In coherence accounts of the justification of patients' evaluative judgments about their own well-being or good, these judgments are subjective in the sense that they are justified just in case and to the extent that they survive the process of reaching reflective equilibrium by that person. That process, however, is a complex one, the details of which cannot be explored here. Suffice it to say that there are many places in that process at which a person's initial moral judgments may undergo revision and correction. No plausible coherentist view gives any reason for physicians confronting treatment choices with patients to accept as incorrigible patients' judgments about their good, or even the ultimate values by which patients define their good. Incorrigibility is never achievable for moral judgments since the best that individuals can hope for is to reach wide reflective equilibrium in their moral judgments at a particular point in time.[11] There is no assurance that new experience, considerations, or arguments may not in the future upset that equilibrium and cause some of the moral judgments it encompasses to be revised. Coherence accounts of justification in morality do make justified moral judgments ultimately subjective in the sense that the moral judgments that are justified for a particular person are the judgments that person makes in reflective equilibrium. Since reflective equilibrium is only an ideal at which a person can aim rather than a state one could be assured of being in before considering a significant ethical choice, there is never reason to assume at the outset of shared decision making that the relevant values a patient brings to that decision making are maximally justified for him or her in having survived reflective equilibrium.

C. Incorrigibility Based on Normative Subjectivism

It is important to distinguish this meta-ethical subjectivism concerning the epistemic status of a person's judgments about his or her good or well-being from normative subjectivism about those judgments. By normative subjectivism of moral or value judgments about the good for persons, I mean the view that what is valuable or good for a person consists entirely in or depends importantly on contingent psychological facts about that person, such as what makes him or her happy or what he or she desires.[12] Normative subjectivism about value is also thought to provide support for the facts/values division of labor in shared decision making with patients supplying the values or conceptions of their good or well-being for evaluation of treatment alternatives. However, there are at least two serious difficulties in this use of normative subjectivism about value or the good. First, even leading subjective conceptions of individual good or well-being do not make a patient's evaluation of treatment alternatives incorrigible. Second, the most plausible theory of value or the good for persons is not fully subjective. Both of these difficulties can be brought out by considering briefly three broad alternative theories of the good for persons commonly distinguished in the philosophical literature— what I will call hedonist, preference satisfaction, and ideal theories of a good life.[13] Hedonist and preference theories are normatively subjective; ideal theories contain normatively objective components.

1. *Hedonist Theories of the Good for Persons.* What is common to hedonist theories is that they take the ultimate good for persons to be certain kinds of conscious experiences. The particular kinds of conscious experiences are variously characterized as pleasure, happiness, or the satisfaction or enjoyment that typically accompanies the successful pursuit of our aims and desires. Particular states of the person that do not make reference to conscious experience, such as having diseased or healthy lungs, and particular activities of the person, such as studying philosophy or playing tennis, are a part of a good life in this view only to the extent that they produce the valuable conscious experience. Hedonist views have been widely rejected for failing in serious ways to match most persons' considered moral judgments about a good life.[14] Nevertheless, even if a subjective hedonist view of the good were correct, it would not justify an uncritical acceptance of the values a patient brings to shared decision making. Persons are often mistaken about what will bring them pleasure or make them happy and others are often in a better position to determine this. No incorrigibility assumption about the patient's evaluation of treatment alternatives is justified on hedonist theories of the good.

2. *Preference Satisfaction Theories of the Good for Persons.* Preference satisfaction theories take a good life for persons to consist in the satisfaction of their desires or preferences. Desires or preferences have objects and are satisfied when their objects are realized; for example, my desire to see the sunrise tomorrow is satisfied just in case I see the sunrise tomorrow. This is to be distinguished from any feelings of satisfaction or pleasure, understood as a conscious experience of mine, that I may experience if I see the sunrise tomorrow. The difference is clearest in cases in which the object of my desire is not an experience of mine and so my desire can be satisfied, but I either do not or could not know that it is and so receive no feelings of pleasure or satisfaction from getting what I desire. Preference theories share a subjectivity with hedonist theories since they make a person's good depend ultimately on what that particular individual desires or prefers.

Nevertheless, just as with hedonist theories, preference theories of the good for persons do not support any assumption of patient incorrigibility in the evaluation of treatment alternatives. In this theory, what is good for persons is what they desire for its own sake, which I will call their basic desires, as opposed to what they desire only as instrumental, or as means, to the satisfaction of their basic desires. It might seem that patients' basic desires are incorrigible, though, of course, patients can be mistaken about the factual question of what courses of treatment will best satisfy those basic desires. But a person's basic desires would incorrigibly determine his or her good on a preference theory of the good only if that theory defined a person's good solely by that person's *actual* basic desires. No defender of the preference theory, however, defends it in this form. For preference satisfaction theories of the good for persons to be at all plausible, they must allow for some correcting or "laundering" of a person's actual preferences.[15] The most obvious example is the need to correct for misinformed preferences; for example, a person's desire for a particular treatment based on a false belief about his or her medical condition. But apparently basic desires or preferences will sometimes require correction as well; for example, a preference to avoid medical care deriving from a frightening experience in a hospital as a young child. Corrected preference theories of the good for persons are difficult to evaluate decisively because what corrections should be made to actual preferences is controversial. Nevertheless, the need for corrections of preferences makes clear that even the basic desires or preferences patients express in treatment decision making have no claim to incorrigibility in defining their good until they have either been corrected or it has been determined that they need no correction.

3. Ideal Theories of the Good for Persons. We have seen that even in normatively subjective hedonist and preference theories of the good for persons, no presumption in shared decision making that patients' values are incorrigible is warranted. The second difficulty with appeal to hedonist or preference theories to support normative subjectivity and the facts/values division of labor in shared decision making is that neither a hedonist nor a preference theory is the most plausible theory of the good for persons. Ideal theories hold that at least part of a good life consists neither of any conscious experience of a broadly hedonist sort nor of the satisfaction of the person's corrected preferences or desires, but instead consists of the realization of specific ideals of the person, including possession of certain virtues and character traits. For example, many have held that one important component of a good life consists in being a self-determined or autonomous agent, and that this is part of a good life for a person even if he or she is neither happier as a result nor desires to be autonomous. Ideal theories will differ both in the specific ideals, virtues, and character traits the theories endorse, and in the relative place they give to happiness and preference satisfaction in their full account of the good for persons. Ideal theories are normatively objective, or at least contain objective components, in the sense that they hold a good life for a person to be, at least in part, objectively determined by the correct or justified ideals of the good life, independent of the psychological states of the person.

The most plausible theory about the good for persons, and the theory that best fits the considered moral judgments of most members of our society, is an ideal theory, though there is not space here adequately to develop, much less defend, these claims. But I want to say enough about this conception of the good to make at least its broad outlines clear and to show its relation to the incorrigibility thesis and the division of labor assignment of values to the patient. One fundamental ideal is the exercise of a person's capacity as a valuing agent, what I have called self-determination. This ideal is central in a good life in the sense that it organizes and determines many other important components of a theory of the good for persons. The exercise of self-determination in constructing a relatively full human life will require in an individual what I have called elsewhere primary functional capacities.[16] By primary functions I mean human functions that are necessary for, or at least valuable in, the pursuit of nearly all relatively full and complete human life plans and lives. There are four broad types of primary functions: biologic, for example, well-functioning organs; physical, for example, mobility; mental, for example, a variety of reasoning and emotional capabilities; social, for example, the ability to communicate. There are not sharp boundaries between these broad types of primary functions, and they can be specified in different ways. The important point for my purposes here is that in an ideal theory, they are normatively objective components of a good life. Their value does not depend on contingent psychological facts about a particular person, though their relative weight within any particular life may be in part subjectively determined in this way.

Besides primary functions, there are what I call agent-specific functions, again specifiable at varying levels of generality and detail, which are necessary for a person to pursue successfully the particular purposes and life plan he or she has chosen; for example, the capacity to do highly abstract reasoning required in mathematics or the physical dexterity necessary to a musician. The relative values of these functions can vary widely among persons and will depend on the particular life plan chosen by the person in question. Because of their role in making possible a significant range of opportunities and alternatives for choice, primary and agent-specific functions are both necessary in an account of the good life that gives centrality to the valuing and choosing agent.

At an even more agent-relative level are the particular desires pursued by particular persons on particular occasions in their valued aims and activities. These will be more subjective still in their dependence on the specific aims of a particular person. As one moves from primary functions to agent-specific functions to agent-specific desires, one simultaneously moves across a continuum of objectivity to subjectivity in the normative content of a person's good. Also at the subjective end is the final important component of the good for persons—the hedonic or happiness component of a good life: that aspect which represents a person's subjective, conscious response, in terms of enjoyments and satisfactions, to the life he or she has chosen and the activities and achievements it contains. The happiness component is subjective both because different things make different persons happy and also because reasonable persons can and do disagree about the relative importance of happiness in a good life.

The importance of what I have called the objective-subjective continuum in a full ideal theory of the good for persons is that it explains why the incorrigibility thesis regarding the patient's values is mistaken at the objective end of the continuum and why that thesis becomes increasingly more plausible as one moves to the subjective end of that continuum. The more the patient's values and choices in shared decision making appear to be in conflict with his or her objective good, that is, ideals and functions at the objective end of the continuum, the stronger the case for the physician being an advocate for those ideals and functions and seeking to insure that the patient's values and choices do not, in fact, conflict with them. This is not to say that the physician should ride roughshod over a patient's values and choices that appear in conflict with his or her objective good. As already noted, the importance of self-determination for a competent patient militates strongly against doing that. However, it is to say that the incorrigibility thesis about the patient's ultimate values is mistaken and cannot justify any sharp division of labor between physician and patient along facts/values lines. If physicians and patients are exploring alternative treatments when the selection of treatment is genuinely problematic, it is a mistake to believe that the only appropriate role for the physician is the delivery of facts. On the contrary, the physician can have a responsibility to explore, together with the patient, the values by which alternatives should be evaluated and, if necessary, to help in a joint process of critical reflection on those values. Proponents of shared treatment decision making should not defend it with appeal to the incorrigibility of the patient's values. Physicians are rightly skeptical of that appeal and it can unnecessarily undermine instead of strengthen shared decision making by resting it on unsound foundations. It is personal self-determination, not incorrigibility regarding the ultimate values that define one's good, that is the central foundation of ultimate deference to competent patients' choices in shared decision making.

IV. The Physician as Facts-Provider

The other side of the division of labor in shared decision making assigns to the physician the role of gatherer and presenter of facts regarding the patient's diagnosis and prognosis with alternative treatments. The aim is to place the physician in a value-neutral role so as to leave the evaluation of alternatives to the patient and the patient's values. One central reason for this is the extreme subjectivism about values or, in other words, the incorrigibility thesis. I have argued that that thesis, in both its meta-ethical and normative ethical versions, is mistaken. As a result, physicians sometimes should play an active role in a collaborative process with patients in examining and assessing the values that will guide treatment choice. Nevertheless, what of the role that the division of labor assigns to the physician as provider of the facts about diagnosis and prognosis? Can that role be value neutral? Or, instead, does it, or must it, carry value and ethical commitments?

Several versions of the claim of value neutrality for the physician's role should be distinguished, each of which raises different issues. The first version concerns whether *in practice* it is possible for physicians to provide to patients the information relevant to treatment decision making in a value-neutral form. There are a number of ways in which physicians can and do fail to achieve this value neutrality in practice. First, the language they use to describe treatment alternatives may itself be in part evaluative: for example, when a family is told that continued treatment will only prolong the patient's suffering, the suffering is presented as bad for the patient. Second, even when the language used is ostensibly value neutral, physicians may convey in a host of other ways, such as body language, tone of voice, and emphasis in presenting information, their own positive or negative evaluation of various alternatives. Third, physicians nearly always couple the process of informing the patient about treatment alternatives with a recommendation that a particular alternative be pursued. Moreover, providing a recommendation is not simply an unfortunate slip from the role of value-neutral information provider, but is understood by both physician and patient as a proper and important part of the physician's professional role and responsibility. For a variety of well-known reasons, sick patients are often extremely vulnerable to being strongly influenced by these treatment recommendations. Fourth, physicians commonly see a part of their role as securing patient compliance with the treatment that has been decided on and the means to securing compliance often involve physicians acting as strong advocates for the treatment. Fifth, since it is never possible in practice to provide all possibly relevant facts about treatment alternatives, a value judgment must always be made about which facts are most important.

For evaluating actual professional relations between physicians and patients, and the roles of facts and values in those relations, the respects in which physicians commonly fail in practice to conform to a value-neutral role are probably of greatest importance. However, the facts/values division of labor might still be defended by maintaining that at least *in principle* physicians can and should maintain the role of value-neutral facts provider, even if in practice they often fail to do so. There are several different levels at which the very possibility and/or desirability, even in principle, of the value neutrality of physicians can be challenged. The first level is in the most basic scientific theories of physical chemistry and biological science on which medical science builds. Is theory choice at this level fully determined by the facts about the world, as a simple empiricist view would have it, or is theory choice not fully determined by the world and so inevitably influenced by values, whether they be scientific values or broader social values? In what sense, if any, are the concepts employed in these scientific theories value free or do they carry value commitments? Is the truth of major alternative scientific theories and paradigms, and changes in them over time, dictated solely by facts about the world or are such alternatives instead incommensurable and dictated in part by values and other noncognitive factors? These questions raise extremely complex scientific, philosophical, and historical issues in the philosophy of science. There is no consensus on what is the correct view, although few defend a simplistic empiricism according to which science and scientific theory are fully governed by a value-free and concept-neutral world and data. But this is not the level at which the physician's role most clearly embodies value commitments and so I will set these basic issues in the philosophy of science aside. Even if basic physical chemistry and biological science are in some significant sense value neutral and value free, that still leaves us a far distance from the conclusion that the physician's role in shared decision making is, or could be, value neutral.

Let me make a relatively crude distinction between the basic physical and biological sciences on which medicine builds and medical science itself. It is fairly widely agreed that medical science is concerned, in the most general terms, with health and disease, or the normal and pathological, in human beings. There has been considerable debate in the philosophy of medicine about whether the concepts of "health" and "disease" are value-free empirical or factual concepts, or whether instead the determination of the healthy and diseased inevitably and ineliminably involves appeal to certain values or value judgments. Defenders of a naturalistic, value-free account of health and disease like Christopher Boorse and Leon Kass generally appeal to an understanding of health and disease in terms of normal and abnormal function of the organism.[17] Taking disease in an organism to be roughly equivalent to the pathological, Boorse argues: "the essence of the pathological is *statistically species-subnormal part-function*, or more carefully: A condition of a part or process in an organism is *pathological* when the ability of the part or process to perform one or more of its species-typical biological functions falls below some central range of statistical distribution for that ability in corresponding parts or processes in members of an appropriate reference class of the species."[18] Functions of an organ, in turn, can be understood as "its species typical causal contributions to the organism's survival and reproduction."[19]

Critics of this view hold that the classification of a particular condition as healthy or diseased is not determined solely by functional, biological facts in nature, but requires imposing a value judgment on facts about conditions and functions.[20] In this view, diseases are not simply deviations from species-typical functions, but are deviations that are judged *bad* for the organism. These critics point to admittedly extreme historical examples in which masturbation, desires of slaves to run away from their owners, and homosexuality have been classified as diseases on the basis of an evaluation of these practices, desires, and conditions as bad for their possessors.[21] In this view, the classification of homosexuality as a disease reflected a negative social evaluation of the condition. The removal of it from the classification of diseases by the American Psychiatric Association resulted from an ethical and political challenge to its negative evaluation, not from the discovery of any new scientific facts.[22] Even in more common everyday cases of disease, it is argued, mere deviation from normal function does not entail disease when the deviation is in a positive direction or has a positive effect on the organism's function. Moreover, normal function is not just statistically normal function, but valued function, and concerns more than just survival and reproduction.

If determination of what constitutes well-functioning requires, at least implicitly, appeal to value judgments, and may vary in different social contexts and historical periods, then "health" and "disease" seem not to be value-free concepts. The import of this debate for the understanding of the physician's role in the division of labor of shared decision making should be evident. If the physician's role is to determine and communicate to the patient whether the patient is diseased and what treatments of that disease are possible, the physician could not do this in a value-free way if what are diseases themselves are not value-free scientific determinations. If, instead, a particular condition is only classified as a disease in part on the basis of the evaluation of it as bad for those who have it, then provision of information to a patient about his or her diseased condition implicitly invokes and carries with it the value judgment about its badness.

Whether or not the concepts of "health" and "disease" are themselves value neutral, physicians commonly do understand themselves, in their role as medical professionals, as committed to preserving, promoting, and restoring health, and preventing and treating disease. Because the professional commitment of physicians includes a central commitment to the value of health and the disvalue of disease (even if it is possible to understand "health" and "disease" themselves in value-neutral terms), physicians cannot be understood simply as value-neutral providers of the facts. Their provision of the facts must be understood as in the service of the value of their patients' health. Moreover, this is not simply an unfortunate deviation by physicians from the ideal of value neutrality. The role of advocate for their patients' health is a central part of common ideals for physician-patient relations and treatment decision making.

More generally, the professional understanding of the role of physician is substantially defined by *ethical* commitments which are, to a significant degree, special to medicine and not found in other social and commercial relations. Unlike commercial relations in which profit maximization is accepted as a proper motivation, the professional ethos of physicians requires that the interests of their patients must first and foremost guide physicians' behavior. This altruistic commitment of physicians to their patients' interests, and the concomitant setting aside of the interests of all others, including their own, is perhaps the most striking defining norm of medicine. The requirement of gaining the patient's informed consent for treatment likewise adds to the commitment to the patient's health and well-being, the ethical commitment to respect the patient's self-determination. The requirement to be truthful with and not to lie to patients about their medical conditions and treatment is a further ethical commitment that sets the medical profession apart from most other social and commercial relations. The point is not that we don't expect any truthfulness elsewhere, but that the *strength* of the physician's ethical commitment to truthfulness with his or her patients is relatively unique. Related to truthfulness is a very strong requirement of confidentiality governing information provided by the patient to the physician; this too must be seen as an ethical commitment contributing to the defining norms of what it is to be a physician. Finally, there are professional norms of medicine governing access to health care. Access to at least basic health care should not be determined by ability to pay, but should be determined by medical need. Of course, all of these ethical norms are far more complex and controversial than the simple formulation I have given them here would indicate. It should also go without saying that all physicians do not always live up to and act in accordance with all of these professional norms. The point is rather that physicians commonly understand what it is to be a physician as entailing a commitment to a related and coherent body of ethical norms and that the profession judges itself and asks others to judge it in part by these ethical norms. These norms give substance to the general ethos of the medical profession as a "high calling." An ethically driven calling must be understood as serving an important good, and not entirely ethically neutral about the results of the practice of the profession. That important good is health, seen as ultimately in the service of the patient's well-being.

Now it might be argued that this ethically defined role of physician still requires physicians to attempt as much as possible to be value-neutral presenters of the facts to patients in treatment decision making. The ethical definition of the role of physician might itself require striving for value neutrality. But I think that cannot be correct. The various ethical commitments that I have suggested substantially define the physician's role do not make sense except as in the service of important values. The central value, I have indicated, is health, seen as ultimately in the service of the patient's well-being. To say that the value is "health, ultimately in the service of the patient's well-being," is to underline that the medical intervention best for a particular patient need not always be what is best for other patients with similar medical conditions. As noted earlier, different human functionings that are a part of the good for persons fall at different points on an objective-subjective continuum. The more subjective the value of the functioning affected, the more advocating for patients' health is perfectly compatible with, indeed requires, a recognition that treatment that best serves "health, ultimately in the service of the patient's well-being," may differ for different patients suffering from the same disease.

I believe physicians are correct to see themselves as advocates for their patients' health. This advocacy, however, must be seen as limited by respect for the self-determination of competent patients. It is this interest of patients in making important decisions about their own lives that requires physicians to respect and not interfere with patients' treatment choices, even if those choices will be bad for them. If a patient's decision-making capacities are sufficiently defective to warrant a determination that he or she is incompetent to decide for himself or herself, a surrogate must make the decisions. The two values of patient well-being and self-determination together require a balancing in the physician's role between value-committed, nonvalue-neutral advocacy for the patient's health and a willingness to accept a choice that fails best to secure the patient's health.

Nevertheless, there will be some choices made by the patient that are in sufficiently serious conflict with the value of health to which the medical profession is committed that the physician may reasonably be unwilling to participate in carrying out that choice and must withdraw from the care of the patient. When patients withdraw from the care of their physicians, or from particular aspects of that care, with likely serious adverse consequences for their health, those physicians are not, nor would we want them to be, merely value-neutral onlookers. Instead, they are active advocates with those patients for the patients' health, and when this breakdown in the physician-patient relationship occurs in the hospital, the patient must sign out "AMA"— against medical advice. This practice is not just for the protection of the physician and the hospital, but reflects the value-committed role as advocates for our health that we want our physicians to play. My general argument throughout his paper has been that the professional role of physicians and also the underlying basis for that role are not value neutral in the way the facts/values division of labor between physicians and patients would have it.

Notes

1. See, for example, President's Commission for the Study of Ethical Problems in Medicine and Biomedical and Behavioral Research, *Making Health Care Decisions* (Washington, D.C.: U.S. Government Printing Office, 1982).

2. One of the classic and most influential general accounts of positivist positions is Alfred J. Ayer, *Language, Truth, and Logic* (New York: Dover Publications, 1936).

3. Perhaps the most influential account of ethics along these lines was Charles Stevenson, *Ethics and Language* (New Haven: Yale University Press, 1944).

4. Though for an account of how far we remain from full patient participation in treatment decision making, see Jay Katz, *The Silent World of Doctor and Patient* (New York: Free Press, 1984).

5. Michael Bayles, "Physicians as Body Mechanics," in *Contemporary Issues in Biomedical Ethics*, ed. John W. Davis, Barry Hoffmaster, and Susan Shorten (Clifton, N.J.: Humana Press, 1978).

6. Robert Veatch, "Models for Medicine in a Revolutionary Age," *Hastings Center Report* (June 1972).

7. Richard Sherlock, "Reasonable Men and Sick Human Beings," *American Journal of Medicine* 80 (January 1986):2-4.

8. Geoffrey Sayre-McCord, *Essays on Moral Realism* (Ithaca, N.Y.: Cornell University Press, 1988) and David Brink, *Moral Realism and the Foundations of Ethics* (Cambridge: Cambridge University Press, 1989).

9. The difficulties in both intuitionism and naturalism will be familiar to philosophers. Those unfamiliar with them can find an account of these difficulties that places the development of both intuitionism and naturalism in historical context in W.D. Hudson, *Modern Moral Philosophy* (Garden City, N.Y.: Doubleday, 1970).

10. John Rawls, *A Theory of Justice* (Cambridge, Mass.: Harvard University Press, 1971), section 9.

11. Norman Daniels, "Wide Reflective Equilibrium and Theory Acceptance in Ethics," *Journal of Philosophy* 76 (1979):256-82.

12. This is the characterization of subjectivism employed by Brink, *Moral Realism*, pp. 217-36.

13. I discussed these theories some years ago as alternative accounts of utility in "Recent Work in Utilitarianism," *American Philosophical Quarterly* 19 (1973):241-76. A more recent treatment is in my "Quality of Life Measures in Health Care and Medical Ethics," in *The Quality of Life*, ed. Amartya Sen and Martha Nussbaum (Oxford: Oxford University Press, forthcoming). One of the best accounts of these alternative theories and the difficulties of each is James Griffin, *Well-Being* (Oxford: Oxford University Press, 1986).

14. Griffin, *Well-Being*, chap. 1.

15. Robert Goodin, "Laundering Preferences," in *Foundations of Social Choice Theory*, ed. Jon Elster and Aanund Hylland (Cambridge: Cambridge University Press, 1986).

16. Brock, "Quality of Life Measures in Health Care and Medical Ethics."

17. Christopher Boorse's account is developed in: "On the Distinction between Disease and Illness," *Philosophy and Public Affairs* 5 (1975):49-68; "Health as a Theoretical Concept," *Philosophy of Science* 44 (1977); "Concepts of Health," in *Health Care Ethics*, ed. Donald VanDe Veer and Tom Regan (Philadelphia: Temple University Press, 1987). Leon Kass's account is in his *Toward a More Natural Science* (New York: Free Press, 1985).

18. Boorse, "Concepts of Health," 370.

19. Ibid., 371.

20. For example, Peter Sedgwick, "Illness—Mental or Otherwise," *Hastings Center Studies* I (1973):30-31.

21. H. Tristram Engelhardt, Jr., "The Disease of Masturbation: Values and the Concept of Disease," *Bulletin of the History of Medicine* 48 (Summer 1974): 234-48.

22. See Ronald Bayer, *Homosexuality and American Psychiatry* (New York: Basic Books, 1981).

Discussion

Dr. Pellegrino: I would like to clarify the notion of the corrigibility or incorrigibility of the patient's assessment, as to what would lead to good in this circumstance. I am not quite sure what criteria you used to judge the corrigibility of someone's assessment of his own good. I think that I might accept your conclusions that the physician might have to step out of that relationship, and so on. But, so far as judging the patient's determination of his or her interest or self-interest, I find it difficult to know what the criterion is going to be in light of the fact that you suggest that the distinction is not a dichotomy but a continuum, as I understood that.

Dr. Brock: The judgment about whether the patient's view of his or her own good can be corrigible, will depend on what one takes to be the most justified theory of the good for persons. I sketched three main alternatives. My own view would be that physicians do, in fact, often use the most plausible alternative, which is some kind of ideal theory of the good for persons, as the standard by which to test whether the values that a patient is applying to the decision-making process correctly define that patient's good.

Whatever one's account of the most plausible theory of the good for persons is, would be the criterion one would use. And I think the one that physicians often, in fact, do use is some version of the one which I think is the most plausible.

Dr. Pellegrino: But, when medical professionals face the situation where they have a hierarchy of values and the medical value, or health, which they are advocating is not the highest value, how can the professional know whether the patient is correct?

Dr. Brock: That obviously is difficult.

Dr. Pellegrino: Patients are saying that there are things more important to them than the medical good, which the physician is advocating.

Dr. Brock: I believe that when physicians use an account of the good for persons and when they are judging whether this patient is right about what is best for him or her, they need to be using a broader account of good than just medical good. They need to be, in effect, appealing, though only implicitly, to some general theory of good for persons.

I take it that any plausible general theory will allow for particular patients giving differential value to health as opposed to other goods and more specifically for giving differential value to particular aspects of health vis-à-vis other goods. So, any plausible theory will have to allow for variation in the importance of health or particular components of health within a particular full conception of the good of life for an individual person.

Dr. Pellegrino: I happen to agree with that and have argued that extensively. But it does weaken the notion of the corrigibility of the patient's determination of his or her own self-interest.

Dr. Brock: Well, I guess I agree with you because this analysis says, if we could say health is exactly this important and no different, no more and no less for everybody, the patients are going to be able to be mistaken, much more than they will be if we accept variation in the importance of health.

Dr. Veatch: The Jehovah's Witness example makes Dr. Brock's case very nicely. In fact, most of the disagreement about Jehovah's Witnesses is an empirical disagreement about facts, not a disagreement about the good. When medical professionals are confronted with a Jehovah's Witness child needing a blood transfusion, they are extremely confident that they know objectively what the good for that child is. They have no trouble intervening. The doubts we have about intervening in the case of the Jehovah's Witness adult are not about the theory of the good at all. It is about our willingness to respect the autonomy of the individual while he fouls up the good for his life.

The cases involving children are clear. We are confident that we know objectively what the good is for such individuals.

Dr. Brock: I certainly agree with you about the difference between the way in which we treat the children's and the adult cases. What I had in mind when I said that the Jehovah's Witness case is a hard case, is the sense in which it is right that we take it to be a disagreement about facts. This is oversimplified, but because they are religious beliefs they are beliefs which, in a sense are acknowledged to go beyond any available evidence to determine them decisively. That is just why one might say they have a fixed belief about facts, and there is not any evidence that can be brought forward as to whether they are mistaken.

In some cases, when we find such fixed beliefs about facts that are impervious, so to speak, to new evidence, we call them psychotic delusions. That is, it is not just holding false beliefs but holding fixed ones which cannot be changed by the evidence.

It is because of some of the similarities between the beliefs of Jehovah's Witnesses and their relation to the available evidence and to these other cases where we would call into question the person's competence in making a judgment on the question that I find the Jehovah's Witness case a hard one with respect to their use of what are reported to be facts.

Dr. Pellegrino: Faith is not fact determinable. That is the crucial issue, epistemologically. It vitiates the objection.

Dr. Meilaender: I am not altogether sure that we are confident that this person is fouling up his life if that is the right way to put it. And I am not even sure that it is simply about religious beliefs, although I do not doubt that that is important.

But the person stands within a kind of community of discourse. And within that community, not as an individual alone, there is a kind of intelligibility, a tradition of discourse, in fact, that helps us to understand belief as an intelligible claim, however little we might share it.

Might it not be that, over a period of time, some of these beliefs will begin to sound like not just single individuals stating their scale of values, but like a tradition of discourse? And it will perhaps be possible to distinguish some such claims from others that are more purely idiosyncratic.

Dr. Brock: It is a way of testing if those beliefs fit within the general community that has some historical continuity to it, and it is a way in which we feel justified in giving more credibility to the patient's particular expression of them on a particular occasion, because we think these do, in fact, fit the sort of stable, coherent, life plan defining values of the patient.

I think, when beliefs have that kind of community setting, it gives us more grounds justifiably for giving weight to and being willing to rely on them, in defining that person's good.

Dr. Gorovitz: My question is rooted in agreement with your thesis that the patient's judgment is cardinal, and that the generalized theory of the good is used to test that patient's judgment.

My question is about the corrigibility of the physician's application of that test of the patient's judgment by that criterion. Unless there is reason to believe that the application of the criterion is more reliable than the corrigible judgment to which it is applied, there is little defense of that application.

Dr. Brock: Yes. That is an empirical question, the answer to which in general I have to say I have not the slightest idea. We can only answer it by narrowing down the context in which we are asking it. And even then I am not sure we have a lot of evidence to make us very confident about the answer to your question of how reliable the physician is as opposed to the patient.

All I want to insist on is that when we begin to narrow it down to more specific contexts, there are going to be some where we may grant that the physician may be good enough in an application of the criterion at least to justify a role which has him or her in discourse, so to speak, with the patient about the values that are to be applied.

Perhaps the issue is whether the professional should leave the facts and the values to the patient or whether he or she should have a role in discourse about them but, nevertheless, ultimately accept the choice that the patient comes to. If that is the issue we are talking about as opposed to the physician applying his account of the good for that patient and insisting on the treatment that would follow that application, then we can accept a higher degree of corrigibility on the physician's part because he or she is not going to insist that treatment necessarily follow its application as well.

Dr. Gorovitz: We are clearly not only talking about the level of reliance on the criteria when we include cases like the Jehovah's Witness case for children where there is an overriding perception of their good.

Dr. Brock: But that is a case where it is not just the physician's judgment about corrigibility, but the general social view with regard to that child's good. And the account is justified.

Dr. Gorovitz: Is that not, in fact, part of the answer, that it rarely is in the application of this criterion just the physician's view? Idiosyncratically? But, rather it is reliance on broader social appeal and on a larger community of individuals reflecting on the case? There is usually consultation with a nurse or other players.

Dr. Brock: All I was trying to do in the paper is to question a division of labor. The things you point to quite rightly would only be used to strengthen the case of the physician. It is not just his idiosyncratic application of the criterion. His application is checked by other players, like the nurse, and his application is not just one that he thought up all on his own but one that came from the complicated ways of broader society.

Dr. Buchanan: I would like to come back to something Dr. Meilaender said that I think is extremely important. That is, the belief of a patient that stems from the individual's participation in a group or a community with a tradition different from ours is more justified than if we thought the belief to be just an idiosyncrasy that that person happened to have.

I agree with what Dr. Meilaender was suggesting and with what Dr. Brock said, that *prima facie*, we might be willing to give more weight to a belief that was embedded in the community. But, I think, at most, we only want to give a little more weight to it initially, unless we were able to find out that the tradition of that community included certain conditions for the correction of belief. That is, there has to be some kind of mechanism for internal criticism within that community in the development of its distinctive views. Otherwise, I see absolutely no reason to think that those beliefs have any more going for them than the beliefs that individuals might happen to have because of some strange chemical introduced into their neocortex.

Dr. Brock: I would even go a step further. I agree with essentially everything you just said, but it may be that when we look at the community, in which we find the belief embedded, we might have even less reason to give credence to it.

Imagine that what we find is a person who has been within Jim Jones's community and there have been various forms of indoctrination used to induce beliefs in members of the community. I would give less credence to it.

Dr. Meilaender: I do not disagree entirely, although I simply want to note that I would be surprised if you could find communities that existed over a considerable period of time—Jim Jones's group really did not—in which there had not been internal processes of argument and criticism.

It does not mean that its official views necessarily were changed, but we underestimate the critical and argumentative capacities of ordinary folk if we too quickly assume that a community that exists for a sizable period of time has none of these capacities.

Dr. Buchanan: It is a matter of degree. Maybe the jury is still out on fundamentalist Iran at this point. It is hard to know how much self-criticism is going on, but we know there are deliberate measures taken to minimize self-criticism.

Fr. Sokolowski: But I wonder what the criteria for self-criticism are. It is not necessarily the case that a Popperian view or a particular eastern American establishment view of self-criticism is the right one to take into account.

Dr. Buchanan: I would like to leave that open. There may be a lot of variation. There has to be some kind of revision of belief that involves rational faculties in some way.

I think that the clearest, uncontroversial example of this is the kind of model of scientific reasoning of theory succession—of how better theories are identified and lesser theories are weeded out. But I am not assuming that that is a paradigm that you could just transport.

Fr. Sokolowski: And, in fact, the very notion that theories are what are operating in moral discourse is another assumption.

Dr. Buchanan: In the sense it is implied in this talk about what he takes to be the corrective conventional view about justification of moral beliefs.

Fr. Sokolowski: But, in moral matters, things might look incoherent precisely because you do not elevate them into an abstract system. You're coping with more situational things. You might not be able to relate coherence as an essential criterion.

I would also like to make one final point regarding reflective equilibrium. Do you still want to say that it is a matter of coordinating and finding a reflective equilibrium within the judgments a person has made? Or would it also be between some judgments and what the person is?

Dr. Brock: I am not sure I understand what you have in mind in the difference between the judgments. You mentioned also what the person is. But I think I want to accept your broader interpretation because I think many of the relevant judgments that would be a part of this process are judgments the person makes about himself or herself and what they are, what ideals they are committed to, what things they find satisfying, and so forth and so on.

Fr. Sokolowski: Because there might be a lot of judgments that have not been made yet or that ought to be made, but have not been.

Dr. Brock: I take Rawls and others, and certainly my use of "reflective equilibrium," to be an ideal of justification against which we always fall somewhat short at any point in time, because I take it to be a very strong condition of justification. I take reflective equilibrium to have required that one consider the possible arguments against the particular views that one holds justified in reflective equilibrium. And there are always limits on the degree to which we have considered not just what can be said in favor of the judgments we are making, but what can be said against them.

GILBERT MEILAENDER

Are There Virtues Inherent in a Profession?

I. Introduction

The investigation of almost any moral question invites us to assume that we not only can but also need to work out an answer. My aim in this essay, however, will be to suggest that we need not worry too much about answering the question in the essay's title. For the answer is going to turn out to be rather obvious. It is: "Yes, of course there are. But, then, it is also true that these are not the only virtues human beings ought to seek."

I will make my way toward this conclusion by (1) describing two quite different kinds of morality; (2) arguing that morality is not confined to claims that can be universalized; (3) offering two examples of ways in which virtues might be said to be inherent in a profession; and (4) considering the dangers of a view that admits a place for inherent professional virtues.

At the outset, however, we need to set aside certain concerns. One might argue that, within a profession, there will always be disagreements among practitioners about the meaning of their practice—and that these different conceptions will of necessity suggest different visions of any virtues thought to be inherent in that profession. As an empirical claim this may be faultless—but also, not very significant. For a profession does not consist simply of the sum total of its members, nor does the definition of virtuous practice depend solely on the opinions of current practitioners. There will always be something of a gap between the opinions of individual professionals and the purposes claimed to be inherent in the profession. If this gap becomes too large, we are rightly concerned.[1] Indeed, at some point we might have to conclude that the very meaning of the profession ought to be reconceived. But that would, of course, require normative argument, not surveys of current opinions. We might also conclude that what was really needed was better initiation and socialization into the norms of professional practice—that is, better moral education of beginning practitioners. To suppose that the visions of professional virtue could be as many as there are practitioners would seem rather like giving up entirely the notion of a profession as a social institution. Professional commitment would be reduced to authenticity; one would profess simply, "Such is my life and character." But the moral virtues—both those inherent in particular professions and those needed by human beings generally—are not that variable, even though the path of virtue can never be fully specified in advance.

II. Oakeshott's Forms of Moral Life

It may be best to begin very generally. What is the moral life, and how is it transmitted? In an essay titled "The Tower of Babel" and written almost four decades ago, the British political theorist Michael Oakeshott masterfully depicts the enduring nature of this problem.[2] Oakeshott outlines two different forms of the moral life, each an ideal construct unlikely to be found anywhere in pure form. But if neither can be lived in undiluted fashion, the crucial question for any society will be which predominates. Oakeshott had in mind political communities, but his types can apply to other societies as well—including professional societies.

For some societies, during at least some part of their history, the moral life may be chiefly what Oakeshott calls "a habit of affection and conduct."[3] That is, moral decisions are not the product of reflective thought, nor are they made by applying a moral ideal or principle to a particular situation. Rather, when this form dominates, we act from habits of behavior—habits taken for granted in society and inculcated in the young (or, keeping in mind our topic, the beginning practitioner). Ideally, decisions are reached almost without reflection, just as we learn to speak our native tongue without, on every occasion of speech, pausing to review the rules of grammar and syntax. For this pattern of behavior, Oakeshott writes, "most of the current situations of life do not appear as occasions calling for judgment, or as problems requiring solutions; there is no weighing up of alternatives or reflection on consequences, no uncertainty, no battle of scruples. There is . . .

nothing more than the unreflective following of a tradition of conduct in which we have been brought up."[4]

The moral life, conceived in this way, is transmitted in a manner appropriate to its form. Certainly, this transmission will not be done chiefly in a classroom, or by learning—and then learning to apply—a set of moral rules. We might learn a foreign language that way, he says, but "we acquire habits of conduct in the same way as we acquire our native tongue."[5] We learn from those around us—from living with people who habitually behave in certain ways, and from being thereby initiated into a tradition of conduct. The moral life is essentially a reflection on practice, and we are drawn into such reflection as we learn from skilled practitioners. Again, the analogy with language is illuminating. We have learned to speak English, but there is no moment to which we can point and say, "then I began to learn the language." For it was habitually spoken by all around us. It was the form of life in which we were immersed. To be sure, our language will also have its grammatical and syntactical rules, and the day will probably come when we learn them. Perhaps on one occasion or another these rules will help us over a difficult point, but this sort of learning has little to do with making us skilled speakers of the language. Education in our native tongue cannot be confined to particular moments. It is the sea in which we float and then, perhaps, swim. "One may set apart an hour in which to learn mathematics and devote another to the catechism, but it is impossible to engage in any activity whatever without contributing to this kind of moral education, and it is impossible to enjoy this kind of moral education in an hour set aside for its study."[6] From this perspective we might say something similar about the meaning of professional virtue.

The chief characteristic of this first form of the moral life may be the stability it provides both to individuals and their society. This does not mean that no moral change occurs; indeed, it takes place constantly within such a tradition of conduct. Stability comes precisely from the fact that such change is constant, always adjusting to what is new, but never collapsing all at once (in the way a theory can collapse when confronted with a devastating counterexample). We can even recognize the possibility of fairly radical change. A few members of the society may turn out to be gifted poets with a genuine "feel" for the language, and they may speak or write in ways which, though to outward appearances quite contrary to the rules of the language, in fact extend and enrich it.

If this form of the moral life is not likely to suffer sudden collapse, its chief danger lies in the possibility of gradual degeneration. Precisely because it offers the ability to act without hesitation or doubt, it does not provide the critical ability to evaluate the shape of the society's moral life—to transcend it, as it were, and think of it from some more universal perspective. As Oakeshott notes, "from this sort of education can spring the ability never to write a false line of poetry, but it will give us neither the ability to scan nor a knowledge of the names of the various metric forms."[7] As a consequence, lacking self-critical powers, the society may be unable to distinguish its vision of virtue from "the way we do things," and may be unable to deal with an external challenge based on some more universal claim.

Oakeshott's second form of the moral life is one in which "activity is determined, not by a habit of behaviour, but by the reflective application of a moral criterion," whether in the form of ideals or rules.[8] From this perspective what we need is the ability to set out the proper form of the moral life in systematic, connected fashion and then seek to apply it to practice. Particular activity is merely the specification of the more universal, systematically developed vision. This approach requires of us a kind of critical, self-reflective ability to defend our moral claims against all challenges. If, in the first form, conduct tends to be unreflective and free of hesitation, here there must be constant criticism and analysis to determine whether our practice adequately reflects the principles we have adopted.

In such a society, Oakeshott says, education into the moral life cannot come primarily from observing and practicing the appropriate behavior of others. Instead, we will need an intellectual training in the principles themselves: training in how to apply and defend them. The aim is that each moral agent should act self-consciously, aware of the grounds upon which he or she acts and prepared to defend those grounds. The proper analogy for this second form of moral life cannot be that of a language slowly and continuously developing, perhaps even changing considerably when reshaped by one who loves his native tongue and alters it in the spirit of the language itself. Rather, the analogy useful to describe this second form is of a language developed for a specific purpose—changed in idiom and structure whenever such change will serve certain specifiable interests.

People whose moral life takes this second form are not likely to permit it to become a mere tradition of "how we do things"; their life is far too self-critical for that. The weakness of this form lies elsewhere. It cannot offer the same certainty about how to act that the first form gives. Its adherents will be confident about the criteria for moral decision, but "together with the certainty about how to *think* about moral ideals, must be expected to go a proportionate uncertainty about how to *act*."[9] The constant tendency to analyze practice in the light of purportedly universal standards undermines the ability to act habitually and confidently. The pause of reflection that is always needed before one acts can be paralyzing. If this second form of the moral life collapses, it is more likely to happen suddenly than by slow and gradual degeneration. For although its adherents may have acquired considerable ability to resist external, critical challenge, should that resistance be broken, little is left (since their moral life is not undergirded by habit and custom). Mores are likely to change suddenly and rapidly. For example, thinking about professional practice from this perspective, we can imagine how physicians might very quickly shift from hesitation to do abortions to widespread endorsement of them.

The moral life of any living society is, of course, likely to combine these two forms. And, as Oakeshott himself notes, this is for the best. "Neither, taken alone, recommends itself convincingly as a likely form of the moral life, in an individual or in a society; the one is all habit, the other all reflection."[10] The one supposes that virtue never requires us to transcend the communities in which we learned to be virtuous. The other supposes that the virtuous life is that of the moral virtuoso who stands on neutral ground willing universally, or legislating for humankind, and fashioning entirely the self that he or she will be. The very fact that I can be asked to write on the topic of this essay's title suggests the degree to which Oakeshott's second form of the moral life has triumphed in our culture. Indeed, professions may be among the last bastions in which remnants of the first form are still found among us. But if they, too, find themselves uncertain of the meaning of professional practice and the norms of professional virtue, Oakeshott's analysis should suggest to us that help may not be found in universal moral principles. Although those principles may provide a kind of necessary check on the tendency of professional norms to become ingrown (as I will suggest in the final section of this essay), the moral life—together with the rich background it provides for deliberation and decision—is neither created nor sustained by universal principle. Indeed, I want now to move beyond Oakeshott's suggestion that there simply *are* two forms of the moral life and argue that the sphere of morality ought not be equated with norms that are universalizable.

III. Universalization in Ethical Reflection

Although extreme cases are not always best for making a point, it may prove instructive to consider the case of Captain Oates, who walked out of his tent to die in the Antarctic. W.D. Hudson once argued that if Oates had said to himself, "I ought to walk away," he would by that use of moral language have ben committed to requiring the same of all persons similarly situated. Hudson wrote: "Would Oates have rejected that implication? I doubt it. Surely a man in his position, acting as he did, we presume from a sense of duty, would think that anyone in the same position who failed so to act would be blameworthy."[11] It is possible—though I am not sure even of this— that Oates (were he to wax philosophical at such a moment) would think that any person similarly situated, who held the same set of ideals which he himself held, ordered and balanced those ideals in the same way, and had committed himself to the same way of life, would also be committed to walking out of the tent to die. But even if this should be true, it would still be quite different from the sort of duty that is universalizable in any strong sense.

Suppose, for example, Captain Oates had decided that, in order to make his own food supplies last longer, he should take his companions by surprise and kill them. We would, I think, condemn that act in the case of Captain Oates and anyone else who held his ideals. But, more important, we would condemn the act by anyone at all who ventured to take this way out of his predicament. We would feel relatively little need to inquire into the way of life he had chosen before rendering our moral judgment. To see this is to see the sphere in which universalization properly operates. Although certain fundamental moral duties are universalizable in a way that is not context dependent, this is not true for the whole of the moral life. Indeed, I suggest that, if we thought Oates' act should be required of anyone similarly situated, we would not suppose it told us much about Oates' character. It could not have the meaning it does for us if we thought, as Hudson does, that Oates himself would assume that anyone else in his position would be blameworthy for not doing the same.

The case of Oates points us simply to one action taken in very unusual circumstances. But almost all of us make vocational commitments to particular ways of life—of which commitments to professional practice are one sort. These vocations bind us to care in particular ways for certain people, but they do not bind others or define for others the virtues they must seek. We may all share certain basic, universalizable moral duties that limit the way in which we ought to pursue our vocational or professional commitments. But within the space those duties leave, we are free to seek to discern the virtues required of us in our calling. And these virtues may be quite different for, let us say, the physician and the hangman.

J.L. Mackie distinguished three stages at which one might require universalization in ethical reflection.[12] First, such a requirement might mean simply that all merely numerical differences between one person and another should be deemed irrelevant. Thus, Mackie writes, the ascetic could not say, "I cannot allow myself such indulgences, but I do not condemn them in others."[13] At this first level, therefore, nothing would prohibit a strong man from adopting and universalizing a principle endorsing rigorous competition and survival of the fittest. Second, universalizability might require that we seek imaginatively to put ourself in the place of the other. Thus, the strong man would ask himself what life would be like for the weak person in a rigorously competitive world, and whether he would want such a life to be his. Third, universalization may mean that we not only imagine ourself in the other's place but imagine that—while in his or her place—we share his or her preferences, values, and ideals. Thus, the strong man would not consider that, even in a harsh world, *he* prefers to be self-reliant. He would instead consider the preference of the other person.

The third of these stages is clearly a substantive moral position, not simply a logical requirement, and, though it may perhaps be useful as a device for achieving political compromise in a pluralistic society, it is quite unsatisfactory as a moral stance. For it makes it impossible for us to adopt a way of life that we consider peculiarly our own; it forces us to regard our life as would an observer. Indeed, only the first of these stages can, with any plausibility, be said to be a requirement built into the logic of moral language, and even that is questionable. "One of the marks of a certain type of bad man," C.S. Lewis once wrote, "is that he cannot give up a thing himself without wanting everyone else to give it up."[14] To be such a bad person is what even Mackie's first stage requires of us. In making vocational or professional commitments, we give ourselves—but not everyone else—to a way of life. If we want to know what virtues that way of life calls for, we must simply look and see. We cannot spin them out of the nature of morality itself.

IV. Virtues Inherent to Professional Commitments

We can turn now from these general arguments to more particular instances in order to think about what it might mean to suggest that there are virtues inherent in certain professional commitments, virtues that are not simply specifications or applications of a universal morality. I take my examples somewhat arbitrarily from two of the original professions—ministry and medicine.

In 1935, the German Lutheran pastor Dietrich Bonhoeffer was called to serve as principal of a seminary at Finkenwalde, founded by the Confessing Church in Germany. While there, Bonhoeffer wrote some of his early works—among them the little known *Seelsorge*, recently translated into English under the title *Spiritual Care*.[15] As Bonhoeffer understands it, the spiritual care offered by pastor to parishioner is governed by no "method" and is directed not at human beings in general but at fellow believers within the Body of Christ. It is simply "a special sort of proclamation"—applying to the life of the individual believer what is contained in the public proclamation of the church for which the pastor is authorized to speak.[16]

This means that the activity of the pastor in providing *Seelsorge* is decisively determined neither by his or her gifts, nor by the desires and needs of his or her parishioners, nor by any general theory of human well-being. Still less is such care to be understood as personal guidance or counsel, in which one person submits to the wisdom and insight of another. Spiritual care, Bonhoeffer holds, "comes down 'from above,' from God to the human being."[17] It aims, in the words of Bonhoeffer's translator, "to arrange the contingencies for an encounter with the Divine"—an encounter that governs both pastor and parishioner.[18] This purpose defines the meaning of such care, as the following passages demonstrate:

> The goal of spiritual care should never be a change of mental condition. . . . I do not provide *decisive* help for anyone if I turn a sad person into a cheerful one, a timid person into a courageous one. . . . Beyond and within circumstances such as sadness and timidity it should be believed that God is our help and comfort.[19]

> Spiritual care does not want to bring about competence, build character or produce certain types of persons. Instead it uncovers sin and creates hearers of the gospel.[20]

In one sense, there is no difference at all between the pastor who provides spiritual care and the believer to whom it is given. The difference between the two is not at all a difference of ability or power but of office; the pastor is commissioned by God to fill this role.[21] "To those who come to us for spiritual care our ability has less than no authority. Only the mission binds and calls us together."[22]

It is clear, therefore, that Bonhoeffer takes a definite view of what the profession of ministry is and involves. It is not a matter of any particular technique that can be learned and then applied to the needs of those who present themselves to the pastor. Indeed, the "pastor remains fundamentally premethodical and prepsychological, in the best sense naive."[23] That is, the pastor remains simply prepared "to arrange the contingencies for an encounter with the Divine." As the physician serves physical and emotional wholeness in human beings, as the lawyer serves justice in human relations, so the pastor serves the Word of God as it enters human lives to judge and save. And the meaning of the profession—and of good professional practice—is determined by that understanding.

This view colors and permeates everything Bonhoeffer has to say about particular acts of pastoral care. Thus, for example, the pastor must guard his or her tongue, lest the members of the congregation lose confidence in their ability to speak confidentially with the pastor when seeking spiritual care. Such care in speaking is inherent in faithfulness to the pastor's calling, and it is absolutely crucial when the parishioner comes to confess sin.

> The confessional seal is a divine commandment. Its breach must result in loss of office. In the confessional the salvation of the soul is at stake. The other person only confides in me and puts himself in my hands because I act "in God's stead." I must keep this secret as God keeps it. No worldly power must be allowed to tear it from me. God will require the soul of the confessor from the one who reveals the confidences made in the confessional. . .Only on the day of judgment will what was spoken in the confessional be revealed.[24]

We should note the sort of appeal Bonhoeffer makes here. In talking about the need to guard one's tongue, Bonhoeffer has been able to give rather ordinary, practical advice. For example: The pastor who gossips about her congregation is likely to find herself the topic of the congregation's gossip. Or again: Gossip poisons trust and is the worst evil in a congregation. But when Bonhoeffer seeks to make clear why the confession made to the pastor must be kept in utter confidence, he appeals to no general principle about trust, harm, or the like. He appeals to the peculiar nature of the office. The pastor hears this confession and offers absolution in God's stead. No one but God may reveal what has ben spoken there. And this is so integral to the office that failure here "must result in loss of office."

Not all spiritual care takes place in the confessional, however. The pastor may also visit parishioners in their homes, showing "through a visit that Christ wishes to come to this house."[25] But this is not done casually or without permission. "That the pastor may do this must be reckoned in every way as an extension of trust. It is a special privilege that comes with the office."[26] And with this privilege comes special responsibility. The pastor does not come into the home as an observer seeking the secrets of others in their privacy. Nor does he or she come as one desiring friendship. By inviting him or her into their homes, others welcome the pastor into the sphere where they are most truly seen as they are. They disclose themselves and make themselves vulnerable before the pastor—who, it must be added, does not do the same. Hence, Bonhoeffer writes, "utmost reserve is called for. The pastor never speaks about what he has seen in a home."[27] To do so would be to forget the role he or she fills as Christ's representative there.

The sense in which ministerial practice must be governed by submission to the Word of God can be seen in another way in what Bonhoeffer says about funeral practices. Proper practice must be understood in the light of what is really taking place. "The intent of Christian burial is not to eulogize the deceased, nor is it a farewell to the deceased . . . Christian burial is a recollection of the hope which is given our body . . ."[28] What of occasions when the pastor functions at the burial of one who, though perhaps baptized, had not been faithful and active in the life of the church? The norms governing such functioning are not determined by respect for the dead, nor even by the wishes or needs of the mourners. The pastor is governed decisively by the fact that this too is an occasion for proclamation of the Word to which the pastor has submitted in taking up the profession.

> One should not be silent about indifference to Christian faith or opposition and hatred toward the faith. Thus the pastor, at the interment of Hofmann von Fallersleben, said, after the recital of many positive things, "yet this man was a fool because he did not recognize the presence of Christ in his life." Such a judgment, naturally, can proceed only from a firm knowledge of the deceased and only after continual and earnest pastoral efforts with him. Interment is more than a proclamation to the congregation. It is an activity having to do with the dead.Truth must override all other considerations, especially false respect.[29]

Certainly, this conception of pastoral practice could not be described as a specification of the more general and well-known piece of wisdom: *de mortuis nil nisi bonum*!

Some will, of course, want to disagree with Bonhoeffer's understanding of what ministry as a profession means and requires. If, however, they disagree as those who are essentially outsiders to the faith, if they hold that the sort of ministerial practice Bonhoeffer commends can scarcely demonstrate true compassion or serve human well-being, their disagreement will be beside the point. For Bonhoeffer has not taken his start from any such point. He has begun with the Call of God. If critics disagree as insiders, they may well want to argue that Bonhoeffer has gotten the understanding of ministry wrong in one way or another—perhaps he is mistakenly Teutonic, hierarchical, or inflexible in his understanding. But the argument then will have to proceed not on the basis of any purportedly universal meaning of "care," but with specific attention to the meaning of "spiritual care" as the Christian church ought to understand it.

We turn now to an example taken from medicine, another profession with a long and distinguished history. Just as Bonhoeffer believed that being a pastor has, as it were, its own meaning and significance—a meaning that did not depend on what parishioners wanted from their pastor, nor even on the pastor's desire to be helpful to them—so, Leon Kass has argued, being a physician has *its* own essential meaning. Kass has argued this view with considerable eloquence in some of the chapters of *Toward a More Natural Science*.[30] Here I will trace a few strands of his argument in a still more recent article, "Neither for Love nor Money: Why Doctors Must Not Kill."[31]

For Bonhoeffer the central virtue of the pastor is faithfulness to the Divine Word that encounters human beings through the pastor's ministry. In a structurally similar way, for Kass the physician is essentially a healer—committed to seeking wholeness (physical and emotional) for his or her patients. Physicians may well be—we hope they are—benevolent, but benevolence is not their central commitment; for, on Kass's understanding of the profession, they ought not kill even for love, even when moved by the benevolent desire to relieve suffering. Moreover, physicians may well—we hope they will—respect the freedom of their patients, but, still, they will not think of themselves as "a highly competent hired syringe." There are ways in which physicians will not place their technical competence into the service of patients; they will not kill, even if the patient requests it and promises to reward their service. Neither love nor money should persuade them to kill, since they are healers by the very nature of their professional commitment. And it is important to keep in mind that Kass states very explicitly that he is not here making a general argument against euthanasia; he is arguing only that those who are healers must not aim to kill. [32]

Kass offers a variety of consequentialist arguments in support of this position, but the heart of his argument lies in his understanding of the meaning of medical practice. He explores its significance from two angles—focusing first on the limits of medicine and, then, on its center. The practice of medicine has limits: things a healer ought never do. Kass finds three such limits embedded in the Hippocratic Oath:

"no breach of confidentiality, no sexual relations with patients, [and] no dispensing of deadly drugs."[33] The fact that doctors have the technical capacity to do certain things does not in itself make such actions part of the practice of medicine. It may be that doctors are the best, most efficient executioners. But medicine is not whatever doctors can do best—not if the act is itself incompatible with the virtue of a healer.

In my view, Kass is quite persuasive here, but there are complexities that deserve our attention.[34] A virtue is not simply a disposition to act in certain ways, even though, it is true, some activities do seem well nigh incompatible with certain virtues. We may doubt whether someone who turns and runs from danger can really be moved by the virtue of courage. We may doubt—but we cannot be certain. The person who runs from danger may, in fact, be courageous. This need not lead us to characterize running from danger as an "act of courage," but it is, at least, an act that might be done by one who is courageous. There must be some connection between virtues and external behavior, but there is never a perfect fit.[35]

If virtues are not simply dispositions to act in certain ways, we may come closer to the mark if (following Aristotle) we think of them as rather like skills. They are skills which are learned, not techniques that are taught. It is the difference between learning to cook and following the directions in a cook book, between learning to drive a car and passing one's written test after studying the manual, between living as a Christian and studying the catechism. One might still argue that virtues, unlike skills, engage the will. If I deliberately miss a baseball pitched to me, it does not show that I lack the skill to hit it. But if while playing baseball I deliberately treat the opposing team unjustly, that does indicate the lack of a certain virtue. If someone, seeing me miss the pitch, says that I lack the skill to hit, I can respond by saying that I missed it deliberately. But if someone accuses me of unjust behavior, I cannot excuse myself by saying, "I did it deliberately."[36]

We ought not to press the distinction too far, though. If I deliberately miss the pitch too often, I am likely to develop some deficiencies in my swing (a hitch, moving the back foot) that will make me less proficient as a hitter. Something similar is true of virtues. Contrary inclinations or vice may be gradually learned. To make a moral mistake too often, even to do it deliberately as one might miss a pitch, may gradually engage the will. This was Bonhoeffer's worry when he questioned whether he and those like him could still be of any use after Germany's crisis was over.

We have been the silent witnesses of evil deeds. Many storms have gone over our heads. We have learnt the art of deception and of equivocal speech. Experience has made us suspicious of others and prevented us from being open and frank. Bitter conflicts have made us weary and even cynical. Are we still serviceable? It is not the genius that we shall need, not the cynic, not the misanthropist, not the adroit tactician, but honest, straightforward men. Will our spiritual resources prove adequate and our candour with ourselves remorseless enough to enable us to find our way back again to simplicity and straightforwardness?[37]

To lie in a good cause for the first time may not show that we lack the virtue of truthfulness; it might make good sense to note that we did it deliberately. But Bonhoeffer's concern is a valid one: to do this too often may gradually engage the will in vice, and it may be difficult to "find our way back again to simplicity and straightforwardness."

Kass's claims about medicine suggest a similar concern. To ignore its limits may, at some point, make it difficult any longer to be a healer. And for Kass, such a limit must therefore be built into the meaning of medical practice. Patients make themselves vulnerable before physicians, entrusting their bodies—and, hence, their persons and lives— to the doctor. And since doctors do not similarly hand themselves over to their patients, the relation cannot be symmetrical. Such asymmetry calls for restraint, for limits, if the physician is really to be a healer to whom patients can give themselves with trust. "For the physician, at least, human life in living bodies commands respect and reverence—*by its very nature.*"[38] Not simply because the patient wants or demands such respect. Not simply because the benevolent physician desires to give it. But because the commitment of the healer will be undermined and, finally, destroyed if it is not given.

Not only the limits but also the center of medical practice suggests for Kass that healers must not kill. Physicians practice their art for the benefit of the sick, cooperating with the body's powers in an effort to heal. To care for the sick, to seek their healing, is therefore "the central core of medicine."[39] Physicians do not simply deal with bodies or organisms, but with the persons who are bodily present—who are psychophysical unities.

> The sickness may be experienced largely as belonging to the body as something other; but the healing one wants is the wholeness of one's entire embodied being. Not the wholeness of *soma*, not the wholeness of *psyche*, but the wholeness of *anthropos* as a (puzzling) concretion of *soma-psyche* is the benefit sought by the sick. This human wholeness is what medicine is finally all about.[40]

Whatever others may think or do, therefore, physicians must be committed to the bodily life of their patients, whose personhood "is manifest on earth only in living bodies."[41] For doctors to kill, even in the name of personal well-being of their patients, "is like a tree seeking to cut its roots for the sake of growing its highest fruit."[42] It violates the very central commitment of the healer's art. Thus, the outermost limit of medical practice ("do not kill") is integrally related to its central virtue (faithfulness to the wholeness of a patient whose personal presence is always an embodied presence). Perhaps others in a society—police, soldiers, official executioners, justified revolutionaries, (even conceivably) appointed euthanizers—should sometimes kill, but doctors, as doctors, cannot kill their patients without setting aside the inherent moral meaning of their profession. They would then have to "profess" something quite different.

V. The Unity of the Virtues

The view that I have illustrated in Bonhoeffer and Kass, that there may be in professional practice inherent virtues which are not merely specifications or applications of more universal principles, is not without its dangers. I would, however, locate the principal danger a little differently from where some others might. For some, the chief danger in such a view is the danger of relativism. Robert Veatch has argued that "[s]pecial norms . . . cannot exist for a professional group without collapsing into ethical relativism and particularism."[43] If it could be the case that divulging information revealed in confidence could be "right" for the layperson but "wrong" for the pastor, if there could be circumstances in which it would be "wrong" for a doctor to kill a suffering patient but "right" for someone else, then, so the argument goes, professional ethics would have become an ingrown, relativistic code.[44]

I do not myself think this is the best way to put the problem, though, to be sure, there is a problem here. On Kass's account, anyone—past, present, or future; at any time or place—professionally committed to the healer's role ought not kill. On Bonhoeffer's account, anyone—past, present, or future; at any time or place—professionally committed to listen and speak in God's stead, cannot divulge what is told him in confidence in that representative role. That others may perhaps not be so committed means only that they have a different station and correspondingly different duties, a different profession or calling.

To be sure, such claims to special professional virtue can be dangerous. Recognizing that danger, we may sometimes press the claim for a morality more universal—and to do so represents a demand for fairness, a reminder that professionals, too, may have self-regarding impulses in need of discipline. But the truly important moral question here is not relativism; it is the old question of the unity of the virtues. Can a good physician, a good minister, be a good citizen or a good person? If one possesses the virtues central to pastoral or medical practice, will one necessarily be a virtuous person *simpliciter*? Or, may the virtues of a profession and the virtues of familial or civic commitment (or the virtue of general benevolence) sometimes seem to clash? An emphasis on the unity of the virtues comes naturally to those who believe that the moral life is harmonious, a seamless robe which must either be worn intact or not at all.[45] For adherents of such a view there must be some single best way of life for all human beings, however general may be the terms in which we describe it. Those less persuaded may incline to the view that tragic conflict cannot be eliminated from the life of virtue.[46] Still others may wish to hold that the unity of the virtues can be apparent only in a world quite unlike the one in which we live, a world in which the self has been perfected and the kingdom has come. I have suggested that there are, indeed, virtues inherent to a profession, virtues that are not specifications of some more universal norm. But we should not fail to honor the impulse present in those who want to argue for greater unity and universality in the moral life. We may be moved by those who stress the disunity of the virtues and the tensions of the moral life, but we can also pay a price for savoring the tragic too much. We compartmentalize human character, we settle for isolated virtues, and we lose the sense that to seek virtue is to seek wholeness of the self and not just professional virtue. Whether a universal morality is the savior we need to provide such wholeness is still another question. Perhaps so. But perhaps the universality we seek is best found in some other way—for example, through a larger context in which we learn to think of a virtue and wholeness not entirely confined to our own achievement or profession. It may even be that, apart from such a larger context, professional virtue can never be entirely safe.

Notes

1. P.F. Camenisch, *Grounding Professional Ethics in a Pluralistic Society* (New York: Haven Publications, 1983), 9.

2. M. Oakeshott, *Rationalism in Politics and Other Essays* (London: Methuen & Co., 1962), 59-79.

3. Ibid., 61.

4. Ibid.

5. Ibid., 62.

6. Ibid., 62ff.

7. Ibid., 63.

8. Ibid., 66.

9. Ibid., 68.

10. Ibid., 70.

11. W.D. Hudson, *Modern Moral Philosophy* (Garden City, N.Y.: Doubleday Anchor, 1970), 221.

12. J.L. Mackie, *Ethics: Inventing Right and Wrong* (New York: Penguin Books, 1977), 83-102.

13. Ibid., 84.

14. C.S. Lewis, *Mere Christianity* (New York: Macmillan, 1960), 62.

15. Dietrich Bonhoeffer, *Spiritual Care*, trans. J.C. Rochelle (Philadelphia: Fortress Press, 1985).

16. Ibid., 30.

17. Ibid.

18. Ibid., 23.

19. Ibid., 30.

20. Ibid., 32.

21. Ibid., 37.

22. Ibid.

23. Ibid., 36.

24. Ibid., 40.

25. Ibid., 45.

26. Ibid., 46.

27. Ibid.

28. Ibid., 69.

29. Ibid., 73.

30. L. Kass, *Toward a More Natural Science* (New York: Free Press, 1985).

31. L. Kass, "Neither for Love nor Money: Why Doctors Must Not Kill," *The Public Interest* 94 (1989):25-46.

32. Ibid., 31.

33. Ibid., 36ff.

34. See G. Meilaender, *The Theory and Practice of Virtue* (Notre Dame: University of Notre Dame Press, 1984), 7ff.

35. G.H. von Wright, *The Varieties of Goodness* (London: Routledge & Kegan Paul, 1970), 148.

36. Philippa Foot, *Virtues and Vices and Other Essays in Moral Philosophy* (Berkeley: University of California Press, 1978), 7f.

37. D. Bonhoeffer, *Prisoner for God: Letters and Papers from Prison* (New York: Macmillan, 1958), 27.

38. Kass, "Neither for Love nor Money," 38.

39. Ibid., 39.

40. Ibid., 40.

41. Ibid., 41.

42. Ibid.

43. R.M. Veatch, "Medical Ethics: Professional or Universal?" *Harvard Theological Review* 65 (1972):559.

44. Ibid., 554.

45. See Meilaender, *The Theory and Practice of Virtue*, 19-22.

46. A. MacIntyre, *After Virtue* (Notre Dame: University of Notre Dame Press, 1981), 153.

Discussion

Dr. Buchanan: You emphasized the notion of justification and the central view of the medical profession that understanding what it is to be a doctor includes certain kinds of virtues and certain rules that can be extracted from those. And there is no further justification of a universalistic sort for those rules.

Suppose you take Kass's example of not killing. You would say something like: Everybody committed to this enterprise of being a physician ought not to kill, at least in his capacity as a physician. Maybe in a war, you can kill, but qua physician, you should not do that. And that is inherent in the notion of a physician.

Presumably, that means that to be a physician is to be a healer, and healing is something different from killing. So, if one is faithful to the calling of being a healer, then one should not kill.

But suppose you are a physician in Holland, where there is a certain kind of limited active euthanasia permitted, and you say, "I have a different conception of the calling of being a physician, to be a healer, or where that fails, to provide comfort, or to provide relief from suffering. And sometimes when my patient who is suffering acute respiratory distress in the final stages of a terminal illness, when I have talked to the person in advance, and he or she wants to be given morphine sufficient to suppress the breathing reflex knowing this will be fatal, I am going to do that. It's compatible with my conception of my calling to do that."

If there were a unified conception of the role of physician in a given society that made it clear that a physician was only to be a healer and never a killer even for the sake of relieving suffering, then you might be able to say to someone who was a physician but who thought it was permissible to kill a patient, that he or she is misleading people by saying that he or she is a physician.

But, of course, in the societies where it is a live issue as to whether a physician should kill, there is no such unified social understanding about what the distinctive role of a physician is and what the inherent virtues of being a physician are.

It is a matter of controversy in this society as to whether the proper conception of the role is to be a healer who does not kill or to be a hero when one can in some rare exceptional cases, killing for the sake of relieving suffering.

In cases in which it would not be a live issue and in which justification would not be called for, Kass's view works. Is that a problem or not?

Dr. Meilaender: I think it is a problem, yes. Kass attempts to go a little beyond what he does in *Toward a More Natural Science,*[1] in which he has real problems with the move from what happens when I can no longer be a healer. In this article, he is at least very self-conscious about that problem. I do not know how we sort out completely the normative and empirical elements. If Kass and I say that the profession is one thing, but then eighty percent of the people tagged physicians say it is something else, then something screwy is going on at that point. There are various ways, however, to describe what the screwiness is.

One of the ways would be to say that in this community of physicians we are talking about, there has been an enormous failure to inculcate among physicians what the real virtues of the profession involve. That failure is cause for concern, shame, wondering whether we have really got the same profession around any longer. That is one kind of response. I do not know at what point that does not sound believable any longer. I do not know how one decides that. But I think that is always a possible response to make at that point. I would even have some sympathy with such a response.

Another response borrows from Oakeshott's suggestion that in first forming the moral life, one of the weaknesses it has because of its nonself-reflective character is the difficulty of responding to criticism in some ways. You are, in a sense, asking what happens in a society where there is the criticism. Is that not exactly the moment when this kind of view will not work?

Well, I cannot make up my mind about what is the honest answer. One side of me tends to think that it can be determined definitively what the profession is. Another side of me, however, wonders whether those people are not right who argue that there is no definitive concept of obligation regarding the physician's role. This would imply that the most effective way of responding to such criticism is not trying to meet it by insisting on a definitive conceptualization, but by trying seriously to rethink what the profession is about.

There is a side of me that tends to agree with what you say, but there are other moments when I wonder if we would not be better just to rework Kass again and see if people do not learn to think that way.

Dr. Brock: All you would need to do if you wanted to accept what Dr. Buchanan says, which I guess you would, is show that a dispute over which virtues are inherent in a profession is a useful way of framing the disagreement. We might still find it useful to frame the disagreement in terms of what virtues are needed to practice this profession.

Dr. Sass: In parts of your paper, I was not sure whether you were really talking about virtues or skills, that is, virtues or virtuosity. For example, Bonhoeffer's spiritual care, *Seelsorge*, and soul care are certain forms of skill—praying skills, sermon delivery skills, and soul care skills. Also remember Dr. Pellegrino's article on the virtuous physician, and whether there is a difference between a virtuous physician and skillful physician.

Dr. Meilaender: It is sometimes difficult to distinguish skills and virtues. The analogy has traditionally been one way of trying to get at what virtues are about, that is, to think of them as certain kinds of skills. For example, if somebody throws a hardball toward me from sixty feet away and I hit it once, it does not prove that I have the skill to do it. Though, if I can do it consistently, it may. In the same vein, if I act courageously, it does not prove that I have virtue, but if I habitually act with courage, I may.

So I do not think we would want to claim that there is no connection between our notion of virtues and our notion of skills. It is not a tight fit, however. I say just in passing in the paper that virtue has engaged the will in a way that skills do not. There is a difference between the concept of a virtue and a skill. There are also some virtues that are more general in terms of fitting us for life, and some that are perhaps more role-specific.

Fr. Sokolowski: I have a remark about the previous discussion. It seems to me that one must distinguish between discussion about the end of the profession and opinions about the profession. What is the bottom line? Is it an end or a nature of the profession? Or is it what everyone thinks about the profession?

Note

1. L. Kass, *Toward a More Natural Science* (New York: Free Press, 1985); "Neither for Love nor Money: Why Doctors Must Not Kill," *The Public Interest* 94 (1989):25-46.

ROBERT M. VEATCH

Is Trust of Professionals
a Coherent Concept?

I. Introduction

It is widely held that the problem of contemporary professionals is that they can no longer be trusted. By this it is often meant either that professional self-interest has so captured the professionals' agenda that their clients can no longer approach them with the traditional moral expectation that client interests will be paramount, or alternatively, that societal interests in cost containment, the advancement of research, or other agendas force the professional to sacrifice the client. If this assessment is correct, we would appropriately say that the professional can no longer be trusted. The fiduciary relationship, it would be said, is in trouble. If this is the trouble with the fiduciary relation, however, it is potentially fixable. We could undertake the task of trying to make professionals more committed to their clients or we could make clear morally those cases where conflicting interests are legitimate. There may be a more fundamental problem for the fiduciary relation in contemporary society, however. It may be that the very concept of trusting a professional is not a coherent one. All of the first-order criticisms of the fiduciary relation assume that it makes sense to believe that if the professional were of good character and were committed to the client, then trust could be restored. In short, it is assumed that professionals, at least in theory, can be trustworthy.

The three preceding papers in this section, however, all raise questions about that presumption. While their authors focus on the medical professional role, the problems they address seem to pose a serious threat to the concept of the professional in general as one who, in the ideal, is worthy of a client's trust.

The traditional argument in professional ethics appears to be something like the following: It is the nature of a profession to be client-centered, to expect of its members that they act, not as self-interested business people, but as moral agents committed to serving the interest of their clients. Allen Buchanan, however, shows in his analysis that there may be good reasons why professionals ought not to be able to know what their client's interests are.

The defender of the more traditional notion of the professional might at this point make the move to what could be called the "liberal solution." The professional should at least be trusted to present the relevant facts and the plausible options to the client, who would have the responsibility to choose from those options. Then the professional would have the responsibility to serve the client's interest (with the proviso that he or she should be able to opt out of the relation when the client's choice so violates the professional's conscience that the fiduciary relation can no longer be maintained). Dan Brock makes clear in his paper, however, that the fact/value dichotomy upon which this liberal solution rests is seriously flawed. Not only would it be immoral for the professional to present the value-free facts; it is conceptually impossible, according to contemporary philosophy of science, to present "just the value-free facts" to the client. A final defense of the fiduciary role for the professional is that at least the professional should be trusted (in the ideal case) to act on a set of virtues inherent in the profession and that these virtues cannot simply be imposed on the profession from some general set of universal ones that are not specific to the particular profession in question. Gilbert Meilaender, in his paper, makes a case that virtue sets can be seen as specific to the various professions rather than derived from more global ethical systems.

I am generally sympathetic with the analyses of Buchanan and Brock and would like to bring out the implications of each for a more general theory of trust in the professions, expanding the analysis beyond the medical professional role. For Meilaender's discussion of the virtues, I fear more work is needed than simply an expansion to a general theory of the fiduciary-professional relation. While I have no problem with the claim that the virtues appropriate to various professions must be profession-specific and not simply a repeat of the virtues of the good person generally, I am not convinced that it is possible to have each profession determine what the virtues are that are appropriate to its role. I am not even sure that it makes sense to think of each profession having a univocal set of virtues that are based on practices intrinsic to the profession or even that there is such a thing as a single, definitive conceptualization of how a particular profession ought to be practiced.

To the extent that it is impossible for professionals (1) to know what the interests of clients are, (2) to present value-free facts and behavior options, and (3) to determine a definitive set of virtues for a particular profession, then I am forced to the conclusion that professionals ought not to be trusted. They ought not to be trusted, not because they are morally deficient or lacking in virtue, but rather because knowing client interests, presenting value-free facts, or determining virtues intrinsic to the professional role are impossible.

II. Serving the Client's Best Interest

Buchanan begins his insightful analysis with the observation that, at least in medicine, there are times when serving the client's best interest will conflict with respecting client autonomy. It is by now as well established as anything can be in ethics that sometimes it may be morally necessary to sacrifice the client's best interest in order to respect the client's autonomy. That would seem to apply to all professions, not simply medicine, although medical professionals may have come further in affirming the primacy of autonomy. Lawyers, for example, are sometimes reluctant to concede that in cases where the lawyer knows that a client's interest would be served by a particular legal strategy, that strategy morally ought to be abandoned because the client prefers another course.

That is a preliminary point, however. Buchanan shows that there are important functions a physician can fulfill that are devoted to promoting the client's interest without violating the client's autonomy. Presumably, other professionals have the same range of actions open to them: ruling out reasonably implausible options, preparing a menu of options, making recommendations, and making actual decisions when delegated by the client to do so.

The problem of serving the client's interest cuts far deeper, however. There is increasing reason to hold that modern professionals ought not to be able to know what the client's interests really are. The problem is only partly related to the increasing anonymity of the lay-professional relation. Increasingly, the professional and client are strangers to one another forced together by accident or, at best, by a referral based on something far short of good knowledge of the interests of the client. More fundamentally, the interests of the client have almost nothing to do with the kind of knowledge a professional can be expected to have. The client, insofar as he or she is pursuing his or her own interests, should be striving for total well-being or welfare. That well-being is complex, made up of many subspheres, including the physical, psychological, social, legal, economic, aesthetic, educational, occupational, cultural, and religious. A professional in any one of these spheres can, at most, be expected to know with professional expertise something about the client's well-being in the particular sphere about which the professional is an expert. The physician might, at most, know about medical well-being, the lawyer, about legal well-being, and so forth. But no rational person wants to maximize his or her well-being in one particular sphere of life; he or she wants to maximize total well-being. Whenever well-being in education or aesthetics or law conflicts with well-being in some other sphere, we would expect that the correct course for the client is purposely to decline to pursue maximum well-being in most if not all of the subspheres.

The problem of professional knowledge of client interest is made worse by the facts that not only can a professional in one subsphere be expected to be ignorant about client well-being in the other spheres (and thus incapable of knowing how to promote the total well-being of a client); but also, a professional can be expected to have a unique value commitment to his or her special sphere of well-being. We would expect clergypersons to be uniquely committed to promoting spiritual well-being at the expense of other spheres, the artist to be overcommitted to aesthetic well-being, and so forth. Professionals ought to overcommit their clients to their own subspheres. Thus, if the fiduciary professional is trusted to promote the client's well-being, the professional's choices ought to be wrong insofar as he or she knows nothing about the client's other spheres of well-being and will naturally overvalue the area of his or her own professional commitment.

This is not the end of the problem. One might retreat by saying that the professional can realistically be said to be able only to know the client's interest in the professional's sphere of expertise. Even this is impossible, however. Professions are complex enterprises. A profession will have goals, objectives, or ends that seem intrinsic to it. The problem, however, is that each profession can plausibly have many goals that often conflict. In medicine the goals are variously preservation of life, cure of disease, relief of suffering, and promotion of health. In order to know even the client's medical well-being, one needs to know the correct mixing and balancing of these conflicting goals within the medical sphere. A teacher needs to know whether the student's educational well-being is enhanced by learning reasoning, specific technical skills, or how to pass exams. Assuming each has some place in the student's well-being, one needs to know the correct mix of these objectives.

Professionals in any profession that has more than one legitimate end cannot be expected to know the client's interests even within that sphere unless they know the correct mix of these ends for this particular client. Just as Buchanan shows the impossibility of the physician knowing the patient's medical best interest, so every professional will find it impossible to know the client's best interest within the professional's sphere.

Buchanan's proposal that the professional will have to take on the broader role as counselor poses real problems, however. One might think that the professional should be at least as good a counselor to the client as any other generally educated, concerned friend of the client. However, if I am correct, the professional ought systematically to miscalculate the client's best interest to the extent that he or she is overcommitted to one subsphere of well-being. Anyone who has given his or her life to one such subsphere might well be so overcommitted. The client might better be advised to place trust in less specifically invested friends, colleagues, or relatives who share the client's same general world view and value system than in someone who *ought* to know nothing special about the client's well-being outside the professional's sphere and, in fact, ought to overvalue well-being within that sphere. If it is impossible for the professional to know how to promote the well-being of the client even within the professional's own sphere, then trust of the professional seems misplaced even if the professional is dedicated to the client and is impeccably virtuous.

It is striking that different professions seem to make radically different presumptions about the ability of the professional to know the best interest of the client. At one extreme are the spheres of education, medicine, and law, where professionals seem to believe that clients should know very little about their own well-being. Teachers, at least at lower grade levels, presume that they can determine the student's interest far better than the student can. At the other extreme, where great respect for the independence of the client's conceptualization of the client's interest is manifest, paradoxically we have the military. Whatever else can be said about military ethics, it is generally recognized that the client (the government) is the one that should determine not only overall objectives but strategic and tactical maneuvers. Professionals in the foreign service likewise minimize their claims about their ability to know their "client's" best interest. Rather they are servants of the government, which is expected to make its own best-interest value choices.

An interesting intermediate case is architecture. While lawyers or physicians might routinely say, figuratively or literally, to their clients, "Trust me. I will promote your interest," one cannot imagine an architect saying to the client wanting a house built, "Leave it to me to promote your interest. I will build a Tudor, a wild contemporary, or a two-family box based on my judgment of your best interest." The architect will presume that for most of these major aesthetic choices and for decisions about the price range, the client's choice should prevail. However, in other kinds of tactical choices, the architect may find himself or herself claiming a right to be trusted in determining the client's best interest. The architect may choose the level of safety in the construction methods or the durability of the materials on the presumption that the client should trust the professional to these choices even though they involve trade-offs of one sphere of the client's well-being for another sphere about which the professional knows nothing.

III. Trusting the Professional with the Facts

If the professional ought not to be trusted to know the client's best interest, then can the professional at least be trusted to give the client the facts and the plausible interaction options? Dan Brock shows that trust may even be misplaced at this level. Brock makes clear some of the problems. Most professionals will insist that professionals are moral agents who must act on their own moral commitments. The obstetrician who believes abortion is murder probably should not be trusted to present the option of amniocentesis and abortion for women with a marginal risk of an afflicted fetus. Brock also observes that in medicine what I am calling the liberal solution—what he called the consumer sovereignty model—fails to take into account the reality of sick patients.

The point is limited, however. It is remarkable how frequently analysts of medicine, especially those, unlike Brock, who are defenders of medical paternalism, appeal to the incapacity of the sick as a reason why clients cannot be sovereign. In fact, even in medicine the vast majority of lay decision makers are not so incapacitated by their illnesses that they lack substantial autonomy in decision making. Many are not sick at all. They see the physician for routine physicals, well baby and prenatal visits. Others who are sick have illnesses that are not incapacitating. They see the physician for follow-up of chronic, nondebilitating conditions such as a heart arrhythmia or diabetes, or if they have a serious illness that is stable or in remission. Often they are very knowledgeable about their conditions and not so traumatized that they cannot act rationally. In many other cases, patients are incapacitated, but others who are healthy are their surrogates—parents, spouses, or those designated with durable powers of attorney. Even if the point did hold for medicine, it would not be relevant to other professions where clients are seeking services for conditions that would not affect their ability to reason.

The real problem with the liberal solution is not primarily that clients are incapacitated or even that professionals should act on their consciences. Normally, these should not interfere with the ideal of consumer choice. The real problems are those raised later by Brock. His discussion of the incorrigibility of patient values provides a needed corrective for excessively subjective positions. However, it does not follow that if patient's interests can be determined with objectivity that any one professional can be in a position to determine them. Thus if decision making is to be shared on these grounds, the plausible conclusion would not be decision making shared with the professional, but rather with the person or group that plausibly is in a position to know what is objectively in the client's interest. Even that conclusion requires a subordination of autonomy as a constraint on promotion of the client's objective well-being, a subordination many liberals would not be willing to accept.

The most serious problem with the liberal solution for the claim of professional-client trust is not necessarily this difficulty in professional's knowing client well-being, but rather the problem addressed in the second part of Brock's paper: the problem of providing value-free facts. If the professional ought not to be trusted even for that task, then our understanding of the professional as a trusted informant, as one justifiably in the fiduciary role, will be utterly shaken.

Brock makes a good case for the difficulties for professionals in providing factual information. Whatever Brock says about physicians would appear to apply equally to all the other professionals under consideration. Their accounts of the facts in the law, teaching, architecture, and all other professions must necessarily incorporate theory choice, selection of which observations are important (i.e. valuable), choice of levels of significance in drawing conclusions, and countless other choices in the presentation of the facts.

Once again, the problem is not that professionals are unworthy of trust because of their biases, lack of commitment, or lack of objectivity. Even the most skilled, knowledgeable, and unbiased professional must constantly make evaluative and conceptual choices that must get incorporated into the presentation to the client. The lawyer's summary of the legal history, the teacher's selection of a syllabus of the important literature, and the accountant's choice of an accounting method all cloud the most impeccably devoted, skilled, and unbiased professional's presentations. Professionals cannot be trusted to present the facts objectively, not because of their shortcomings as professionals, but because of the inherent limits in the process of reporting professional knowledge. Brock's conclusions make clear that trust does not make sense if one views the professional as a presenter of facts any more than it does if the professional is seen as the one who makes decisions based on his or her presumptions about the client's interest.

IV. Trusting the Professional to be Virtuous

There is one last defense of the notion that professionals should be trusted. Perhaps even if they cannot know the client's interest and cannot present objective, value-free accounts of the facts, they can at least be trusted, if they are good practitioners, to manifest the virtues inherent in the profession.

This last hope for the notion that professionals should be trusted, however, rests on the presumption that there is such a thing as a virtue inherent in a profession that the members of the profession can be expected to know and articulate to the general public. Gilbert Meilaender considers the question of whether this is possible.

He initially takes on what may be a straw person: his belief that some people hold that there are universal sets of values or virtues and that professional virtues are merely what he calls "specifications of more universal norms." Some critics of professional ethics have argued that the ethics for a profession should be seen as derived from a more universal ethical system rather than created or articulated by the professions themselves. Some, apparently including Meilaender, have mistakenly understood this to mean that holders of this view reject the notion that there can be special norms or rules or virtues for special roles.

I, for one, have long argued explicitly that no one can plausibly deny that there should be special rules and duties—what I have called role-specific duties—for those in professional roles.[1] I have not specifically addressed whether there should be special virtues for special roles, but that seems plausible as well. For example, I assume that the rules of distributive justice for distributing scarce resources are quite different for those who are parents and those who are administrators of food programs to feed the hungry. Parents have a role-specific duty to take care of their own children first; administrators have a duty to distribute food according to some principle that is not particularistic like the parent's duty is—according to need, for example. I assume that each conceptualization of a profession will have a special set of virtues that uniquely fits that conceptualization, just as it has a special set of principles and rules. The real question, though, is how this relates to whether there is a virtue or set of virtues inherent in a profession.

I have argued that the role-specific duties of those in special roles should be grounded in a more universal ethical system. I mean by this that whatever the duty is for one in the particular role, it should stem from a more basic ethical system. For example, a Kantian ethic or a Christian ethic might provide the underpinning for both the egalitarian justice rule of the relief worker and the rule of the parent that there are special obligations to fulfill commitments one has to one's own children. These role-specific duties do not find their ultimate ground in the agreement of relief workers or of parents about their respective roles. Rather, they both grow out of a common moral system. Both Christian relief workers and Christian parents should understand why relief workers should be egalitarian and parents should not. Likewise, the virtues of a relief worker and the virtues of the parent should be different, but anyone who understands a Christian system of ethics should be able to grasp what the virtues of the Christian conception of the relief worker or parent would be.

The implication of this for whether professionals can be trusted to manifest virtues inherent in their professions should begin to emerge. Even though there are different virtues for different roles, it is not that the virtues are inherent in the role, independent of any underlying foundational ethical system. Rather, there may be as many different conceptions of the virtues of a particular profession as there are underlying foundational systems capable of generating a conceptualization of the professional role in question.

It is, according to this formation, a serious mistake to assume that there is any such thing as a univocal concept of the profession of lawyer or teacher or physician. Rather, there are as many different conceptions as there are systems of belief and value that can imagine professionals working in the legal, educational, and medical spheres. Thus, it is doubly a mistake to think of a single set of virtues inherent in a profession. In the first place there are many competing conceptualizations of each professional role. The Talmudic physician's role may have so little to do with the feminist physician's role that they are essentially different professional roles. There is no ideal type role of the professional physician abstracted from the Talmudic or feminist or Hippocratic or Christian conception of physicianing to which a set of virtues can be inherent. Moreover, the varying sets of virtues that are appropriate for each professional role according to the various basic systems of beliefs and values that can conceptualize the roles do not take their origin from the professional images that are thus generated. Rather, each grows out of the underlying system of belief and value that generates it.

Thus, there is no one set of virtues for generic lawyers. Rather, there are different virtues appropriate to the libertarian lawyer, the Talmudic lawyer, and the Buddhist lawyer. These sets of virtues stem from the underlying systems of libertarianism, Judaism, and Buddhism, respectively. These are not general virtues of libertarianism, Judaism, or Buddhism. We acknowledge that the lawyering role should have its own set of virtues in each case. We can have as our goal, trusting the libertarian lawyer to manifest the virtues libertarians see as appropriate for their lawyers; trusting the Talmudic lawyer to manifest the virtues that Jews see as appropriate for their lawyers; and so forth. We cannot trust lawyers generally to manifest the virtues of generic lawyers because, even if they are terribly dedicated and virtuous, there is no such thing as a set of virtues inherent in a profession. The lawyering virtues come in many brands, reflecting the many different conceptions of the lawyering profession, and each of these brands of lawyering virtues takes its roots in some underlying system of beliefs and values. The virtues for the various lawyering roles will not be identical to the virtues for the general good person in these various systems, but they will derive from them and be special manifestations of the virtues as understood by these various traditions.

V. Summary

Thus, it is a mistake to assume that professionals can be trusted to know the best interest of their clients, to present facts and options to them objectively, or to manifest virtues inherent in professional roles. This does not imply that professionals are "untrustworthy" in the sense that they are lacking in dedication, integrity, or good character. It does not even imply that they are self-serving or conflicted by the demands to serve the interests of those other than their clients. Even if the professional is impeccably committed to the client, still, in theory, the professional ought not to be able to know the client's interest, ought not be able to present the relevant facts in a value-free manner, and ought not be expected to manifest some set of virtues inherent in the professional role. Trust requires something far different: a commitment to the client, a confession of inability to present value-free facts, and an acknowledgment of which underlying belief system generates the set of virtues and the role conception under which the professional is operating.

Note

1. R.M. Veatch, *A Theory of Medical Ethics* (New York: Basic Books, Inc., 1981), chap. 2; and *The Foundations of Justice* (New York: Oxford University Press, 1986), chap. 6.

Discussion

Dr. Freidson: I am a little puzzled why you posed the issue as being one of trust in the professional's being able to know the interest of the clients rather than trust in the professional's competence and commitment to the interest of the clients, whether they know it or not.

In other words, a client can tell an architect that he wants a postmodern facade and trust the competence of the architect, who, in fact, does some sketches that show a variety of postmodern facades and does it competently, according to what the client has expressed as his or her interests. I do not know why one has to assume that the professional knows or can know the interests, but whether they will serve the interests is really another matter again.

Dr. Veatch: What I am trying to do, for the purposes of this discussion, is to finesse the very practical and important question of whether professionals will serve the interests of their clients once they know them.

Dr. Freidson: Why do you want to finesse it?

Dr. Veatch: Because I think the important problem is prior to that, the presumption that a professional can know the client's interests.

One might ask why the professional cannot simply ask the client? That, however, presumes that there are a few definitive choice points where we can call time out and have that conversation.

If Dan Brock is right, the penetration of the professional's evaluation into the communication is far more pervasive than is generally realized. I go back to my example of the lawyer. It would take certainly hours, if not years, for the lawyer to understand what the client's

interests are in pursuing a rather complicated and sensitive legal issue—for instance, a divorce or contesting a will. To think that the lawyer can have a ten-minute conversation where the client can spell out
his or her interests presumes much more ability to communicate than
can actually take place. It also presumes that there are only a few key
judgments that are dependent upon articulation of those interests.

In fact, in many professional relationships that conversation does
not even take place at this elementary level. In many professions, the
professional just assumes that he or she can deduce what those interests are.

It is extremely difficult, I believe impossible, for the professional to
learn and comprehend the client's interest unless the professional
comes out of the same systems of beliefs and values as the client. If
they do come from the same tradition, the client can say, "We still
think together on this. I shall turn you loose. You will bias all your
facts and communications, but that is all right because they will be the
biases that I would want to have anyway. We cannot figure out exactly what virtues you are manifesting, but you will be manifesting virtues that are derived from my system of beliefs and values, so it is all
right."

In fact, we do not yet choose professionals that way.

Dr. Pellegrino: I want to make two points of clarification on assumptions that are not necessarily my views but relate to the papers
here. At least when I use the term "medical good," I am using it in a
very narrow sense. I am using it in the sense of that which is scientifically correct to the extent that one can make a fact judgment, and I do
not think you are suggesting that we could not make some fact
judgments.

I think the virtue of Dr. Brock's position is that he saw it as a spec-
trum in which there was a value-loaded end and fact-loaded end. So,
when I use "medical good," it is in the case of a nephrologist saying,
"All right, you have renal failure. The medical good is to change the
natural history of the disease. We can alter the state of mortality and
morbidity in a definable way." That is to say, in a definable way in
terms of the degree of nitrogen and so on. That is a thing that can be
looked at scientifically. That is what I mean by the medical good.
Now, whether in fact, that is good for the patient is a different matter.
It is not subsumed in medical good.

The patient says, "Look, I do not choose to be kept alive when my
heart is failing, my lungs are failing, and so on."

So there are various levels of good. We do not conflate all of them
in one sense, the physician can know that local level of good. That to

me is the lowest level of good. The medical good. The medically indicated. That is the language I am using.

The second point I want to make is that I have never suggested and I do not think it is appropriate to suggest that the predicament of illness necessarily interferes with autonomy. I am merely saying that the patient is, as a matter of fact, anxious, fearful, et cetera, but these conditions do not take away autonomy. But they do provide certain impediments to the expression of the autonomy, and that imposes on the physician an enormous responsibility to enhance that autonomy to work with the altered state of the patient and not deprive him or her of autonomy. I do not agree with those physicians who feel that if you are ill, by that very fact, you cannot be autonomous.

Dr. Buchanan: Talking about medical good in the case of the nephrologist is already lumping together too many things. You seem to want a notion of the medical best interest, but renal function is not the patient's medical good necessarily, because that may come at the price of impairing some other function. There are many cases where even the notion of medical best interest is a very complex, weighted, evaluative kind of summarizing judgment; not only would it be difficult for any one specialist to make such a judgment because it involves weighing things across areas of expertise of different specialists, but it is hard for me even to imagine that there would be an answer that even an omniscient clinician would know as to what is in the medical best interest of the patient in some of those complicated cases.

So I think the problem at what you consider to be the factual level is already more difficult. It is not just that the medical interests are not the most important interests vis-à-vis the human interests, it is that even the notion of medical interest requires evaluative assumptions in some cases. It requires assuming that a kind of aggregated weighted judgment can be made about the beneficial effects of many different kinds of bodily functions, some of which are not hierarchically ordered.

Dr. Pellegrino: Are you denying that there can be any objective statements?

Dr. Buchanan: No.

Dr. Pellegrino: If you are not denying that, then I think we could in individual situations predict that if we did not intervene, a particular outcome would be the natural history, the statistical projection of this particular case.

Dr. Buchanan: But that prediction is not a judgment about good. To say something is good, even medically good, is to evaluate the results of certain events that will occur.

Dr. Pellegrino: I am using the term idiosyncratically in terms of good medicine. I understand that is not the same as good. I am very clear on that. It is an idiosyncratic way in which the physicians use the term.

If you want to reject that, that is perfectly okay. But the evaluation of the natural history of the disease and what you modify is all that I am saying is the good. The medically right might be a better term. Or, the technically right.

Dr. Veatch: I am afraid that even changing to medically right does not solve the problem because right conveys an evaluative judgment much like the evaluation that goes on in saying something is good.

It seems that the preferable strategy would be to use language I know you use elsewhere, that is, to distinguish between a medical effect and a medical good or a medical benefit.

Until we consider the implications of Dan Brock's paper, we might say that what the medical professional can tell is whether dialysis for a particular kidney patient will have medical effect, leaving open the question of whether it promoted the medical good. In fact, there will be several effects, several medical effects. It could prolong life, but also increase suffering. Whether it is a medical good depends upon the evaluative trade-off between prolonging life and relieving suffering.

Dr. Brock's analysis becomes critical at that point. He says, first of all, that there may be an objectively correct answer to the question of what the medical good is. It is going to be hard to figure out what that objectively correct answer is, and I would argue that it is going to be contingent upon what fundamental system of belief and value is used for the assessments. But even conceding for a moment that an objective medical good exists, it does not follow that the nephrologist can figure out what that objective good is.

Furthermore, if we take the position that all the physician can do then is to tell whether the intervention will have an effect and that we will have to use some other strategy for finding out objectively whether it is a good or bad effect, now we are challenged further by Dan Brock's paper. Dr. Brock tells us that even in telling whether the dialysis will have an effect, there is a whole set of evaluations that have gone on for some of these cases. The evaluations may be so obvious and consensual that they are not worth looking at or pursuing, but, nevertheless, there are evaluations.

For example, in explaining the options to the nephrology patient, it is factually correct that putting a gun to the patient's head and pulling the trigger is one intervention strategy. Most clinicians will not present it, even though they can give a factual account of what happens when the trigger is pulled. They will rule that option out in part because it is immoral and in part because they think it is so implausible that the patient will not find it attractive, even though they may make a mistake in that assessment.

All of that leads me to line up with Drs. Brock and Buchanan; as a practical matter, professionals may find themselves explaining the effects and then asking the patient to evaluate, to decide whether the effects are good or bad. This strategy, however, rests on the mistaken assumption that the facts can be communicated without necessarily making conceptual and evaluative assumptions.

Ultimately, the only solution to this is to confess that the values will so penetrate the interaction that neither patient nor professional can understand the process. One's only protection as a lay person is to pick the professional who has bought into the same system of beliefs and values, the same conceptual assumptions the client holds. The same problems arise in teaching.

I know when I write a syllabus for a course I am making all sorts of value judgments for students, and there are students whose interests I do not really understand. I hope that the students for whom I am making all of these value choices somehow share the values that I bring to bear in the designing of the syllabus or the structuring of a lecture. My hope that that is the case probably is not very well founded.

I can also follow Dr. Brock's strategy of saying there is some objective good for these students and that somehow I can figure out what that is and impose it upon them. But that is a very unsatisfactory solution. I am not at all confident that professionals are capable of discerning the client's interest even in the professional's sphere, let alone in areas in which the professional is not an expert.

III.
The Sociocultural Setting of the Professions

SAMUEL GOROVITZ

Professions, Professors, and Competing Obligations

I. Introduction: Fiduciary Responsibility and the Common Good

To consider the conflict between the professional's fiduciary responsibility and the professional's obligations with respect to the common good it is necessary to ask first, what it is to be a professional; second, what sort of fiduciary responsibility is associated with being a professional; and third, what sense can relevantly be made of the notion of the common good. I will address these questions only very briefly, giving the majority of my attention to examples of the conflict between fiduciary obligation and the common good in the academic community. The profession I will focus on is that of the university or college professor.

Although the various professions are quite different from one another, they seem, in large part, to be united in their commitment to serve the interests of a particular person: the client in the case of the lawyer, the patient in the case of the doctor, the parishioner in the case of the priest, and the student in the case of the teacher. This commitment constitutes the foundation of the fiduciary relationship between the professional and the individual served and exists because of the social institution that establishes that specific profession. For example, I could perform a medical procedure, and yet this would not make me a doctor. Even if I removed an appendix properly, the relationship I would have with the person divested of the appendix would not be a physician-patient relationship because I am not a member of the social institution of medicine. Language is misleading on this point because we do speak of a nonphysician "practicing medicine" without a license. Yet, in an important sense, that person is not practicing medicine at all, but doing something else, even though it is medicine-like. He or she is performing medical acts, but not practicing medicine.

I speak of the professions as social institutions because society grants distinctive authorities to professionals and demands particular obligations of them. As many of the contributors to this volume have noted, this network of entitlements and responsibilities is granted by society because the services provided by professionals are deemed to serve the common good. What the common good is taken to mean, however, will vary from profession to profession.

For some, the common good served by the legal profession is the availability to all of the procedural justice that is provided by the adversarial system. Others with a different view, perhaps from critical legal studies, might argue instead that the common good that ought to be served by the legal profession is substantive justice—quite a different matter. But in any case, either is a very different conception of the good than that which motivates the health care professions. The larger good sought by these professions may be defined as the health of the community, but is not likely to have much to do with either procedural or substantive justice. For a physician, the common good may have to do with the hospital as distinct from the individual patient, with the medical specialty, or with some larger collective, each of which in different ways can be in conflict with the interests of a particular patient.

The sense of common good that animates judgments within the professions tends to be profession-specific, rather than some sort of global notion of net aggregate utility across humanity. So in order to understand the conflicts that may arise between professional obligations to the individual and to the common good, we have to understand and interpret both the fiduciary responsibilities and the common good in a way that makes sense within the context of individual professions.

There is an inherent potential for conflict between any professional's obligations of fidelity to individuals, on the one hand, and the common good, on the other; one can readily cite examples, profession by profession, of that kind of conflict. Consider the example of the doctor prolonging the life, at immense public cost, of an irreversibly insensate patient. The professional staff of the hospital may feel a clear and explicit fiduciary responsibility to continue the treatment of such a patient regardless of cost. At the same time, however, it is clear that the financial integrity of the hospital is a necessary condition of its maintaining the ability to provide care at all, and that the common good such an ability constitutes can be in conflict with an unrestrained pursuit of the interests of the individuals to whom the hospital staff feel a responsibility.

The justification of each professional's willingness and even commitment to act in defense of the individual's interests, despite an apparent cost to the common good, is that the social practice which creates those commitments is, on balance, preferable to a social arrangement within which the professional abandons that commitment whenever the common good seems imperiled by strict fidelity to the individual's good. So, for example, we believe that the physician may not properly consider social or personal criteria in deciding whether to treat a patient in need, and may not abandon a seriously ill patient merely because the money runs out. Nor should the lawyer function as a pretrial judge in order to elect only the virtuous to represent. But in general, there are limits, however ill defined, to each professional's commitment to the individual—instances where the professional is expected to place the common good above that of the individual, despite the existence of a fiduciary relationship. The reporting of infectious diseases or gunshot wounds are examples of such limits.

II. The Professor as Professional

I want now to focus on the college or university professor, whose obligation to individual students can conflict with other obligations, either to a class, an institution, a profession, or to society. A full range of issues arises when we consider the professional responsibilities of the faculty, including issues concerning personal relationships with the constituency served, supervisory relationships, and even questions of safety. It is my hope that this discussion of the academic context will shed some light on the other professions as well.

The primary responsibility of professors is to educate their students. Given this, the student should be able to trust not only the faculty member's knowledge, but also the procedural fairness with which the professor conveys this knowledge and assesses student performance. These elements constitute the basis of the fiduciary relationship between professor and student.

The common good relative to an academic enterprise may be defined in terms of the discipline which a faculty member feels an obligation to represent fairly, to advocate, and perhaps to advance. It may also be defined in terms of the class, as distinct from the individual student, or in terms of the college, the university, or even the nation.

Steven Cahn is one of the few writers who has devoted serious attention to the ethical questions that pertain to professorial responsibility. In his book, *Saints and Scamps: Ethics and Academia*,[1] Cahn discusses teaching at both undergraduate and graduate levels, scholarship, service, and personnel decisions. He notes especially the faculty members' obligations to students, which include obligations of competence and impartiality and the responsibility to evaluate the performance of colleagues and to act to prevent or eliminate incompetence in teaching.

In his paper in this volume, Eliot Freidson discusses the subject of peer review with regard to professional work. "Present day etiquette," he says, "makes it inappropriate to denigrate the work of a colleague to a client. Even if one feels that a colleague does poor work, it is not proper to inform the client of that. . . . This reluctance to judge is sustained by an even greater unwillingness to confront apparently erring colleagues, let alone to take any action to punish or otherwise correct them in the interest of the well-being of clients. Even when there is intervention, the dominant rule is confidentiality so as to protect both the reputation and career of the errant colleague and the public face of the profession itself. This etiquette expresses an important part of the ideal typical of professionalism—namely, collegiality."[2] Freidson's observations about collegiality provide an accurate description of much of what goes on in academic life, at least among tenured faculty. There is substantial evaluation of the vulnerable untenured, but for the most part, there it stops.

Syracuse University's College of Arts and Sciences recently passed, after two years of debate, a statement of academic responsibility which affirms that the first responsibility of students is to the academic side of college life and, in like manner, the first obligation of the faculty members is to their classes and students. Faculty members are expected to give careful, competent attention to the full range of their teaching duties, which are then enumerated. They must conclude classes on time and evaluation must be impartial and solely on the academic performance of the students. This document by itself will not radically transform the behavior of the few most problematic members of the faculty, but it at least strengthens the hand of those who want to exert a constructive influence on those whose behavior fails to meet the university's criteria.

If we are going to think about academic ethics in a way that is similar to the way in which medical or legal ethics has been pursued, it will be helpful to have some specific cases to consider. One is very simple, and relatively uncontroversial. Some years ago I had a number of complaints about a faculty member who was chronically late to class. When I confronted that faculty member and said "Students are complaining: you are apparently always late to class," the response was "That is a professorial prerogative. They come into class late. I don't like to have students trickle in, disrupting the start of the class. So I give them five minutes to get in and get settled, then I show up. I don't mind if some of them wait for me, but I am not about to waste my time waiting for them." I suggested that this wasn't the right way to handle the class, but in the end induced punctuality only by a credible threat of suspension of pay. It was not a happy solution, though the tardiness did stop. I take that as an example of a faculty member without a proper sense of a fiduciary relationship to the students.

More recently, a faculty member told a disruptive student to "get out" of her class late in the semester. The student came in to complain about this perceived mistreatment. The complaint was thoroughly investigated, and the outcome was not to the student's advantage.

The young professor, somewhat unsure of her authority, found the student consistently disruptive of the class. He alone held certain views that were opposed by everyone else in the class. Since there were, therefore, two sides to the issue, and he alone advocated one of them, he wanted half the discussion time. He provided that rationale explicitly, and tried to take half the discussion time. All efforts to reason with him, to persuade him to temper his outbursts, were unsuccessful. Finally, in frustration, the faculty member evicted him from the class.

The faculty member originally felt a responsibility to that student, though he was being problematic and disruptive. She felt an obligation to allow him to continue as a member of the class, to let him speak, and to try to educate him. Later, she recognized her obligation to the rest of the class, which was feeling increasingly deprived and oppressed by the disruptive behavior. The student was put on disciplinary probation in response to the complaint he lodged, and told he could return to the class only provided that he kept his mouth shut. Any disruptive behavior on his part would result in his permanent and irrevocable removal from the class. We tried to reinforce the faculty member's sense both of authority and of obligation to the class as a community. This was an example of someone whose interests as a student had to be overridden in the interest of the common good, or the educational environment for the entire class. Of course, it can plausibly be argued that it is in the best interest of the individual student to have been held strictly responsible for the consequences of his unacceptable behavior, and that therefore the action that best served the common good—in this case, the harmonious functioning of the class—was also in the best interests of the individual student in the long run. But not every case admits of such a comforting interpretation.

The next example is one that I found terribly difficult some years ago. A severely handicapped student had earned standing as a junior by virtue of his intelligence and tenacity at a level unprecedented in my experience. He was wheelchair-bound and had minimal communicative capacity; he could not speak or write! He could communicate in just two ways. One was by pecking on an electric typewriter, one key at a time, with a wooden dowel affixed to a kind of hat. That is how he produced his papers. In class, he had a board which had a limited vocabulary of perhaps two or three dozen key words printed on it—the logical connectives, for example, and the alphabet. He had enough muscular control to cause one hand to circle around; if one looked carefully, one could discern what word or letter he was indicating. He raised his hand when he had something to say, and when he was called on, another member of the class would decode his behavior and translate it to the class. This was a slow procedure. It took minutes for his question, or the point he wanted to make, to surface. At the same time, members of the class learned much from the presence of this student—about stereotyping, tenacity, courage, tolerance, and human capacity. At one point this student raised his hand to offer a joke—not a funny or brief joke, but a joke—to the class. It was extremely irritating to the rest of the class, partly because it took so much time. I felt a particular relationship of nurturance, caring, guidance, and encouragement with this student, but I made a decision that day henceforth to discriminate against him on grounds of his handicap; that is, I decided that my obligation to the common good, to the class as a functioning educational environment, made it necessary for me to withdraw from him certain communicative privileges which the rest of the class would retain. Others could quip, others could make a joke. He no longer could. I felt an obligation to explain to him why that decision was made, and, in effect, to put him under injunction to cease and desist from communicating in ways which, because of his handicap, were detrimental to the interests of the class generally. It is not at all clear that his own interests were thereby advanced.

I cite those three cases as examples of the many kinds of conflict that arise in academia. We must think carefully about such matters if we wish to elevate the discussion of professional responsibility in higher education to the level of our concern with ethical judgment in other professions.

In his paper in this volume, Dan Brock argues that professional judgment, at least in the case of medicine, is not value neutral, but that there are certain values which place constraints on the decisions that professionals make. These values constitute the fundamental norms of the profession which it is the professional's obligation to defend and to advocate. Quite the same is true in law and in each of the other professions, including the academic profession. Just as the physician has a commitment to health and a responsibility to advocate health-related values, the academic has a responsibility to defend and advocate certain core values of the academy. So, for example, plagiarism and cheating are violations of those fundamental values, and faculty members have responsibilities, more weighty and pervasive responsibilities than faculty reliably fulfill, to combat such violations of academic values. Academic dishonesty on the part of the student is something like a patient feigning symptoms or denying their presence to the physician. Such deception strikes at the very possibility of trust in the relationship between professional and patient or student. Just as a physician may be trustworthy, but cannot have a mutually trusting relationship with a patient who is lying about symptoms or compliance with prescriptions, the faculty member's capacity to educate is undermined by betrayals of integrity on the part of the student. A firm response to such dishonesty is appropriate, even if the case cannot be sustained that the culprit's interest will be best served as a result.

In some instances, defending the basic values of a profession may require overriding the best interests of an individual, just as those interests may at times be overridden by other aspects of a commitment to a common good. No algorithms are generally available to relieve professionals of the burden of resolving such conflicts; instead, they require the exercise of moral judgment, and can invite challenge and controversy. That such sensitive judgment is required is not due solely to the need to resolve conflicts between fiduciary commitments and the common good, however. It is, after all, the need for the continuing exercise of judgment that is perhaps the single most distinguishing characteristic of those enterprises we count as professions.

One issue that is coming rapidly to the fore in higher education is that the professoriate is a very diverse population, and that many faculty members aren't just teachers, especially at research universities. In some cases, they aren't even primarily teachers. They have multiple commitments and multiple motivations. It may well be that new faculty members are in general not trained in or brought into an ethos which places student interests at the center of their behavior.

In his paper in this volume, Dan Fox asks us to look at the ethos of the profession and how it shapes behavior in health care, as it has evolved over six decades. Similarly, we need to look at the ethos of the profession into which faculty members enter and how that ethos has been evolving, what it is like now, and what future is most probable. It is only in the context of that evolution of a complex professional ethos that we can consider and judge the professional responsibility of faculty members.

Notes

1. S. Cahn, *Saints and Scamps: Ethics and Academia* (Totowa, N.J.: Rowman and Littlefield, 1986).
2. E. Freidson, "Nourishing Professionalism," in this volume, p. 198.

Discussion

Dr. Brock: Your talk surprised me in one respect; that is, I expected the conflicts that you would talk about to be conflicts, say, between the particular individual to whom the professional is committed and broader social goods where the costs or harms to these were, so to speak, not within, not the same kinds of goods that the profession sought to produce. For example, in cases where a newspaper publishes information that is supposed to be protected by national security, you have a conflict between individual rights and another good outside the good of freedom of the press that was at stake.

I wonder if the analysis would be different and in some ways harder because the goods I think are less measurable, if you had conflicts between your commitments to your individual student and to some broader social good that wasn't a piece of the same good that you were promoting in education.

Dr. Gorovitz: What would be an example of that? Let's see, perhaps someone who had a student—suppose you had a student who wanted to be a more successful advertising copywriter for the tobacco industry.

Dr. Brock: That would be an example. I don't know whether it would be a hard case or not.

Dr. Meilaender: Can I give you an example? Suppose you had a student in a class who is a neo-Nazi and was putting forward an argument just as a piece of reasoning and getting dumped on by other students. Would you conceive of yourself as entering into the discussion, in a sense on his side, helping to explore the argument he was providing the rationale for, even at the possible cost of having some other students see that he had a point?

Dr. Brock: It is not clear to me that that is the sort of thing I was getting at. My thought is that the goods are not as commensurable if you are just trading off the same kind of goods with particular individuals in the same area. For example, in medicine you may trade off goods regarding three people's health more reasonably than you can trade off interest in public parks against Jones's health.

Dr. Gorovitz: The difficulty we are having coming up with examples tells us something. The fact that we haven't been able to come up with an example that prompts you to say, "Yes, those are just the parameters of the conflict," shows us that that is not the kind of conflict that is very salient in the actual practicing lives of the teaching profession; whereas, conflicts of values *within* the profession actually are.

Dr. Pellegrino: I have three people with questions. Would you be willing to have them make their comments and then take them as a group?

Dr. Gorovitz: Yes.

Dr. Zaner: I have a very brief comment. It has to do with the kind of conflict that might violate the very nature of the student-teacher relationship. In medicine, for example, Eric Cassell points out conduct that seems to many physicians to undermine the very idea of the physician-patient relationship. Two examples would be the seductive patient and the deceptive patient. As Cassell explains it, the patient who is lying to the doctor is not lying to you. He is lying to the doctor, the social role. The same with the seductive patient. The patient is seducing the doctor; that is to say, to put it slightly differently, those modes of conduct themselves are medically significant and must be taken as such.

I wonder if some of these examples of the student-teacher relationship might have that kind of mode of analysis appropriate to them.

Dr. Veatch: I think it is very helpful to the project to have the teacher example highlighted because it seems to me to show that it is logically necessary in some cases to serve the individual interest of at least some of one's clients. If you stop and think about it, it is equally true for any other profession, assuming that the professional has more than one client at a time. If that is true, the corollary is that trust at a certain point is inappropriate, and it would be morally misleading for clients in those spots to trust their professional to be serving their interests when they are in head-on conflict with the interests of other clients, possibly with the interests of third parties outside of that relationship.

That seems to me to suggest that it is logically necessary and sometimes that it is morally appropriate to abandon the client in special circumstances. If that is true, then trust can no longer be an automatically assumed good without limit. That being the case, I think we can press one step further. I think it is also plausible that if you ask the profession what those limits are, you will get systematically structured answers that would be quite different from the answers you get if you asked the society generally what the limits are.

For example, if you asked the psychiatrist when it is appropriate to violate confidence, he will give you some class of cases. You ask the society generally, they will give you a different class of cases.

Ultimately, I am interested in the question of what one should do if the professions will not only admit that trust is inappropriate, but give systematically biased answers to the question of when that limit is incurred.

Dr. Brock: Could I put a footnote on that? That will especially be the case in conflicts with third parties because we can expect them systematically to overvalue the good produced.

Dr. Freidson: I can be brief, also, but there are distinctions to be made when we discuss the profession, a profession, or a paradigmatic profession. Dr. Buchanan in some sense protested about that, and I think one thing Dr. Gorovitz will almost certainly agree on is that he was talking about people in research universities, major universities, and it is possible to argue that the academic profession, as people have argued about the legal profession, is really several different professions.

The Heinz and Laumann study of the Chicago Bar[1] concluded that there isn't a single legal profession. There are at least these two hemispheres, and you can, in fact, claim that various specialties are separate professions that have little in common or that what they have in common seems to be of relatively little importance.

So the issue does come down in a sense to empiricism, as Dr. Buchanan keeps insisting, what I think it is *actually* like as opposed to what is the *paradigm*. I think we can't do without these kinds of paradigms because they keep us in some sense enclosed in a kind of universe that we can begin to explore and that doesn't simply fall apart. In the case of the academic profession, I think it is possible to say that it is the one profession that isn't clearly divided into three really separate roles of administration, scholarship and research, and practice.

But generally speaking, there tend to be really quite distinct differences in the everyday lives and overall performances of people within professions that divide them and also make whatever ethical problems they have different, insofar as they have different clientele or no clientele at all.

But as I say, this is, I think, a matter that Dr. Gorovitz will agree on and might usefully elaborate on.

Dr. Gorovitz: First, I do think that student behavior that violates the values and commitments of the academic profession is educationally relevant behavior. Our first responsibility is to educate students with respect to those kinds of issues rather than simply to resort to the guillotine.

Now, how we do that is one question. Another question is to what extent can you do that student by student without regard to a separate issue, and that is deterrent value.

There is a need, I think, to some degree—and determining that degree is part of the job—to be intolerant of certain kinds of behaviors and for it to be visibly known that one is intolerant. For example, I publish in the student newspaper the litany of convictions that have been made for violations of academic integrity. It think it is important for people to know that this occurred and what is the penalty. At the same time it is a violation of educational responsibility to the offending student not to try to get that student to understand the imprudence, from his own point of view, of certain types of behavior, and so on.

I guess I stand with Cassell on the general point, but how it plays out in any particular case can itself generate conflicts, not the least of which has to do with allocation of resources at a particular time because these cases can be tremendously time-consuming. We spent eight months, in one instance, to prove that a student hired another student to go in and take an exam in his place and in his name. To get a conviction, we had to go back to hundreds of admissions applications, match handwriting samples, etc. It took eight months and I don't know how many hours, and we finally got them both. But those kinds of things do place tremendous demands on resources, and that, too, was an ingredient in the conflict.

On Dr. Veatch's point, my example didn't, I think, show that it is logically necessary to fail to serve the individual interests of at least some of one's clients. I think it showed that situations can occur in which it is logically necessary.

Dr. Veatch: Some of the time.

Dr. Gorovitz: That puts me in mind of Bernard Williams' phrase, though he used it in a somewhat different context, "moral luck." I felt when I was dealing with that handicapped student that whatever I did would give me legitimate grounds for regret and possibly for feeling guilty about what I had done, and it is a piece of bad moral luck. No matter what I did, there would be some moral remainder that manifested itself in my agent-regret.[2]

So I want to embrace a somewhat softer version of the point that Dr. Freidson made. I do agree entirely with your remark about the complexity of the profession of being a faculty member.

There are 3,300 colleges and universities in the United States, and there is almost nothing that is true of them all. Virtually anything that is true of one or more of them falls into at least some of them, and there are many, many different ways of being a part of the profession, but I do think that the constituency I am focusing on is large enough and central enough and influential enough that it constitutes a subclass of the entirety that is really very important.

Dr. Brock: It strikes me that there are implications for trust in the cases of disruptive students or students to whom we cannot give adequate time. When you think about what you can give your students in terms of attention, we always know if we have even a modestly sized class that we don't do all that we could do for those students to educate them, and we don't think that somehow undermines their trust in the kind of relationship we have. Well, why is that? One reason, I think, is that there is an implicit, rough understanding that we are dealing with scarce resources. There are a lot more of them than there are of us in any one class, and so they don't expect that much of us.

I think that shows that where trust might be undermined is where students get something different from what they have been led to expect they would get by norms of the profession.

For example, I suppose in the *Tarasoff*[3] case, it is hard for me to be sympathetic to the complaint of the patient there for the violation of confidentiality, but if that patient had had a very clear affirmation that everything that was said to his physician was absolutely confidential and would not be disclosed under any circumstances whatever, then when that expectation was violated, that is when you would expect to have the erosion of trust.

So, I think the matching of what one gets and the expectation of what one will get when one enters the relationship is probably going to be at least one of the key features of trust, not just the mere necessary limitation on what we can give individuals.

Dr. Gorovitz: I think that is right. It reminds me of a story by Bruce J. Friedman—you may know it—on precisely that issue, where the patient is very skeptical about the physician's commitment to confidentiality, which the patient, therefore, keeps testing. One of the ways he tests it is by revealing that he is having an affair and, indeed, that the affair he is having is with the psychiatrist's wife. The psychiatrist absolutely maintains flawless psychiatric propriety, treats the patient with uncompromised dedication. Finally, the patient is cured and dismissed from therapy, at which point the psychiatrist shoots him.

Prof. Kimura: Were there any cases that students brought to court?

Dr. Gorovitz: Yes. I have not been involved in any. There was one in Virginia. Dr. Brock has talked about the betrayal of expectations. Of course, there are two kinds, expectations legitimately engendered and expectations otherwise. In the case that I am thinking of, someone brought suit against a faculty member and institution on the grounds that the course offered did not correspond to the catalog description, that it cost money and it cost work, and it didn't provide what was advertised, and it was a successful litigation.

Dr. Qiu: Can you identify the common good? In some cases it is very difficult because what is the common good is value laden. In China, many people used to think of the control of the population as the common good. Others disagree. So how can we identify it?

Dr. Gorovitz: Part of what I was suggesting is that that is an important question and the answer isn't uniform. The question has to be asked within each profession and then more specifically within professions. The relevant sense of the common good from which are drawn the parameters of choice may be different at a research university and a college, and in a public versus a private university, and so on.

One of the things we have to ask is not what is the common good, but in this context, what is the relevant sense of common good, and that may be quite controversial.

Dr. Meilaender: This does not relate precisely to your theme of the common good and potential conflict there, but I just wanted to note this is also an area in which, however, the relation has been interpreted in the past, there is a kind of commodification issue that arises sometimes.

Now, I am at a teaching-intensive institution where students have certain expectations, but we have actually had students say to faculty members: "I am paying $18,000 a year for your time, and that is not just your time in the classroom."

I don't know what one makes of this and how it impinges on what we would be calling a fiduciary relationship, but the understanding of that could be transformed. Also, it is a little different from your precise topic, but I think it is happening to some degree in this area, also.

Dr. Gorovitz: But it really isn't so different. It is directly connected with this notion of expectations and what kind of expectations are legitimate, and we hear it often, often from parents who call up and say for $18,000 I expect—then you fill in the blank with whatever your imagination will produce—and what is expected is sometimes a clear violation of academic values or a clear violation of what we consider the educational responsibilities that we have in regard to the student in question.

So, yes, I try to get students to function as sophisticated consumers of education, but not in the sense of the commodification. Rather, I think the most effective way to get a faculty member to be conscientious about commenting on student work is to have students who simply won't stand for work that simply has a grade without critical commentary.

Dr. Zaner: I want to know when you say that there is this relativity, in the significance of the common good, the concept specifically of each profession's understanding and articulation, whether these are specific renditions of the common good from the perspective of a particular profession or whether you are trying to say there is no such animal as the common good.

For law, there is only the access or availability to procedural justice. There may be disputes about that, but what medicine takes for the common good has nothing to do with that. Are these two ways of articulating some more embracing notion of the commonweal of society?

Dr. Gorovitz: At the very least, I am saying that I don't think anything useful and insightful about the functioning of professions is going to flow from a generalized conception of a common good, writ large. Each profession focuses on a different slice of social direction and if we want usefully to understand the conflicts within that profession between fiduciary obligation and the sense of a large responsibility, we will understand that that larger responsibility is understood within the profession, in a profession-specific way.

Dr. Veatch: Shouldn't the profession have a systematically distorted view of that slice of the common good such that the society ought to discount the profession's assessment accordingly?

Fr. Langan: Common good has a particular place within Catholic social teaching, representing a kind of general harmony of interests within society, a harmony in which the norms are observed. As a result, it becomes a notion which is very evocative and not at all easy to unpack in a precise way.

For that reason, I suppose, I was inclined to feel a little bit of sympathy for the notion that it should simply be broken down into a series of professional specifications. But it does seem to me that that won't work, partly because even if we think about a relatively specialized segment of our society—something like the health polity that Dan Fox talked about this morning—we will find different professional groups with conflicting notions of what the good of the polity is and that they will be specified in professionally different ways.

One would still like to have the notion of common good in this polity, this health polity, or at least perhaps, if the notion of common good is too puzzling, to talk about the good of a community recognizing that people are going to belong to a variety of different communities. Things on the level of the health polity and the entire civil society.

And the notion, granted its vagueness and its scrambling over various incremental things, will continue to be something that needs to be appealed to in the resolution of conflicts between more specific conceptions of what is appropriate to a particular profession or common practice.

Notes

1. John P. Heinz and E.D. Laumann, *Chicago Lawyers: The Social Structure of the Bar* (New York: Russell Sage, 1982).

2. B. Williams, "Moral Luck," in *Moral Luck* (Cambridge: Cambridge University Press, 1981), 20-39.

3. *Tarasoff v. Regents of the University of California*, 17 Cal Rep 3d 425 (July 1, 1976).

ELIOT FREIDSON

Nourishing Professionalism

I. Introduction

In the United States today, the professions are going through great changes in their composition, numbers, and political influence. At the same time, their customary practices and privileges are changing. Law is struggling with both internal changes and vociferous public questioning of its ethics, accountancy is coming under increasing pressure from regulatory authorities, research science faces growing criticism of its capacity to assure the integrity of its members' work, and engineering is taking its licks. Medicine has been going through the most profound changes, perhaps because it deals with universal needs and its bills are being paid by the state and a handful of powerful, private "third parties." Its position today exemplifies what is typical about professionalism as a social problem—namely, the tension between the provision of affordable and conscientious service to others, and the economic interest of those who provide it.

Serious as the problem may be, physicians, lawyers, and other professionals continue to hold a special position in our political economy. Unlike many areas of our economy which have been deregulated, the professional arena continues to be characterized by quasi-monopolies over core services, often sustained by exclusive licensing.[1] Only at the margins of their jurisdictional boundaries has competition by other occupations been allowed. However, recent shifts in the ideological winds in the United States have led to pressure to reduce professional control over the way practices are organized and the way professionals compete with each other. Many professionally imposed restrictions on advertising were struck down by the Supreme Court while other restrictions were whittled away by the Federal Trade Commission's threat of antitrust action. New forms of ownership and control of the institutions in which professionals practice have been emerging and while many legal barriers remain,[2] we can now conceive of circumstances in which it is possible for individual professional practices to be drawn into large-scale, nonprofessional, corporate institutions. Medicine in particular seems likely to undergo such "corporatization," and prominent commentators like Paul Starr[3] and Arnold Relman[4] warn of its consequences.

In this paper I wish to appraise the potential effects of corporatization on professionalism. I shall argue that the simple fact of employment of professionals like physicians and lawyers by large-scale public or private organizations does not, in and of itself, threaten the spirit and ethos of professionalism. The major threat, I shall argue, comes from more particular policies that are not intrinsic to large-scale organizations and that, in fact, also influence the professionalism of self-employed practitioners. But first, let me discuss the meaning of professionalism.

II. Professionalism

It is not uncommon to use the term "professional" to distinguish someone who is competent to perform some kind of productive activity. In contrast, the "amateur" is comparatively less competent. Using the term this way, virtually anyone who performs some productive activity reliably and well can be considered a professional. But that usage is too narrow. We also wish to assign social value to a professional activity: what is performed is of value to other people, and is not merely a private skilled pursuit as can be, for example, a hobby. An additional distinction between "professional" and "amateur" uses monetary value as a measure of competence. Professionals perform so reliably and competently that others are willing to pay them for their work. In contrast to an amateur, a professional gains a living by the practice of a specialized skill. This is possible because others value it enough to pay for it. In this somewhat larger sense, then, "profession" is synonymous with "occupation": it refers to specialized work by which one gains a living in an exchange economy.

Even if we cannot see many of the important connotations of professionalism in that rudimentary distinction, their germ is there. One does a particular kind of work well; one does good work. But it is not just *any* kind of work that professionals do well. The kind of work they do is esoteric, complex, and discretionary in character: it requires theoretical knowledge, skill, and judgment that ordinary people do not possess, may not wholly comprehend, and cannot readily evaluate. Furthermore, the kind of work they do is believed to be especially important for the well-being of individuals or of society at large, having a value so special that money cannot serve as its sole measure: it is also Good Work. It is the capacity to perform that special kind of work which distinguishes those who are called professional from most other workers.

The character of professional work suggests two basic elements of professionalism—commitment to practicing a body of knowledge and skill of special value and to maintaining a fiduciary relationship with clients. A relatively demanding period of training is required for learning how to do esoteric and complex work well. That course of training tends to create commitment to knowledge and skill so that the professional's work becomes a central life-interest which provides its own intrinsic rewards. Professionals develop intellectual interest in their work, so they are concerned with extending and refining it and they believe in its value to society. They do not merely exercise a complex skill, but identify themselves with it. What they do is not labor solely for the income but for the pleasure of something more, something that may on occasion be considered to be play.[5]

Second, what professionals do is of special value to their clients. But their knowledge is sufficiently complex and esoteric that clients are not able to evaluate it accurately. Therefore, as other contributors to this volume have observed, clients of professionals must place more trust in them than they do in others. A fiduciary relationship must exist between professionals and their clients. Professionals are expected to honor the trust that clients have no alternative but to place in them. The client's needs and benefits must take precedence over the professional's need to make a living.

III. The Professional Market Project

What I have said so far is singularly unsociological, for I have talked only of knowledge and skill, motives and meanings, values and commitments. In portraying professionals' relations with clients, I painted an image of one individual consulting another. It is true that our experience rests primarily on our qualities as individuals and on our interaction with other individuals. Nonetheless, one cannot make adequate sense of that experience without explaining how it is that thousands of individuals can be identifiable members of the same profession, that their interaction with hundreds of thousands of clients has pretty much the same form and content, and that they all share common characteristics. It is the institutions of professionalism that provide that commonality. Furthermore, they produce the circumstances that encourage and reinforce professionalism in individuals.

Because the professional, unlike the amateur, does sufficiently good work to warrant getting paid for it, a critical fact about professionals in our day is that they depend on their work for their living. This dependence is neither universal nor inevitable,[6] but in our nation it is the norm. It was made possible during the late nineteenth and early twentieth centuries when the modern professions established their present-day economic position.[7] In the United States, they developed institutions designed to control the selection, training, and credentialing of their members, and to gain privileges providing marked advantage in the marketplace.[8]

This was not accomplished easily, for both in the United States and elsewhere the political climate opposed constraints on the market for services and goods. Indeed, during the Jacksonian period in the United States, earlier colonial legislation granting privilege to the professions of medicine and law was repealed in many states on the ground that all should be free to practice whatever occupation they wished. The reinstitution of professional privileges by state legislatures came hard for the traditional professions, and similar privileges remain an as yet unfulfilled goal for many aspiring occupations today. However, when they *are* legislated, they are typically justified by a series of assumptions about the nature of professional work, the characteristics of the potential consumers of that work, and the operation of professional institutions.

The argument supporting professional privilege is fairly standard. First, it asserts that the occupation's body of knowledge and skill deals with problems of great importance to the public good, whereas that of other occupations does not. Second, its body of knowledge and skill is so esoteric, specialized, and complex that lay people cannot be expected to be able to act as rational consumers capable of protecting their own interests by making well-informed choices among those competing to provide them with service in the ordinary open marketplace. For the public's own protection, therefore, only the profession's members should be allowed to offer such services. Third, the occupation is worthy of public trust because it is a profession rather than an ordinary occupation. Because its members are properly selected and trained, they may be trusted to put the good of their clients ahead of their own material interest. While a very few may abuse that trust, the profession conducts itself in such a way as to discover them quickly and discipline them effectively.

On the basis of such assurances, professions gain a privileged legal position in the marketplace which seriously handicaps their competitors even if it does not always completely exclude them. And by those assurances, as well as by their higher education and middle-class status, professions gain general public esteem and trust without which legal support alone would be inadequate. Thus, an implicit contract is made between a profession and both the state and the public: "Protect my members from the unfettered competition of a free market, and you can trust them to put your interest before their own. I will select them carefully and train and organize them to provide competent and ethical service." It is that implicit contract between the corporate profession and society which both allows and requires us to trust the individual professionals we consult.

IV. The Professional Maintenance Project[9]

The "market project" of the modern professions looks outward to the broader marketplace, seeking to establish a secure jurisdiction in the social division of labor,[10] a "labor market shelter,"[11] or, in Max Weber's terms, a "social closure"[12] that excludes potential competitors from outside the profession and protects its members from dominance by clients or employers. But the professions also engage in another necessary project—namely, maintaining sufficient cohesion of the profession as a whole to be able to undertake common action both to sustain its status and privilege and to advance its own "cultural" projects.[13] This might be called its "maintenance project" of adapting to the changing political and economic environment so as to be able to continue to control its own affairs.

A number of things contribute to the maintenance of its cohesion. First, the members of all professions, unlike most other occupations today, have a distinct public identity that provides a foundation for solidarity and mutual sympathy. Second, when training is attached to the university, lengthened by requiring a college education as a minimum prerequisite, and standardized, all members of a profession share a common socialization experience. Furthermore, the relatively long period of training required to enter the professions encourages their members to commit themselves to a life-long career.[14] Although life-long professional careers are not quite as common as some claim,[15] the very fact of investing a much longer than average part of one's lifetime in training creates a "sunk cost" that encourages commitment to a career in the profession and creates another bond joining its members.

A critical but often ignored method of sustaining the solidarity of the profession lies in norms governing relations among its members and between its members and lay people. They may be written as rules or practiced as unwritten custom. They may be called "etiquette" or even "ethics." Many are designed not so much to *prevent* competition among members as to *control* it. Rules establishing minimum fees, for example, do not prevent price competition among members, for some charge less than others for their services. They are designed to prevent "cut-throat competition" by which a determined price-cutter can literally drive colleagues out of the market. Similarly, rules governing advertising do not prevent competition among members, but rather restrict its content, form, and mode of circulation. Before many of those restrictions were abolished by the Supreme Court, advertising consisted of brief public announcements, the display of a nameplate within prescribed dimensions, speaking out at local community meetings, and socializing at churches, clubs, lodges, and the like, followed by the parting gift of a business card. The rules restricting advertising reflected in part genteel conceptions of a professional dignity or status, but their greatest significance lay in their effort to mute the quality and intensity of competition between colleagues and assure a minimum income for all.

In addition to rules designed to reduce the intensity and publicity of competition so as to preserve a modicum of equality and solidarity among members of a profession, there are the rules of "etiquette" expected to guide relations between professionals and their clients, and among colleagues. Unlike earlier times, present-day etiquette makes it inappropriate to denigrate the work of a colleague to a client. Even if one feels that a colleague does poor work, it is not proper to inform the client of that. Indeed, one should be reluctant to judge the work of a colleague when one lacks direct experience with the case and its circumstances. "There, but for the grace of God, go I," "Who am I to judge?" or "It may be my turn next" may be said to explain the suspension of condemnatory judgment.[16] This reluctance to judge is sustained by an even greater unwillingness to confront apparently erring colleagues, let alone to take any action to punish or otherwise correct them in the interest of the well-being of clients. Even when there is intervention, the dominant rule is confidentiality so as to protect both the reputation and career of the errant colleague and the public face of the profession itself. This etiquette expresses an important part of the ideal typical of professionalism—namely, collegiality.[17] But because it tends to prevent the use of adequate regulatory procedures which protect the public, it violates the profession's implicit contract with the state and the public. There may be an intrinsic conflict between the profession's efforts to maintain the solidarity of its members and its fiduciary relationship with society.

Finally, I may note a number of devices by which professions attempt to prevent control of their members by lay people. In the United States, professionals may incorporate their practices, but what is legally defined as a professional corporation (P.C.) requires that only the practitioners themselves may hold stock in the corporation, not lay people or outsiders, and that should they retire or die, their stock may not be passed on to heirs or sold to those who do not practice. Another device makes it "unethical" for the member of a profession to enter into a partnership agreement to practice with the member of another profession. Still another requires that the executive officer and supervisors of a professional practice organization be members of the profession and not lay people.

The institution of tenure is also employed to protect professionals from external interference with their work. Tenure is similar to seniority rights in conventional union contracts, but there are important differences. In unions, seniority differentiates members only by length of tenure, providing greater security to those with the greatest seniority and specifying that when jobs are to be eliminated, the most recently hired go first. By contrast, tenure sharply dichotomizes professionals into those who are on probation and can lose their positions at any time, and those who have tenure and may not lose their positions except under stringently specified circumstances. The justification for union seniority is job security. Tenure also provides professionals with economic security, but its justification is different: it lies in protecting the intellectual independence and discretionary judgment of professional employees. It is assumed that employers could use economic threats to suppress disapproved ideas or actions. Tenure is intended to protect the academic, clinical, or scientific freedom of professionals, whose schooled freedom of judgment is assumed to be of benefit to both clients and society at large.

V. Ordinary People in Practice

Thus far, I have tried to sketch a synthetic portrait of the various institutional devices by which organized professions have attempted to create a broad set of social and economic circumstances in which the spirit and ethos of professionalism would not be discouraged, even if not necessarily assured. By creating prestigious social identities to which an ideology of high purpose is attached, young people may be led to aspire to them. Extensive hurdles for entry and a demanding course of training, once surmounted, encourage long-term commitment to the profession as a career. Fairly stable and firm jurisdictional boundaries that minimize competition from other occupations and rules that control competition between colleagues create conditions of sufficient economic security (if not necessarily great wealth) to make long-term commitment feasible. And a number of devices are aimed at preserving independence of judgment from the interference of colleagues, clients, and the lay world in general. Within this portrait, we can distinguish the elements of both the market and maintenance projects. The object of the market project is to gain collective economic protection from external competition. The object of the maintenance project is to preserve solidarity among members, protect the profession's public face, and deflect efforts by clients, employers, and others to exercise control over its members' work. With such protection, professionals can afford to be devoted to the integrity of their craft and to use it for the benefit of others.

It may seem inappropriate for an analysis intended to address the ethos of professionalism to devote so much attention to the materialistic aspects of professionalism, dealing more with protectionist devices than with devoted service. I do so, however, in order to establish the nature of the institutions that provide conditions under which it is reasonable to expect ordinary or a bit more than ordinary people to sustain something resembling the high purposes claimed for professionalism. While the extraordinary person may very well rise above discouraging circumstances to be an exemplar, if their very living is threatened it is unlikely that most professionals—which is to say the profession as a whole—will put the good of their clients and the public before their own.

To buttress the plausibility of that statement, we need not look to the distant past for complaints about unscrupulous practitioners by such honorable professionals as Sir John Securis[18] and, much earlier, the writers of the Hippocratic corpus. It also applies to modern times. Carlin's classic studies[19] of the insecure and sometimes desperate "lower hemisphere"[20] of the legal profession show how the pressure of circumstance degrades practice. The struggle for clients, the need to gain as much income as possible from what "business" they can get, and the shady temptations offered in the lower courts where they work allow us to understand many (though not all) of their ethical lapses. Auerbach[21] rightly castigates as hypocritical those leaders of the bar from the "upper hemisphere" who, themselves in secure and lucrative practices serving the corporate elite, deplore the behavior of "ambulance chasers" and counsel for personal injury plaintiffs.

In my writings on the subject, I deliberately choose the neighborhood, self-employed lawyer in mid-century Chicago and New York as my example in order to stress that the gross form or organization of practice does not in itself pose a threat to professionalism. However, most who write of the professions labor under an unquestioned prejudice against employment. Self-employment is thought to be the ideal state in which professionalism can flourish. Some anticipate that professionalism will perish when professionals are employed by others. We may think about self-employment this way because the two powerful professions that we tend to keep in mind when we talk of professions, law and medicine, have traditionally been self-employed in the United States, serving individual clients on a fee-for-service basis. Even now, the majority in both professions work either alone or in very small partnerships.

What is true of doctors and lawyers in the United States today is not true of professions in general, however. We need only think of clergymen, military officers, professors, engineers, scientists, schoolteachers, social workers, and most other occupations that have been called professions. Professionals in these fields have been employed from the start, but this fact has not made them any less professional. The gross forms of self-employment and fee-for-service payment, or of employment and salary payment, matter far less than the particular circumstances in which they exist. In the case of the self-employed, it is extremely important to remember that history shows how self-employment under unfavorable market conditions discourages professionalism. Nor does fee-for-service or piecework assure independence when the rates are low. Similarly, the mere fact of employment by large, corporate institutions owned and ultimately directed by nonprofessionals need not be hostile to professionalism. To show this, let me discuss the characteristics of large-scale institutions in theory and then how, in practice, those characteristics change when they depend on the skills of professionals.

VI. Professionalism and Formal Rationality

Contemporary organizational theory is in a state of flux, but in one way or another both the formal structure of authority within organizations and the "human relations" among their members remain central to it. Max Weber's ideal typical model of rational-legal administration, or bureaucracy, remains vital to our thinking about large, modern organizations. While it has been accurately criticized over and over again for its failure to deal with many of the empirical characteristics of organizations, it continues to serve as an essential intellectual resource for conceiving of the essence of the spirit and structure of both private corporations and the civil service agencies of the state.

The spirit of those organizations is to reduce everything to the predictable and calculable so as to gain a stated set of ends with the greatest possible efficiency. The structure and practices of such rational-legal bureaucracy express that spirit of formal rationality. In the case of private commercial organizations, we might not be too far off the mark to say that the end is the production of saleable goods and services at the lowest possible cost so as to either increase profits or sustain growth. In the case of public or state organizations, the end is the production of politically acceptable goods or services at the lowest possible cost to the treasury.

Most people have seen the pine-tree-like charts which are meant to portray the formal organization of firms and agencies—who is in charge of what and responsible to whom, the major departments or divisions, the relationships of subordination and superordination, and the "channels." The structure is hierarchical and monocratic, divided vertically into different levels of authority and responsibility, with the ultimate authority held by a single officer who is accountable to those outside the organization itself who own or are otherwise responsible for it. This structure is divided not only vertically but also horizontally into a variety of specialized tasks, positions, or jobs which constitute its division of labor.

The structure of rational-legal bureaucracy is designed to create an efficient division of labor, codes of supervision that can effectively control and coordinate a complex variety of specialized tasks, and channels that freely and fully transmit commands, appeals, and information up and down the hierarchy. In constituting that structure, a number of practices are critical for predictable and successful functioning. The personnel of the organization are chosen solely on the basis of their competence to perform a particular kind of work, and they are limited to performing that work alone. Their rights, duties, and responsibilities are delineated fairly precisely, as is their authority over and subordination to others. The authority they are entitled to exercise over others is strictly limited to the position they hold and the tasks they are authorized to perform. Arbitrary authority is proscribed, and all activities are governed by the rules of the organization. Indeed, formal written rules are a major characteristic of rational-legal bureaucracy. Ambiguity of task and arbitrariness of authority are prevented, and rational ordering of a complex division of labor yields the greatest efficiency possible.

By and large, Weber's discussion of rational-legal administration was based on the German civil service of his time and he was concerned more with its difference from patrimonial and charismatic administrative practices than with the actual tasks of its officials. He emphasized staffing practices and the ordering of authority and paid little attention to how efficiency is related to the ways in which tasks are formulated. It is precisely this relationship that Adam Smith, Karl Marx, and others had analyzed in industrial organizations, showing that when jobs are made into minute, detailed, repetitive tasks that any normal adult (or even child!) could perform after a short period of training and practice, both greater productivity and greater control over workers could be attained. Tasks of this meaningless and degraded character are the antithesis of professional work.[22]

Those who perform such tasks are by definition the industrial proletariat, and the historic process by which once skilled and independent workers were brought to that position has been labeled proletarianization. Some analysts now believe that the continued development of ever more refined specialization and rationalization of professional work, combined with employment in large-scale bureaucratic organizations, is proletarianizing the professions.[23] Others see the extension of formal rationality as a deprofessionalizing force.[24] If this is so, then surely professionalism is doomed. But is it so?

Elsewhere[25] I have argued against the usefulness and accuracy of imputing either proletarianization or deprofessionalization to the professions today, so I shall not repeat myself here. Instead, I wish to suggest that the perceived[26] nature of professional tasks imposes practical political barriers to a continuous movement toward proletarianization or deprofessionalization. In essence, I wish to suggest that because there has been little inclination to accept the substitution of highly predictable, mechanical activities for the basic professional tasks, managers have had little choice but to expect those tasks to be performed on a discretionary basis and to give professionals the leeway that discretion requires. Thus, managers act quite rationally in adapting the organization accordingly.

VII. Professionalism and the Trusted Servant
Since the middle of the century a large literature on professionals in organizations has accumulated. Perhaps the earliest studies of

importance were of engineers and scientists employed in industry, followed by studies of physicians in hospitals and clinics, social workers in social agencies, and lawyers in law firms.[27] They may now seem to be out of date, but over the past decade studies of engineers,[28] lawyers in public and private practice organizations,[29] and others[30] have come to many of the same conclusions reached in earlier studies. By and large, the concrete authority structure and practices by which we characterize rational-legal bureaucracy are systematically modified and hybridized in organizations devoted to the provision of professional services. In virtually all studies, it was observed that professionals had a special position in the organization, either working in units separated from the organization as a whole and headed by a member of the profession, or arrayed in a "staff" or professional hierarchy that was separate from and parallel to the conventional "line" or production and support hierarchy. Furthermore, while some work was structured by "formats" and "standard operating procedures," and all of it (like all work everywhere) limited by available resources, professionals exercised a considerable amount of discretion in the way they performed their work. Indeed, the principal investigator of a recent study of a variety of employed professionals had originally formulated it as a study of what he expected to be proletarianization. In reflecting on its findings, however, he conceded that unlike the industrial proletariat, most employed professionals had considerable autonomy in performing their work—"technical autonomy." He sought to salvage the relevance of the concept by pointing to what he called their "ideological proletarianization,"[31] their loss of the capacity to determine the policies governing their work. He did not, however, examine critically his unquestioned assumption that in the past the self-employed professional in fact possessed and exercised such a capacity.

I believe that the technical autonomy of professional employees, even when unsupported by strong professional institutions, is most plausibly explained functionally. The core tasks of professionals are thought to *require* discretionary judgment, so that ordinary mechanization or bureaucratic rationalization is not possible. In addition, such tasks are believed to be beyond the capacity of untrained lay people to evaluate, so those who perform them must be supervised by one of their own. In essence, the work of professionals is believed to be such that they must be trusted not only by clients but also by employers Those who are employees of an organization and serve individual clients therefore have a *double* fiduciary relationship. Peter Whalley's interesting study of British engineers who, unlike Americans, start at the bottom of the technical worker scale and work their way up to quasi-professional positions, shows how the policies employed by firms lead them to play the role of "trusted employees."[32] And Goldthorpe,[33] following Renner, suggests a "service class" to which professionals as well as managers belong, in positions of trust by virtue of either their specialized knowledge or their exercise of delegated authority.

By and large, the empirical evidence is that large-scale, bureaucratic organizations do not reduce professional work to the detailed, mechanical tasks that preclude the spirit and ethos of professionalism. Because of the influence of professional institutions, lay conceptions of professional work, consumers' demands of professional work, and perhaps, in some instances, the intrinsic character of the work itself, professionals are given considerably more leeway than most other employees in deciding what tasks to do and how to do them. However, while both this modified structure of authority and reliance on discretionary judgment are prerequisites for professionalism, they are not by themselves sufficient.

When we turn from broad issues of organization and overall policies of formulating professional tasks to more concrete internal policies that can vary considerably from one organization to another, we gain a fuller understanding of the structural conditions required to sustain professionalism. Indeed, these conditions are just as important to professionalism in individual, self-employed practices as they are in organized, large-scale practices, whether controlled by professionals themselves, by the states, or by private enterprises. Among the most important structural conditions that influence professionalism are policies that (1) determine the allocation of resources; (2) define the obligations of professional employees toward their employing organization, their clients, and the public in general; and (3) establish the standards for evaluating professional work, and the methods of supervising and controlling it. Let me show the relationship of each of these sets of policy considerations to professionalism.

VIII. Nourishing Professionalism
A. The Allocation of Resources

Professionalism entails commitment to a particular body of knowledge and skill both for its own sake and for the use to which it is put—that is to say, commitment to preserve, refine, and elaborate that knowledge and skill, to do good work and, where it has application to worldly problems, to perform it well for the benefit of others, i.e., to do Good Works. In order to do good work, one must have the nominal freedom to exercise discretionary judgment. And while technical autonomy is perhaps as common among employed professionals as among the self-employed, a critical question is how, in what way, and from what perspective it can be exercised. Without sufficient time, equipment, assistance, and other resources, one cannot do one's work well and one's freedom to employ discretion becomes meaningless.

If there are not enough resources available and the work must be done in any case, it is inevitable that it can be done only by the use of shortcuts and gross formulas that border upon mechanical and only marginally acceptable technique. This threatens the professional character of the work itself. Whatever the nominal right to discretion, severely restricted resources force its use for untoward purposes. Whether a professional works in private organizations devoted to maximizing profits or to growth by minimizing production costs, or in publicly supported organizations required to maximize production with minimal resources (in order to keep taxes and political pressure low), an overwhelming caseload combined with a poverty of resources by which to handle it will at least discourage, if not destroy, both the professional's inclination and capacity to do good work.[34] The same problem can exist in self-employed, individual practices under unfavorable market conditions, when the "free" professional lacks capital for the most basic equipment and assistance, and when a very large caseload is taken on to compensate for the extremely small fees that the market will bear. Under such circumstances, "burnout," "cynicism," and loss of commitment to the work and even to the profession occur.[35] The resources available to the employing organization, therefore, and its policies in allocating them to working professionals, are critical contingencies for the fate of professionalism.

B. The Obligations of Professional Employees

Another critical element of work that comes to bear on professionalism lies in the nature of the relationship between client and professional. Here too, the issue is generic to professional work, however it is organized. In the case of employment in large-scale organizations, policy may endorse the view that customers are always right and that the organization and its members exist solely to serve, even cater to, their desires so long as they are willing to pay. There is a tension inherent in such a policy when it is used to regulate professional work. The tension is revealed when a customer's or client's desire contradicts the better judgment of the professional. Put crudely, policy can favor either the discretionary judgment of the consumer or that of the professional.

This crude rhetorical dichotomy only dramatizes the issue, of course, for most would agree that the professional's relationship to clients should sustain a subtle balance between asserting technical authority and respecting the client's right to self-determination. But if the customer (or the citizen, in the case of publicly owned organizations) is to be *always* right, then professionals are no longer able to exercise the authoritative discretion, guided by their independent perspective on what work is appropriate for their craft, that is supposed to distinguish them. They become mere servants, doing whatever is demanded of them and seeking above all to please. Professionalism can flourish only when practitioners in organizations have firm but by no means absolute support from their employer for the consequential exercise of judgment that is independent of their clients.[36]

Another source of influence on professionalism that is especially important in organizations is very complex because of the multiplicity of interests involved. Those who are employed, professional or not, are, in traditional legal language, "servants" of their employers. The ideas, services, techniques and products resulting from their work as employees are the property of their employers. Furthermore, organizations are authorized to conceal from both competitors and the public those of their affairs that are considered "trade secrets" (or, in public organizations, "privileged information"). How are professionals to behave if organizational policies establish circumstances in which they cannot create a reasonably safe or reliable product or provide what they believe to be a truly adequate service? Do they have the acknowledged right to protest, resist, and even publicize those circumstances? Can they refuse to obey organizational policies that contradict their professional judgment without fear of being fired?

In short, can employed professionals undertake activities that violate established organizational policies that they believe to be against the best interest of their clients or of the public? Does the fiduciary relationship that professionals have with their employers supersede both the fiduciary relationship that they have with their clients and their profession's fiduciary relationship with the public at large? Goldthorpe delineates the service class to which professionals belong as one that is trusted because the nature of its tasks requires trust, and because its members develop a moral commitment to the organizations that employ them. If that commitment is exclusive, it subverts commitment to the well-being of both clients and society that is part of the ethos of professionalism. It also subverts the independence of the professional's responsibility for the integrity of his or her craft.[37]

C. The Evaluation of Professional Work

Finally, I must address the complex problem of regulating the professional's work, a problem that is particularly prominent today in medicine. When formal rationality is employed, every effort is made to eliminate as much discretion from work as possible, and to employ fixed and objective criteria for evaluating it. A great many industrial, office, and service jobs are formulated by engineers, efficiency experts, industrial designers, and the like, and used both to define the tasks of workers and establish the criteria by which their performance is evaluated. Insofar as possible, those criteria are quantitative or measurable in some objective fashion. As I have already noted, this kind of control over work is not characteristic of organizations employing professionals. In few nonprofessional jobs is all discretion eliminated, but the difference between the discretion allowed for semiskilled and professional tasks is marked.[38]

Nonetheless, formal rationality *is* applied to the formulation and evaluation of professional work, though in a special way. It is often visible in the organization of the work of engineers, for example, where at least some assignments are "formatted" or structured in advance. And certainly, elements of formal rationality have long been present in law, where "boilerplate"—standard forms employed for various purposes[39]—has been an essential work resource made even more pervasive now that computerized word-processing is available. Such rationality is being pressed on medicine by both private and public insurers. Records essential for reimbursement by insurers must employ standard forms in which diagnostic and procedure information is precategorized. Quantitative standards are being used to determine whether a physician's performance conforms to statistical as well as absolute norms, and in some cases whether it is appropriate to a stated diagnosis. A significant degree of discretion remains, but its boundaries are becoming more distinct and perhaps more rigid. However, the content of the formats, forms, and standards is created, reviewed, and evaluated not by efficiency experts, industrial engineers, and others outside the profession, but by authorities within the professions. This is one of the circumstances that make the position of professionals quite different from that of the industrial proletariat.

These extensions of formal rationality create a distinct pattern of regulatory procedure, one that in the future is likely to increase both in large-scale organizations and in individual practices dependent on public and private third-party payers who attempt to control the cost and quality of professional services. A framework of formal, often quantitative standards for defining tasks and evaluating their outcome is established by members of the profession who serve as cognitive authorities and provide professional legitimacy to hierarchical methods of regulation and control that are carried out by other members of the profession serving in an administrative capacity. The pressure on practitioners is to restrict the exercise of discretion to the safe limits established by the promulgated norms, which may very well mean, in some cases, forcing the problems of clients into a standardized Procrustean bed. This surely weakens professionalism, for while such standardization may very well be to the benefit of clients in general, it is not likely to be to the benefit of at least some individual clients.[40] Furthermore, such a method of regulating work splits the profession into superior and subordinate, and threatens both collegiality and the cohesion of the corporate body.

The method of regulating work that is most compatible with professionalism is collegiate rather than hierarchical, and is loosely denoted by the term, "peer review." As a method, peer review is interactive and, unlike bureaucratic methods, can employ qualitative judgments finely tuned to variable individual circumstances, problems, and clients. It is, furthermore, a method whose use is facilitated by working in a large-scale organization, where all are familiar with the concrete and often idiosyncratic circumstances connected with their work. By contrast, self-employed, solo practice is a form in which professional work is least likely to be amenable to collegial modes of review and regulation. In any case, wherever peer review is practiced, neither the integrity of the craft nor the well-being of clients is advanced if the process is constrained by the self-protecting etiquette to which professionals are prone. To be true to the claims of professional virtue, peer review must be judgmental and demanding even while being supportive.

IX. The Future of Professionalism

I began this paper by noting that we are living in a time when many are looking closely at the professions, their costs and their benefits, and when a variety of methods are being considered to make their services more accessible to those who need them, and to provide assurance that they are reliable and well considered. Legal barriers to the development of private, for-profit enterprises attempting to provide services at a reasonable cost have been lowered. In medicine, some types of Health Maintenance Organization (HMO) are examples, as are in law the legal clinics of Hyatt and Jacoby and Meyers. In considering whether the growth of such enterprises threatens professionalism, however, I resisted the inclination to react to gross forms of capitalization, ownership, and organization of professional practice. I have argued that organizations employing professionals have accommodated their structure and procedures to the professional need for discretion. Their potential influence on professionalism, therefore, cannot be inferred from ownership and size alone. What is as critical are a number of internal policies which can vary within the general organizational form.

The policies I discussed bear on generic issues of professionalism and are relevant to all forms of professional practice, including individual, self-employed practices; professionally owned and managed partnerships or organizations; nonprofit, community organizations; private large-scale, for-profit organizations owned by lay investors; and agencies of the state that provide professional service. Focusing primarily on large-scale, quasi-bureaucratic organizations, I have suggested that policies about resource allocation, the organization's and its professionals' relation to clients, the loyalty to organizational interest expected of the professional, and the method of regulating professional work all bear on the viability of professionalism.

I hope the implications of my discussion are clear. Without at all meaning to imply that the individual has no personal responsibility to strive for commitment to craft and the well-being of clients, I have focused on the circumstances which encourage such commitment. I have avoided assuming that professionalism requires heroic self-sacrifice: if that were the case, we could not expect to find it in thousands of institutionally certified professionals. I brought the matter down to the concrete social arrangements which make it likely that ordinary or just a bit more than ordinary people will undertake a relatively long and demanding period of training in a professional pursuit and will not be discouraged from performing their work in the spirit that their profession promises.

Central to all the arrangements I have discussed is the question of how practice institutions are to be governed, and the relationship of working professionals to each other as well as to their clients and the executive boards of their organizations. If they are to be mere passive employees, without a strong, organized voice in the allocation of resources that are essential for doing good work, they will find it difficult to remain committed to doing good work. If they are to play the role of merely providing whatever is demanded by consumers and authorized by those who pay for it, they will find it difficult to preserve a sense of the value of their schooled judgment. If they are to be merely loyal servants of the interests of their employers or their own "business," they will have difficulty sustaining any independent commitment to serving the good of both individual clients and the public. And if they are to be required to work within ultimately mechanical, albeit permissive, standards established and enforced by professionals who act as their administrative and cognitive superiors, they will have to forsake the communal or collegiate principle that is distinctive of the professional mode of organizing work.

Notes

1. For a discussion of the institutional characteristics of that set of privileges, see Eliot Freidson, *Professional Powers: A Study of the Institutionalization of Formal Knowledge* (Chicago: University of Chicago Press, 1986), 63-157.

2. For a thorough review of the legal sources of medicine's privileges in the market place, see Mark A. Hall, "Institutional Control of Physician Behavior: Legal Barriers to Health Care Cost Containment," *University of Pennsylvania Law Review* 137 (December 1988):431-536.

3. Paul Starr, *The Social Transformation of American Medicine: The Rise of a Sovereign Profession and the Making of a Vast Industry* (New York: Basic Books, 1982).

4. Arnold S. Relman, "The New Medical-Industrial Complex," *New England Journal of Medicine* 303 (1980):963-70. See also J.B. McKinlay and J.D. Stoeckle, "Corporatization and the Social Transformation of Doctoring," *International Journal of Health Services* 18 (1988):191-205.

5. See Gregory E. Pence, "Towards a Theory of Work," *The Philosophical Forum* 10 (Winter-Summer 1978-79):306-20. Haworth's essay is especially valuable for its emphasis on professionalism as devotion to a craft for its intrinsic value. For example, "[Ordinary] work, then, exists as a means, unpleasant in itself but useful in view of the results of enduring it. When work is professionalized, the circumstances that make it sensible to construe income as an earned reward for having worked are eliminated. For then the person perceives his occupation as making sense in itself, its own reward, and what is wanted is not a pay-off but the means of carrying it on." Lawrence Haworth, *Decadence and Objectivity* (Toronto: University of Toronto Press, 1977), 113.

6. For an argument that under certain circumstances highly skilled professional services can be provided by "amateurs," or unpaid volunteers, see Eliot Freidson, "Professionals and Amateurs in the Welfare State," in *Applied Research and Structural Change in Modern Society*, ed. Lise Kjølsrød et al. (Oslo: Institute of Applied Social Research, 1987), 13-31.

7. For an important history and analysis emphasizing the economic and class-based character of the development of the modern professions, see Magalí Sarfati Larson, *The Rise of Professionalism: A Sociological Analysis* (Berkeley, Calif.: University of California Press, 1977). For medicine, see Starr, *The Social Transformation*.

8. See W.J. Reader, *Professional Men: The Rise of the Professional Classes in*

Nineteenth Century England (New York: Basic Books, 1966), for a general history of the modern professions in England. There is no equivalent for the United States or European countries, but the papers in *The Transformation of Higher Learning, 1860-1930*, ed. Konrad H. Jarausch (Chicago: University of Chicago Press, 1983), describing the development of professional education in England, Germany, Russia, and the United States, provide a helpful comparative view of the development of many professions in those nations.

9. I am indebted to Frederic Hafferty for observing this as a different stage of development for the professions.

10. An important analysis focusing on the struggle with other occupations for jurisdiction is Andrew Abbott, *The System of Professions* (Chicago: University of Chicago Press, 1988).

11. The term is Marcia Freedman's, elaborated in the context of professions in Eliot Freidson, "Occupational Autonomy and Labor Market Shelters," in *Varieties of Work*, ed. Phyllis L. Stewart and Muriel G. Cantor (Beverly Hills, Calif.: Sage Publications, 1982), 39-54.

12. Recent works elaborating on Weber's brief discussion of social closures are Raymond Murphy, *Social Closure: The Theory of Monopolization and Exclusion* (Oxford: Clarendon Press, 1988); Frank Parkin, *Marxism and Class Theory: A Bourgeois Critique* (New York: Columbia University Press, 1979), and Malcolm Waters, "Collegiality, Bureaucratization, and Professionalization: A Weberian Analysis," *American Journal of Sociology* 94 (March 1989):945-72.

13. The phrase is used for want of a better one. Professions do not merely undertake economic projects. They also encourage research and experimentation to advance their knowledge and skill, disseminate information to their members and the public, and organize projects that they believe benefit society. For a study of some of a bar association's cultural projects, see Terence C. Halliday, *Beyond Monopoly: Lawyers, State Crises, and Professional Empowerment* (Chicago: University of Chicago Press, 1987).

14. For some scattered but insightful remarks on the development of a "vertical vision," or life-career orientation among the nineteenth century middle class, see Burton J. Bledstein, *The Culture of Professionalism* (New York: Norton, 1976), 105 ff.

15. For some recent evidence, see Mariah D. Evans and Edward O. Laumann, "Professional Commitment: Myth or Reality?" *Research in Social Stratification and Mobility* (Greenwich, Conn.: JAI Press, 1983), 3-40.

16. For empirical analyses of physicians in this context, see Eliot Freidson, *Doctoring Together: A Study of Professional Social Control* (Chicago: University of Chicago Press, 1980) and Charles L. Bosk, *Forgive and Remember* (Chicago: University of Chicago Press, 1979).

17. Cf. Waters, *Collegiality*.

18. Sanford V. Larkey, "The Hippocratic Oath in Elizabethan England," *Bulletin of the History of Medicine* 5 (March 1936):201-19.

19. Jerome Carlin, *Lawyers on Their Own* (New Brunswick, N.J.: Rutgers University Press, 1962); Jerome Carlin, *Lawyers' Ethics* (New York: Russell Sage Foundation, 1966).

20. John P. Heinz and Edward O. Laumann, *Chicago Lawyers: The Social Structure of the Bar* (Chicago: Russell Sage Foundation and the American Bar Foundation, 1982).

21. Jerrold S. Auerbach, *Unequal Justice: Lawyers and Social Change in Modern America* (New York: Oxford University Press, 1976).

22. See Eliot Freidson, "Labors of Love: a Prospectus," in *The Nature of Work: Sociological Perspectives,* ed. Kai Erikson and Steven P. Vallas (New Haven: Yale University Press, forthcoming).

23. E.g., Stanley Aronowitz, *False Promises: The Shaping of American Working Class Consciousness* (New York: McGraw-Hill, 1973), 312; and Martin Oppenheimer, "The Proletarianization of the Professional," *Sociological Review Monographs* 20 (1973):312-27.

24. George Ritzer and David Walczak, "Rationalization and the Deprofessionalization of Physicians," *Social Forces* 67 (September 1988):1-22.

25. Eliot Freidson, "The Changing Nature of Professional Control," *Annual Review of Sociology* 10 (1984):1-20.

26. I deliberately phrase this to avoid implying that the tasks professionals perform are intrinsically resistant to mechanization. There is no logical reason why a computer cannot diagnose and prescribe treatment for our medical complaints all by itself, nor why all legal problems cannot be handled by predetermined formulas. Mechanization or industrialization of all that professionals now do is quite feasible. It does not occur because people are not willing to have their problems and the solutions for their problems simplified and standardized in the fashion that mechanization requires.

27. E.g., Mary E.W. Goss, "Influence and Authority among Physicians in an Out-Patient Clinic," *American Sociological Review* 26 (1961):39-50; Mary E.W. Goss, "Patterns of Bureaucracy among Hospital Staff Physicians," in *The Hospital in Modern Society,* ed. Eliot Freidson (New York: Free Press, 1963), 170-94; William Kornhauser, *Scientists in Industry* (Berkeley, Calif.: University of California Press, 1963); Simon Marcson, *The Scientist in American Industry* (New York, N.Y.: Harper Brothers, 1960); R. Richard Ritti, *The Engineer in the Industrial Corporation* (New York: Columbia University Press, 1971); W. Richard Scott, "Reactions to Supervision in a Heteronomous Professional Organization," *Administrative Science Quarterly* 10 (June 1965):65-81; W. Richard Scott, "Professional Employees in a Bureaucratic Structure: Social Work," in *The Semiprofessions and Their Organization,* ed. Amitai Etzioni (New York: Free Press, 1969), 82-140; Erwin O. Smigel, *The Wall Street Lawyer: Professional Organization Man?* (New York: Free Press, 1964).

28. Peter F. Meiksins, "Science in the Labor Process: Engineers as Workers," in *Professionals as Workers: Mental Labor in Advanced Capitalism,* ed. Charles Derber (Boston: G.K. Hall & Company, 1982), 121-40; Peter Whalley, *The Social Production of Technical Work: The Case of British Engineers* (Albany: SUNY Press, 1986); Robert Zussman, *Mechanics of the Middle Class: Work and Politics among American Engineers* (Berkeley, Calif.: University of California Press, 1985).

29. Jack Katz, *Poor People's Lawyers in Transition* (New Brunswick, N.J.:

Rutgers University Press, 1982); Lisa J. McIntyre, *The Public Defender: The Practice of Law in the Shadows of Repute* (Chicago: University of Chicago Press, 1987); Eve Spangler, *Lawyers for Hire: Salaried Professionals at Work* (New Haven: Yale University Press ,1986); Robert L. Nelson, *Partners with Power: Transformation of the Large Law Firm* (Berkeley, Calif.: University of California Press, 1988).

30. Michael Lipsky, *Street-Level Bureaucracy: Dilemmas of the Individual in Public Services* (New York: Russell Sage Foundation, 1980).

31. Charles Derber, "Toward a New Theory of Professionals as Workers: Advanced Capitalism and Postindustrial Labor," in *Professionals as Workers: Mental Labor in Advance Capitalism*, ed. Charles Derber (Boston: G.K. Hall, 1982), 193-208.

32. Peter Whalley, "Markets, Managers and Technical Autonomy," *Theory and Society* 15 (1986):223-47.

33. John Goldthorpe, "On the Service Class, Its Formation and Future," in *Social Class and the Division of Labour*, ed. A. Giddens and G. Mackenzie (Cambridge: Cambridge University Press, 1982), 162-85.

34. Perhaps the best general source for discussion of this problem is Lipsky, *Street-Level Bureaucracy*, which is primarily concerned with employees in public agencies that are chronically underfinanced. This problem is also likely to exist among professionals employed by private, for-profit organizations that provide low-cost, mass, professional services, but we know next to nothing about them.

35. C.L. Cooper and J. Marshall, eds., *White Collar and Professional Stress* (New York: John Wiley & Sons, 1980).

36. Loss of independence occurs most likely when clients are sophisticated and powerful organizations. For law, see the discussion in Heinz and Laumann, *Chicago Lawyers*, 365-73. A recent appraisal of the architectural profession notes a marked trend in the importance of such clients and their influence on architectural work. See Robert Gutman, *Architectural Practice: A Critical Review* (Princeton, N.J.: Princeton Architectural Press,1988).

37. For a sensitive discussion of the conditions that sustain the professional independence of the lawyer, as well as the justification for such independence, see Robert W. Gordon, "The Independence of Lawyers," *Boston University Law Review* 68 (1988):1-83. It should be remembered that the problem of conflicting loyalties (only some of which is usually labeled "conflict of interest") also exists among the self-employed. It is an especially thorny problem for lawyers and accountants but physicians and other professionals are by no means free of it. What is special about employed professionals is the addition of yet another fiduciary relationship, with the employing organization likely to have considerably more immediate power to enforce its claim for loyalty than individual clients or the public at large.

38. Conversely, in few professional jobs is discretionary judgment always required, for there is much virtually mechanical routine in all everyday professional work. The difference between the qualities of professional and nonprofessional work is one of degree, with the professional, much more than the

nonprofessional, having to be prepared to forsake routine and exercise schooled judgment whenever that necessity becomes apparent.

39. See David M. Engel, "The Standardization of Lawyers' Services," *American Bar Foundation Research Journal* 1977 (Fall 1977):817-44.

40. For further comments on this issue in health care, see Eliot Freidson, *Medical Work in America* (New Haven: Yale University Press, 1989).

Discussion

Prof. Kimura: I think perhaps that the notion of professionalism has changed since the 1960s, and that you may be using a very classical notion of professionalism.

For example, I think it is quite reasonable to ask for the evaluation of professional companies by having input from clients, but you seem to focus on independent judgment based on the classical notion of the ethos of professionalism.

Dr. Freidson: I didn't mean to imply that there was no room at all. What I was postulating was a circumstance in which there is literally no protection of the individual professional from market forces and from consumer demands. I'll give you an example of one of these depression stories. Namely, a major source of income for a particular doctor came from a patient who had the doctor take his blood pressure every morning.

You know there is no need for anything like that professionally. It's absurd, but this person had the money and could spend the money, and this other person needed the money. That's an extreme circumstance, admittedly.

But I'm really arguing that carrying consumerism and the rights of patients and what's proper for a patient or a client too far, in essence, eliminates the whole notion or the whole justification of the professional's being a professional. It's simply somebody who provides a service that's desired and defined by somebody else, in which case there is no need for a body of knowledge in particular that isn't in fact determined by that demand. That demand could be laetrile. It could be any number of things that are contrary to what is believed to be the correct knowledge. Whether it is or not is, of course, another question.

But I did not mean to imply a totally authoritarian, totally insulated profession that would be to my mind, at least, totally inappropriate.

Fr. Sokolowski: I have a kind of nitpicking remark about Hannah

Arendt. I wonder if her concept of work really applies to, say, professions or medical professions and legal, and so on. It seems to me her sense of work is fairly restricted. It just refers to cases where you produce a product, a sort of stable entity, *homo faber*, the making animal, and that you establish a bunch of things like buildings and furniture.

Dr. Freidson: That's labor, in her terms.

Fr. Sokolowski: No, that's work. Work is when you have a permanent product that remains, whereas labor is a kind of repetitive sustenance of life. It's feeding and nourishing, doing things like that, which has no permanent product.

I always thought she left out something like, say, the healing professions from the analysis. I felt that was omitted. Work for her has this notion—it's from the German, *Werk*—that sense of a product that remains as left over is part of the meaning.

Dr. Freidson: I did not look back at it, but perhaps I should. I intended to suggest a Marxist or Hegelian notion of work as it is discussed by Lawrence Haworth.

Fr. Sokolowski: Can I make one other observation, a brief one? It seems to me that the reason why people like this kind of autonomous activity is precisely because it's an exercise of mind. The best in us is being activated and the independence of judgment is not subordinated to other minds, but really an exercise of independent judgment is one of the reasons why professionals like the work that they do.

Dr. Buchanan: I'd like to emphasize a couple of things that you said that I think are extremely important, and I think they could have been elaborated more than you did.

First, it's a mistake to think that conflicts of interest are new in the medical profession. There may be some differences in degree. Part and parcel of that point is that it's a real mistake to think that for-profit enterprise is the bad guy because if you look at the level of the large-scale organizations, the difference between profit and not for profit is insignificant in many cases.

What matters in for-profit enterprises is how they are organized, who is in charge, and what kind of direct control the corporate heads have over the people who are working for them. There are many organizations that are legally not for profit, which are indistinguishable in their behavior from for-profit organizations. I think that's very important. The other thing I think you said that's even more important is that there is a great deal of mythology about the good old days of fee-for-service private practice, and I think you're exactly right. It all depends on the institutional context, which includes the condition of the market, competition, scarcity of demand for services.

I think there is too much in the current discussion of these issues about conflicts of interest, which is filtered through an assumption that there were "good old days."

Dr. Brock: You stressed the relative economic security of the professional as being important to bear in mind in acting in conformity with the spirit and ethos of the profession.

I wonder if you could tease out, if there are two notions there, how well off someone is and how secure in that level of economic well-being someone is. And if you look at other countries, it seems to me physicians may be less well off economically comparatively within the society as compared to many countries, but perhaps more secure. That is, their job within, for example, state employment isn't threatened, but on the other hand, their level of well-being is.

I wonder if there is any evidence to tease out which is playing the more important role there, the security of their job or the level of economic well-being in protecting their concern with the client's well-being.

Dr. Gorovitz: You've characterized professions as having a sense of the work that they do, as having an importance that other ordinary occupations don't have. That seems just backwards. If we had to do without doctors and lawyers, on the one hand, or farmers and truck drivers, on the other, it seems absolutely clear that it's the farmers and truck drivers we need to keep. So that one of the features of professions is that the importance of what they do is peripheral, rather than central.

Dr. Buchanan: The luxury goods of civilization.

Dr. Gorovitz: That's it. I'm putting it in that stark way precisely because it's one of the traditional views that precisely what is wonderful about professions is that what the professionals do is of central fundamental importance.

Dr. Freidson: First, there isn't much I can say about what Dr. Buchanan said, which was simply an encouragement and reinforcement for which I thank him.

In Dr. Brock's case it's probably an empirical question. I think of professors in Italy or doctors in Israel and I suppose there is very little that I've been able to read about it. Doctors in the Soviet Union are paid rather poorly, and so are doctors in Israel, and so are professors in Italy.

They are apparently paid at a sufficiently low level in the context of stimuli to increase consumption, and, you know, as long as one is eating, the issue is whether you have the stimuli, really, as to what they think they need and what they aspire to for their family as being possible.

In those cases, they scramble around in multiple jobs, moonlighting, soliciting bribes, and, as far as doctors are concerned, at least in the case of the Soviet Union and their economic position, is apparently such as to encourage all kinds of corner cutting in the basic job in which they are secure and all kinds of other enterprises to try to increase income, as well as illegal ones within the job itself, to gain income.

So, it's rather difficult to get an answer to that question that isn't also relative. And I deliberately said relative economic security. I don't think that professionals have to have the level of economic well-being of physicians in the United States, for example, to be able to provide what the lawyers call pro bono service.

It's interesting that lawyers, who on the average are paid considerably lower than doctors and are much less successful, have nonetheless maintained a tradition of pro bono service that doctors seem to have given up twenty years ago, at least. As to Dr. Gorovitz's point about the relative importance of farmers, well, you know, economists including Adam Smith have always struggled with this issue of value and who gets paid what. The problem of value and economics is the basic problem that's never been solved, and in this particular case, my own position has never been that doctors are objectively of greater importance than farmers but rather that they are considered by—what shall I say—those who control the political economy to be more important, to be entitled to greater rewards.

Prof. Kimura: In the modernization process in Japan the state had a very strong policy to encourage the professions. It seems to me that in Western society, the professions have sometimes quite a negative opinion of government regulation.

Dr. Freidson: I would not say Western society. I would say Anglo-American nations. In the case of virtually all European countries, the professions did not arise independently. There was a much greater, strong, central government, although again there are variations between Prussia and Germany, on the one hand, from which Japan borrowed a great deal, and France and certainly Czarist Russia, on the other.

So, there are differences on the Continent, but nonetheless, the state was always more important in every Continental nation in forming professions. In fact, independent professional societies arose rather late in some countries, after the professions were established as part of the civil service bureaucracy. England, with a fairly weak central government, deviated markedly from nations on the Continent of Europe in the corporate independence of professions.

Fr. Langan: I think that one of the many instructive aspects of Professor Freidson's paper is that we should have a deeper recognition of the diversity within professions. But how can we do this without the concept collapsing into pure diversity?

One notion that may be helpful in a kind of middle range is the notion of the value of different exemplars or exemplary individuals. That's a significant part of our moral learning in communities, that we focus on the practitioners whom we regard as imperfect, but interesting and instructive and encouraging, exemplifications of an ideal.

This is, I think, related to the discussion we had this morning, at the end of the session. You say, well, the ideal isn't completely impossible, but it's partly realized in certain people. And that can be specified in different ways—partly, I'd say, looking at different medical specialties, looking at patterns of practice within different types of legal firms, and so on.

Now, that pushes us in a very anecdotal direction and requires comprehensive knowledge of values and practices within a profession. But, something like that kind of notion may well be helpful.

Also, one of the things that a lot of people in professions have to go through is the process of adjustment between certain ideals of the professions that they form in the process of their education and the actual patterns of practicing in the profession as they move into it. And sometimes that leads simply to a kind of disappointment.

People didn't get into the kind of practice at the level that they wanted to as a professional and, as a moralist, I guess I am concerned that they miss an opportunity to grow where they actually are, rather than saying that there is a certain pattern of what I really aspire to, which was to practice at Massachusetts General, or to function on a certain plateau, and I didn't get that.

Sometimes the exemplars that are put before people in the process of professional formation can, I think, be very morally misleading. Another notion that maybe should be looked at a little more is the question of hybrid identities. People going into several different professions.

There are a couple of us around the table who are involved in this in different ways. I am sensitive to this, I guess, because a couple of years ago I spent most of the semester running seminars on ethics for Navy chaplains. There are people who are very conscious of the tensions, some of them bearing directly on questions of future responsibility between the norms that govern them as naval officers and norms that apply to them as chaplains. And in fact, they had to have a kind of dual accreditation as officers and as chaplains and roughly, some of the same things hold for the people who function as lawyers and as medical people in the military context.

One final comment on Professor Freidson's paper that I'm a little surprised nobody picked up: the point made about the inability of the clients to evaluate the performance of the professional. I can think of a sense in which that is true. There's also a sense in which I think it is simply not true.

On the one hand, the professional can well say, you don't understand this enough, and, you don't appreciate that I am giving you the best performance of which well-trained professionals are capable in this area. It's also the case that in many, many situations people can be profoundly dissatisfied with professional performances and for good reasons.

We are not simply dealing with clients, but also with potential critics. But I would think that some attention to the critical element within the practitioner-client relationship is important because it does seem to me something that's legitimate and that may well create tensions with the carrying out of fiduciary responsibilities.

JOHN LANGAN

Professional Paradigms

The paradigm for our thinking about trust and fiduciary relationships in professional life is usually conceived in terms of a relationship between two individuals: the independent practitioner, who charges a fee for service, and the client, who seeks the advice and work of the trained professional. We can place these individuals—in the doctor's office or the attorney's office. We can readily tell stories about their needs, their problems, and their dilemmas. We can formulate ethical norms about what each owes to the other and describe the virtues that should be manifested in their interaction. But focusing our attention on this familiar paradigm, a paradigm which is regularly renewed in the midst of many of us whenever we return to the office for a consultation, is likely to blinker our vision and to limit our understanding of trust and the fiduciary relationship.

It can do so in three different ways. First, it can cause us to overlook professions that have always had a more complex structure, or at least a structure that did not take the interaction of the individual practitioner and the individual client as central and characteristic. The teacher, for instance, customarily dealt with a group of clients or students and was employed by an institution. The priest, the minister, the rabbi served a congregation and, in most cases, a hierarchy as well. The accountant had as client a firm or corporation rather than an individual and had a special responsibility to groups such as shareholders or creditors whose interests required a full and honest reporting of the firm's financial condition. The journalist was employed by a business organization, was expected to serve the general public, and was not expected to pay or to receive money from either readers or sources. Second, focus on the single-client, single-professional paradigm combines all too readily with an effective neglect of critical questions about how the professional-client interaction has come to be structured in the way it has, and of larger issues about how the practices and standards of a profession affect those who are not within the one-on-one interaction of the paradigm. Third, reliance on the single-client, single-professional paradigm can make it more difficult to develop a clear focus on the moral issues arising from social and economic transformations of professional life. These have affected even the most well-established professions, as we can see by looking at the development of national law firms or health maintenance organizations.

Affirming the truth of these observations about the limitations of the single-client, single-professional paradigm does not imply that it is not of fundamental importance or that the problems to which it directs our attention are not themselves interesting and complex. Rather, the point of these observations is to make clear the incompleteness of such a paradigm and the need we have to reflect on the broader social and cultural setting within which we develop our expectations about the work of professionals. This broader social and cultural setting is not itself something that can be briefly described or encapsulated in a single paradigm. But it is surely relevant to our understanding of the moral demands on professionals in a changing society and to the task of resolving some of the dilemmas which arise from changes in these moral demands. For these reasons, the conference turned in this session from the historical, philosophical, and theological examination of the fiduciary relation to reflection on the sociocultural setting of the professions.

Samuel Gorovitz, a philosopher who, after many years of teaching at the University of Maryland, now serves as dean of the School of Arts and Sciences at Syracuse University, began the session with a presentation on the professional and the common good. After arguing that the professions are linked together by a series of family resemblances and relationships, he observes that each profession has its own sense of the common good which is specified by the work of the profession. Even though Gorovitz does not believe that professional judgments are made on the basis of a "global notion of net aggregate utility across humanity," he wants to retain the possibility of significant conflict between the requirement of fidelity to the individual patient or client and the demands of the common good as understood by a specific profession. As the title of his paper indicates, he is particularly interested in reflecting on this conflict as it arises in the teaching profession. Failure to meet classes on time, balancing the claims of students for opportunities to participate, and responses to student dishonesty are all problems that in some way or other have an impact on the fiduciary relationship between the teacher and the individual students. In working out these problems, the teacher will on occasion be justified in subordinating the interests of the individual, even a handicapped individual, to the interests of other students. Gorovitz further observes that teachers are not asked to function only as teachers; particularly in major research universities, they have a multiplicity of responsibilities which are not easily harmonized with each other. Professor Freidson later observed that the teaching profession should be seen as divided into several distinct groups and not treated as an undifferentiated unit when it comes to determining the precise roles and responsibilities of academics.

Professor Brock urged the relevance of cases that reached beyond the ethical framework of a particular profession and the involved conflicts between individual rights and larger social goods. In such cases there would be greater difficulty in commensurating the various goods involved. But according to Dean Gorovitz, examples of such conflicts are not easy to point to and are not commonly encountered within professional practice, in which most conflicts involve goods that are internal to the profession. Dr. Veatch argued that the focus on the teaching profession with its normal multiplicity of clients showed the rightness of abandoning the interest of the individual client in certain situations and therefore the limited value of trust. In Veatch's view, professionals and the public are likely to set the limits on trust at different points; the possibility that a profession will be systematically biased in setting these limits needs to be examined. Professor Zaner suggested that some of the troubling and disruptive behavior of students may itself be educationally significant and may provide an opportunity to instruct them about the reasons for limits on behavior and about better ways to resolve the questions that concern them. In this way, many cases may be resolved without harm to their interests but in a way that involves the redefinition and satisfaction of their interests.

Professor Brock argued that the inevitable limitations on the attention that professors can give to their students are unlikely to produce an undermining of trust, since students implicitly understand that this is an inescapable problem when resources are scarce, but that trust is much more likely to be undermined when there is a gap between legitimate expectations and actual performance by the teacher. At the same time, it is necessary to educate students about just what expectations are legitimate and to prevent them from regarding education as a commodity that they are purchasing.

The common good, however one may try to specify it theoretically and to make it practically effective, is certainly an evaluative notion. The other major concept that drew extended attention is not so easy to place in moral terms. It is the increasing control which large-scale, nonprofessional, corporate institutions now exercise over large areas of professional practice. This increasing control by organizations, most of which are profit-oriented, raises more specific questions about likely impacts on the spirit of professionalism and on the element of trust within fiduciary relationships.

These questions were addressed in the paper of Professor Eliot Freidson, a sociologist at New York University. He defines the professional in terms of specialized work requiring a high degree of skill and having a special value to society and individuals. The requirement of trust is present from the beginning, since the client cannot properly evaluate the work of the professional. Trust is placed by the client in the professional, who is certified by the state, which confers a monopoly or quasi-monopoly on the group of professionals and gives them a certain independence. In Freidson's view, a profession characteristically develops a "maintenance project," which aims at preserving the profession's control of its affairs in a changing social environment and which requires members of the profession to adhere to a set of rules, written or unwritten, in order to maintain professional solidarity. This project sustains the economic position of members of the profession and protects their independence of judgment.

The spirit and ethos of professionalism, in Freidson's view, can be sustained even within bureaucratic organizations and does not require self-employment and fee-for-service—or what this paper has called the single-professional, single-client—paradigm. Bureaucratic organizations, which, as part of their rationality, have to recognize the diverse skills of their personnel, customarily acknowledge the need for professional discretion and accord their professional personnel considerable leeway in their work. By itself, this is not enough to sustain the spirit of professionalism, which also depends on adequate resources, the character of the relationship between the client and the professional, and appropriate policies for reconciling conflicts among the multiple interests that professionals are called to serve. Freidson thus rejects the view that the form of social organization is decisive for the maintenance of professional values, including the sense of trust and the fiduciary relationship. For he thinks that markets, large-scale for-profit organizations, and large-scale nonprofit organizations can all threaten professional values. He directs our attention to the variety of social circumstances that will make the maintenance of such values more likely. At the same time, as he acknowledges at the end of his paper, these changing social conditions need a moral response which is not self-interested or unduly passive.

The subsequent discussion offered confirmatory evidence for Professor Freidson's refusal to give a decisive role to any one form of social organization in sustaining the spirit of professionalism. Freidson underlined the greater independence of the professions from the state in English-speaking countries.

Father Langan urged more careful scrutiny of the ways in which the professions were represented in earlier periods of our culture, and argued for the continuing relevance of the concept of the common good. While it is difficult to make this notion specific enough to guide policy, it should not be dissolved into a series of values that are differently understood in different professions, as Gorovitz had argued. For many problems fall within the domain of overlapping or even conflicting professions, for instance, between doctors and nurses or between doctors and lawyers. We need to look to the common good of institutions or communities, such as the entire community or polity of those concerned with health care. Beyond that, we need to be able to make arguments about the common good of society as a whole. If we need more specific guidance about reconciling the conflicting moral demands put on professionals, we should examine the role of exemplary individuals in the professions. The reference to exemplary individuals (saints, heroes, well-regarded practitioners) is an important part of the moral learning and teaching we do in our various communities. Some professionals, in fact, belong to more than one professional community—for example, chaplains and medical personnel in the armed services.

Professor Meilaender expressed uncertainty about just what groups should be counted as professions; and Professor Zaner pointed to the existence of larger numbers of practitioners, particularly in earlier periods, to whom professional standards had little relevance. Father Sokolowski proposed that we speak of arts or *technai* in place of professions. But this seems to leave out the element of public undertaking or commitment, which Dr. Pellegrino pointed out, has been present in the Stoic use of the term, as well as the interactive aspect of the profession in which there is responsibility to the client. Father Langan noted that the professions traditionally could be undertaken by gentlemen without loss of status, whereas trades and crafts could not.

Professor Buchanan called attention to the importance of self-regulation as a central feature of professions. We need to ask whether the according of professional status to a group is a good bargain for society to enter into. Principal-agent relationships now form a complex web in medicine, and there is need for safeguards for the individuals at risk. Major normative differences can develop between a profession and the larger society, as the Tarasoff case shows in psychology.[1]

Father Sokolowski raised the possibility that the interactive aspect of professional activity might be replaced by more transient and impersonal encounters. Professor Meilaender, in contrast, pointed to the expectation that the professional be available to students, to patients, to those in need of help.

The discussion taken as a whole illustrated the truth that the morally relevant understanding of what a profession is, is not a constant that remains fixed while the social, cultural, and institutional setting for professional activity is changed. The social and institutional shape that is given to the moral commitments undertaken by the professional—commitments that are made both to individual clients and to professional colleagues as well as to society at large—is clearly subject to change as the result of larger social transformations. The values which are served in the fiduciary relationship of the professional and the client are not to be absolutized or given one perennial form, but there was no sentiment for abandoning them in the face of historic changes.

Note

1. *Tarasoff v. Regents of the University of California*, 17 Cal Rep 3d 425 (1 July 1976).

Discussion

Dr. Meilaender: I confess, during the course of the day, an increasing puzzlement in some ways, not so much about the concept of fiduciary responsibility precisely but about that of a profession. Why should we call everybody a professional who happens to engage in an endeavor that is aspiring to some status or other? Is there no way to slice through this in such a way as to rule certain things in or out?

It's just become increasingly baffling to me. I think there might be some ways to do it. Whether they work or not, I don't know. I would like some help on that, I guess, because I confess I never in my life thought of engineers as professionals and I don't plan to start.

Dr. Zaner: I have a similar question, but now expressed within a so-called profession. The concern is not unlike that Galen had. For some physicians, Galen held, austere, august standards, the finest of the fine, and their moral education, and so on, was a theme of the day. But, the vast majority of physicians were simply humdrum peasant practitioners. So Galen's high standards could not reasonably be said to apply to the majority. The trouble with this way of thinking, that I see with it anyway, is that it led Galen—and I suspect that it may lead others of us who want to make these kinds of distinctions—to an internally contradictory kind of position. He wants to call both groups physicians, yet, for one, morality is held to be an integral component of the practice of medicine itself. For the other, morality is totally extraneous. Someone can enter the practice of medicine for fame or any number of reasons, and that does not matter one whit. But they are not the important physicians. The important ones are the elite that give definition to the practice of medicine, and so on.

But, another way of looking at it is, for example, to say that some lawyers who are not really professional in their conduct are still to be called lawyers; or some others—engineers, perhaps—are really "professional" in terms of moral approbation, anyway, whereas others are not. I worry about making those kinds of distinctions, but perhaps for different reasons than you, Dr. Meilaender.

Fr. Sokolowski: To continue this same kind of skeptical direction, suppose I put down a very skeptical position and say, well, what's wrong with this? Let's just abandon professions as a real name for anything that has anything in common.

Suppose we go back to the ancient idea of an art and say that there are definitely arts. There is an art of medicine. There is an art of oratory. But profession—what would be wrong with saying that the whole modern notion of profession is just a kind of etymological fluke? Something that grew out of that late medieval and Renaissance idea of certain things being called professions, partly because of religious contexts, and maybe we're trying to squeeze a lot of things together simply because of this word. Maybe it would be better to go back to art, or *technê*, as a substitute.

Would that somehow blow out of water the fiduciary relationship?

Dr. Pellegrino: The word *professio* first appeared in the first century, A.D., in a treatise by a Stoic, and it was used in the sense of the strict etymology of the word: *professio*, to declare aloud, to make a profession. It had nothing to do with the sociological structure of the people.

Fr. Langan: Just some brief replies.

It may be that the line between experts and professionals might help on the engineering question, and one could consider recognizing expertise here. And that also gets you close to a *technê*.

There are almost certainly vast differences in the kind of motivations that are characteristic of people going into professions today. But it would almost certainly be regarded as invidious to make these fundamental. We somehow treat that as an accident, and perhaps regrettable, even dangerous. And the effort, say, to introduce ethics into professional education is trying to cope with that.

The traditional professions are the kinds of things that gentlemen were allowed to do without great loss of status. That was not always true of medicine, I understand, but certainly not true of surgery. And we may be stuck with a category that really in many ways took shape in early modern society, where people were very status conscious. This is, of course open to historical correction.

The other thing, but which would push me in the opposite direction—and this is where the notion of fiduciary responsibility is very important—the fact that professions are all interactive in a way that some of the *technê* might very well not be, and that you have in this interactive process a clear responsibility to the client.

Dr. Buchanan: I'd like to go Fr. Sokolowski's suggestion one further; that we consider not just the possibility to eliminate the term "profession" from the debate, but eliminate professions from organizations.

Think about the ideological uses of the term "profession." What is the group doing when it identifies itself as a profession and seeks the status of a profession? A couple of different things are going on, several different things, but among them are these: First, there is a claim of special knowledge but also a claim of the ability and willingness to engage in some kind of self-regulation or self-policing. Second, there is a kind of quid pro quo, a kind of claim that if you, society, will recognize that we are a special group with special knowledge, we will police ourselves. Then you should keep your hands off us. Certainly, there is a kind of bargain.

We will police ourselves, and we will maintain these standards, these mores of competence and of technical conduct, in exchange for your recognizing that we should be autonomous. That our group should be, to some degree, autonomous beyond certain other forms of social control that otherwise would apply.

If you look at it that way you can ask, well, when is it a good bargain for society at large to recognize a group as a profession?

Clearly, the internal policing of norms promulgated by the group is one kind of safeguard for individuals who are, in this case, in medical situations where they need an agent. This is a principal-agent situation where the principals lack certain kinds of information, or it would be very costly for them to get the kinds of information needed to evaluate the performance of the agent.

In some cases, it may be a good bargain for us as a society to recognize something as a profession because of the kind of safeguards that are provided by the internal policing. They may be the most economical, most efficient safeguards for us.

But in other circumstances, it may not be a good bargain. I think many of us are quite suspicious as to whether the medical profession in particular has done a good job of policing itself. To say I'm suspicious is just a wild understatement.

I'm convinced that, in fact, the medical profession has done a horrible job of self-policing, and I speak mainly in terms of clear incompetence of drug-addicted physicians, demented physicians, criminal physicians—that kind of thing, to take the extreme cases, of which there are many.

When you look at the ideological uses of the term and look at it as a kind of social bargain, I don't think there is any kind of implicit basic right of physicians to be autonomous from social control. It's a question of whether it's a good bargain, given what our overall values are.

And we might end up concluding that it's not such a good bargain and that we should get rid of the idea of a profession entirely and think instead of people who are competent to do certain kinds of technical things, for whom we have expectations of normal morality—normal in terms of standards that apply to the rest of us, nothing special—and then rely on other kinds of safeguards, institutional safeguards of one kind or another to imbed them in the context that will make it safe to have them around.

Dr. Zaner: Is it your view that this has already occurred to some degree?

Dr. Buchanan: I think we're developing very complex webs of principal-agent relationships, and that, de facto, people are beginning to rely upon many individuals and agencies other than their physician. They are making out durable powers of attorney for health care and appointing surrogates. Certain institutions are using the case manager approach to track patients through the complex web of seeing people from different specialties. Less exclusive reliance is being placed on the one physician who is in charge. Second opinions are being encouraged, even by the medical profession. There is a whole range of ways in which the agency risks that the principal is involved in are being shared, and there are checks and balances among many different agencies.

Fr. Langan: I would think that at least part of the idea as to how the medical profession would react to that would be to say, you might have a variety of other forms of checking and regulation, but we would regard it as absolutely crucial that physicians be central in that process and that even if there are mixed investigations or committees, or whatever, that there has to be a physician present.

Dr. Buchanan: The question is, why? The answer to why has to come, it seems to me, not from some analysis of what the essence of healing is but rather from a larger view of what the appropriate trade-offs are. What are we getting out of the situation which gives primary responsibility to the physician to look out for the interests of the profession?

Dr. Veatch: It seems that granting the professional to be one actor in that mechanism, along with others, would depend on our assessment of not only how well they do their own internal regulation, but the extent to which the norms articulated by the profession are compatible with the society's understanding of what that professional role entails.

If it turns out that the reason a professional group does not do what society considers to be a good job is that the society and the profession have an unarticulated disagreement about what the norm should be, then it would be terribly irrational for the society even to permit the professional group to be one of the regulatory agents.

I'm convinced that in the *Tarasoff*[1] case, there's a flat-out disagreement between the profession and the society about what the norm for the psychology profession ought to be.

Dr. Buchanan: There is always a danger that there will be a disparity between norms of the larger society and the professional group because, by claiming its status as a professional group and establishing its success in that claim, it will become a subculture. It will come to have its own values, to some extent. The success of its being accepted as a profession will make it prone to some extent to develop its own internal norms. These may get out of sync with those of the society it's supposed to be serving.

Dr. Veatch: Or even its own understanding of what the professional role is, the concept of healing or the equivalent.

Fr. Sokolowski: Father Langan, you mentioned that the professional relationship is interactive at some point. I take it that that's where you salvage the fiduciary relationship. I mean, you can't do without that. Of course, there are a lot of people who aren't directly interactive. Jonas Salk, let's say, theoretically didn't treat patients, but he did something which at some point links up with an interactive relationship so that he can participate in it splendidly.

But, let me raise the possibility that it's medicine that's being applied here. Does it have to be an interactive activity between two or even a small group of people? Could it not be more bureaucratized, or more anonymous even than it is sometimes now? So you really have a system that's taking care of sick people when the thing becomes so routinized after a while. Is it not conceivable that the art will sort of subsist on its own at a certain point if it becomes rather routine and mechanical?

Fr. Langan: Something like computerized diagnosis?

Fr. Sokolowski: Or people can come and go. You get one guy working with you for a while and someone else later on. Is it essential that the fiduciary relationship between people be at the center of this application of, say, medicine and law?

Dr. Meilaender: Having asked the question that started us off down this road, I'm not sure I like where we ended up.

I'd just like to say I still do not have a clear notion. I'm not prepared for some definitions of professionalism. But, to set aside that notion of the commitment of self—that's what the word profession involves—to a calling or a vocation would seem to entail great loss.

Granted, if we can get back to a lot of the things that we've been talking about, many professionals will fail to live up to that standard to which they might aspire. For instance, students sometimes call faculty members at times of the day that we would prefer that they did not call us. And they often say as a start something like, I hope it's not too late to call. To which I always say, no, that's all right. I may grumble afterwards to my wife, who says, well, why do you say it's all right? But, it seems to me, that's the obligatory response, in a way.

Now, I might be wrong about that, but in a very simple-minded way, it seems to me that one of the essential features of a professional is to be available. That may have come from growing up in a parsonage, actually. But to lose that aspect of the word "professional," it seems to me, would be a considerable loss, and I think that's probably why I resist incorporating certain other very expert kinds of work into the concept of a profession.

Dr. Zaner: I have to add a comment because of the other side of this. Namely, the centrality of the fiduciary signifies in large part or in essential part the importance of the phenomenon of trust. And that takes it directly to the one being served by the professional.

For that, it seems to me, it's critical to keep some sense of this relationship between professing and being served by those who profess. It's always that relationship I want to keep there, however it is contextualized.

Note

1. *Tarasoff v. Regents of the University of California*, 17 Cal Rep 3d 425 (1 July 1976).

IV.
Fiduciary Relationship:
Several World Views

Rihito Kimura

Fiduciary Relationships and the Medical Profession: A Japanese Point of View

I. Introduction

I would like to begin by briefly describing the Japanese conception of human relatedness as it is reflected in Japan's medical profession. Following this, I shall offer an analysis of cultural and historical facts that illuminate the fiduciary relationship as it exists in the practices of Japan's medical profession. Finally, I should like to outline recent trends in bioethics in Japan that suggest a rather unique approach to cross-cultural encounters. I hope this will lead to new insight regarding the fiduciary relationship in Japan's medical profession in contrast to such relationships in the professions of other nations.

II. "Between-ness" in Japan's Cultural Context

The notion of a person is different in various cultures. Although we tend to use similar terms interchangeably, sometimes we are unable to avoid basic misconceptions due to our failure to appreciate the language and concepts of other cultures.

Ningen, the Japanese term for person, is composed of two Chinese characters; the first one means "human" and the second one means "between-ness." This combination reflects the Japanese understanding of a "person" as a human being existing in a situation of between-ness or relatedness. The individualistic Western notion of self does

235

not reflect the uniqueness of Japanese human identity that exists in be-tween-ness. The character for between-ness reflects the basic ethical character of human life. When a person lives between persons or *neighbors, worlds, spaces,* and *times,* he or she becomes a human. It is not accidental that the character for between-ness appears in each of these Japanese words which express the four basic dimensions of hu-man responsibility.[1] A sense of relatedness to another person is impor-tant and the individualistic "I" is typically avoided in Japanese daily conversation.[2]

Of course, it might be true to say that the Japanese are group-oriented, and thus tend to suppress their individuality. However, there is more to be said here, because of the differences between vari-ous notions of personhood rooted in other premises concerning hu-manity in the Western cultural tradition. This is one reason why cross-cultural analysis of personal relationships, including the fiduciary re-lationship, becomes so difficult to describe.[3] Thus, even though it may be an effective tool for analysis, the simple dichotomy of individual and group does not adequately explain the particular cultural phe-nomenon of human personhood. I would like to propose a framework for contrasting two cultures in terms of health, medicine, and other values that typify Japan and the United States (see Table 1). It is with-in this context of cultural differences displayed in Table 1 that we need to analyze the real meaning of person-to-person encounters in the medical profession.

III. The Fiduciary Relationship in the Traditional Medical Context

The phrase "fiduciary relationship" would be translated *Shinrai-Kankei,* which, in Japanese, always connotes the most important posi-tive value between people. The Japanese use this word in their conver-sation as well as in professional relationships between an expert and a nonexpert who seeks some service.

Due to traditional social attitudes, the Japanese have a tendency to trust and adhere to professional advice. Total dependency on those who have expertise is regarded as positive and good. As the *Shinrai-Kankei* should be respected, it is considered rude to raise questions which might be regarded as casting doubt on the judgment of the expert.

The teaching of Confucius, so central to the Japanese, has had an enormous impact and influence on the Japanese psyche, which seeks to achieve harmonious human relatedness. The key notion of *Jin,* which means "loving kindness" expressed as *person* and *two* combined

Table 1. Health-Related Values, Facts and the Cultural Contrast between Japan and the United States

	Japan	United States
Culture	Homogeneous	Heterogeneous
Problem solving	Consensus decision making	Confrontation; open debate
Conflict resolution	Out of court resolution	Litigation
Personhood	The structure of *amae* (interdependence) human relatedness (passive)	Individuality (independence); human relationship (active)
Community	Community based on family unit	Community based on individual unit
Cooperation	Family/relative cooperation; volunteer organizations are not well organized	Individual cooperation networks in community; volunteer work through church, etc.
The aged/ elderly	Aged live with family	Independent elderly
Aging	Aging regarded as positive	Aging regarded as negative; youth-oriented society
Disease	Coexistence with sickness	Emphasis on health
Professional authority	Confucian-based paternalism; patient dependency regarded as positive	Professional ethics favors patient autonomy
Treatment of patients	Second opinion shunned; physician as decision maker	Second opinion encouraged; shared decision making
Dispensing of medicine	By physician; liberal prescription of drugs	By pharmacist; cautious prescription

into one Chinese character, is based on the fiduciary relationship which is at the core of Confucius' teaching.[4] The ethics of *Jin* that dominated during the Tokugawa era continues to prevail—it is quite natural for many medical doctors to study Confucian theory. Indeed, some Confucian scholars have become medical doctors in order to more fully realize Confucianism. One of the most famous Japanese Confucian scholars, a physician in the seventeenth century, Ekiken Kaibara (1630-1714), has written as follows:

> Medicine is a Humanitarian [*Jin*] art [*jyutsu*]. A physician should have a humanitarian heart and be motivated by the desire to help people. He should not be engrossed in his own interest ... Anyone who aspires to become a doctor should become well versed in the Confucian classics. If he cannot understand these classics, he will not be able to read medical books or master the art of medicine.[5]

"*Jin* is nothing other than love itself, and it is the basis upon which all good rests," according to another great Confucian scholar, Jinsai Itoh, in the seventeenth century. He also commented that "Benevolence is in fact the greatest of all virtues. Therefore, although Confucius and his disciples spoke of both benevolence and righteousness, it was benevolence which served as the foundation for all their teaching."[6]

This traditional notion of *Jin-jyutsu* as a basis for medical practice was actually integrated into the "Physician's Ethics" (1951) of the Japan Medical Association which states the following:

> Basically, the practice of medicine should be a sacred profession, thus the foundation of a physician's conduct rests on "*Jin-jyutsu*." (General principle, 1)
> The Physician should give priority to being a man of character, skill and trustworthiness (*Shinrai*).[7]

As I mentioned before, the *Shinrai-Kankei* is the basis for Japanese human relationships, and it is exactly this Japanese word *Shinrai* that is taken into the Japanese physician's ethical code. Physicians are expected to practice by earning the people's trust.

The historical and cultural background of Japanese medical development has shown us the uniqueness of its character in many ways. Traditionally, there was a tendency to justify medical practice on the basis of religious and ethical traditions such as Shintoism, Buddhism, and Confucianism.[8] The idea of *Jin* became dominant as a basis for medical practice toward the end of the nineteenth century among the traditional Japanese physicians who were practicing Kanpo (Chinese) medicine.

The Meiji government, in the process of modernizing Japan, has decided to accept the Western idea of medicine particularly influenced by Dutch and later German medical science.[9] Even though this new system of medical education and practice has been introduced and effectively developed, the classical notion of *Jin* which evolved in the context of feudalistic medical practice has retained its authority. However, among some physicians, a true understanding of *Jin-jyutsu* is fading away in the process of rapid modernization of traditional medicine. It is still the case that physicians continue to relate to patients in a paternalistic manner and, because of the science-oriented paradigm of modern medicine, to regard patients as objects rather than subjects. As the public has become more aware of medical profit making, in the form of unnecessary treatments and surgery, the word *san-jyutsu*, which means "mathematics," has been cynically used to refer to the medical art.[10] These paternalistic and self-interested practices on the part of physicians are contrary not only to the notion of *Jin* but also to the notion of the fiduciary relationship between physician and patient.

According to article 5 of the Nihon Ishikai Teikan, "Members shall respect the ethics of the profession and must at all times strive to win the respect and confidence of the general public."[11] In addition, article 9 also states that:

> A member to whom any of the following items becomes applicable shall be judged by the arbitration committee which shall reprimand him either by a warning or by dismissal from the Association:
>
> a) A member who violates the doctor's ethic, who disgraces the honor of the Association.
>
> b) A member who violates the constitution of the Association or whose conduct may be unduly disorderly.

The notion of a professional community and its role is a rather new idea for many professions in Japan. Traditionally, professions have been identified with independent families or particular schools or groups under an eminent teacher. In many cases, these groups have not been open to public criticism or even to the mutual exchange of opinions among members of the same profession. Thus, only if the idea of the fiduciary relationship is supported by broad public sentiment will the professional community gain the power to discipline its members accordingly.

Given Japanese society's emphasis on human relatedness, it is usually very important to have some sort of "connection" to be introduced to strangers, including professionals such as physicians or lawyers. The person who introduces two parties has an important role in extending his or her original fiduciary relationship to both people. So, in many cases, clients and professionals will react to one another positively or negatively depending upon the person or institution in charge of their introduction.

IV. The Growing Concern with Bioethics and the Fiduciary Relationship in Japan

Japanese society has undergone significant change since the 1960s. In 1969, a radical campus conflict began in Japan when students rebelled against the authorities at the Medical School of Tokyo University. This initiated gradual change in morality and values among the younger generation, who wanted to reconsider the nature of the patient-doctor relationship, to question the old feudalistic tradition of *Jin*, the rapid advancement of new medical technology, and the significance of the emerging malpractice suits which were being reported by the media.

In January 1983, the Japan Hospital Association issued a booklet entitled "Hospital Physician's Manual." Chapter 1 points out the necessity of the effort to secure *Shinrai-Kankei* (fiduciary relationship) between physician and patient and to gain the confidence of the local community.[12]

One unique example of *Shinrai-Kankei* can be seen in the growing progress of the Japanese movement for medical cooperatives since the 1930s. In order to promote the health and life of the members of the cooperative, there are group activities and discussions on preventive medicine, management, and organization. The community organization of medical cooperatives based on local need has not only become a source of new fiduciary relationships between physicians and local people, both healthy and sick, but has also radically changed the people's role in health care from passive to active participation.[13]

On 9 December 1984, the declaration of patients' rights was adopted at the national conference on patients' rights in Tokyo. One of the foci of the discussion at this meeting was the issue of the fiduciary relationship expressed as *Shinrai-Kankei*. A lawyer explained the need for *Shinrai-Kankei* by saying that the obedient patient is not necessarily a "good patient." Mutual respect between physicians and patients as persons was discussed openly at this meeting.[14]

The notion of the fiduciary relationship is now taking on a broader significance in its application not simply to the individual physician and the patient but also to the total medical system itself.[15] In this regard, the medical cooperative movement in Japan, which now covers one million households by 118 organizations, represents a positive step toward the future health and welfare of the nation.[16]

V. Concluding Remarks

Since the 1980s, there has been a growing public awareness of and advocacy for bioethics in Japan.[17] One catalyst for this awareness was the appearance of a series of articles on bioethics and patient's rights, which appeared in the *Japanese Journal of Hospitals*.[18] These articles were the first of their kind, and had a significant impact on physicians as well as on patients. The Japanese Hospital Association, in 1983, took the issues seriously and announced its version of the principle of patients' rights in its official handbook for hospital-based physicians. The first national conference on the "Patients' Rights Declaration" took place in December 1984 in Tokyo.

Thus far in Japan, as in the United States, bioethical decision making has placed great emphasis on the importance of each patient's right to make particular decisions based on his or her own values and moral standards. This has been viewed by lawyers and bioethicists as an expression of the principle of autonomy and the patient's moral right to make his or her own treatment decisions. However, the notion of autonomy, one of the fundamental principles of Western-oriented bioethics, does not apply suitably to the Japanese sociocultural tradition, particularly within its paternalistic medical tradition. In Japan, each human being (as well as all living beings) is dependent in that every person is obliged to suppress his or her ego and to cultivate social "relatedness."

Because the Japanese are influenced by the way fellow human beings are related to one another and to nature, a subtle sense of new "relatedness" is thus the key element if one hopes to recover one's true humanity within nature. In rediscovering their cultural heritage via fiduciary relationships, Japanese medical professionals are currently modifying their long-standing paternalistic attitudes and working toward a more positive way of sharing information and establishing new *Shinrai-Kankei* between members of the medical profession and people in the community. This is the importance of the Japanese principle of "sharing"—sharing life with others, including all living beings who suffer, are sick, or dying. This positive, creative, living principle is critical to human empathy and is grounded in a new understanding of *Jin* (loving kindness), *En* (relatedness), and *Aida* (between-ness) which should be the three basic elements of the Japanese notion of fiduciary relationships.

Notes

1. Masao Takenaka, *God Is Rice: Asian Culture and Christian Faith* (Geneva: World Council of Churches, 1988), 49.

2. Mitake Katsube, *Nihonjin No Shiso Taiken (Japanese Thought in Experience)* (Tokyo: Kadokawa Shoten, 1979), 29.

3. Eshuun Hamaguchi, *Kanjin Shugi No Shakai Nihon (The Society of Betweenness-ism)* (Tokyo: Tokyo Keizai Shinbun, 1982), 10.

4. Herbert Fingarette, *Confucius—The Secular as Sacred* (New York: Harper & Row, 1972), 37.

5. Ekiken Kaibara, *Yojokun—Japanese Secret of Good Health* (Tokyo: Tokuma Shoten Publishing Co., Ltd., 1974), 122.

6. K. Yoshikawa, *Jinsai, Sorai, Norinaga* (Tokyo: Iwanami Shoten, 1975), 19-21.

7. Japan Medical Association, *Physician's Code of Ethics* (Tokyo: Japan Medical Association, 1956).

8. Yu Fugikawa, *Nihon Igakushi (Medical History of Japan)* (Tokyo: Nisshin Shoin, 1944).

9. Tomoo Oshima, "The Japanese-German System of Medical Education in the Meiji and Taisho Eras," in Teizo Ogawa, ed., *History of Medical Education* (Osaka: Saikon Publishing Co., Ltd., 1983), 211-35.

10. Hideichiro Nakano, *Gendai Nihon No Ishi (The Medical Doctors of Modern Japan)* (Tokyo: Nikkei Shinsho, 1976), 25.

11. Nihon Ishikai Teiken, "Articles of Incorporation" (Tokyo: Japan Medical Association, 1 November, 1947).

12. Japan Hospital Association, *Kinmu Ishi Manual (A Hospital Physician's Manual)* (Tokyo: Japan Hospital Association, 1983), chap. 1.

13. Japan Co-op Medical Association, *Iryoseikyo No Rekishi To Tokucho (The History of Medical Cooperatives)* (Tokyo: Japan Co-op Medical Association, 1988), 88.

14. National Committee on "The Declaration of Patient's Rights," *Kanja No Kenri Sengen (The Declaration of Patient's Rights)* (Tokyo: National Committee on "The Declaration of Patient's Rights," 1984).

15. Takemune Soda, *Shakai Igaku No Harukana Michi (The Long Way of Social Medicine)* (Tokyo: Igaku Shoin, 1985), 89.

16. Japan Co-op Medical Association, *Iryoseikyo No Rekishi To Tokucho (The History of Medical Cooperatives)* (Tokyo: Japan Co-op Medical Association, 1988), 92.

17. Rihito Kimura, "Bioethics as a Prescription for Civic Action: The Japanese Interpretation," *The Journal of Medicine and Philosophy* 12 (1987):267-77.

18. Rihito Kimura, "Bioethics and the Function of the Hospital," *Japanese Journal of Hospitals* 40 (1981):50-53.

Discussion

Dr. Buchanan: What's the major force for change, do you think, in Japanese medical culture, in the move away from paternalism?

Prof. Kimura: I think one of the big forces for change has been the impact of the mass media. My point is that media influence from outside is one of the positive elements to change our system, if we think of this change as positive. In addition, international journals will not accept papers on research which has failed to satisfy the protocols of informed consent and institutional review board authorization. Institutional review board approval and the informed consent of research subjects are necessary if research reports are to appear in the international journals.

But, even so, Japanese medical schools have set up ethics committees, or institutional review boards, to get papers published in international journals, and the committees are composed of only medical professionals. So despite the fact that these committees might have the same name as those here, there are no ethicists on them.

Dr. Sass: I am interested in the semantic and cultural connotations of the term "autonomy" in Japanese. In German, we have three different terms to express the notion of autonomy. *Autonomie* means that you give your own rules, you write your own ticket. That means at least political independence or economic independence, independently wealthy, landed feudal class, in this sort of sense.

Second, is the notion of self-determination, which is a right. It is close in meaning to self-development, self-emancipation.

Third, is the notion of being myself, the right to be left alone, to withdraw, not to get involved in your discussions.

Dr. Gorovitz: I'd like to hear a bit more about the payment aspect. Is anybody excluded from coverage? And what kinds of access and limitations are there, and how are public and private sources of funding divided?

Dr. Brock: You mentioned cancer in two or three examples, and I wondered if that isn't treated specially in Japan with regard to informing patients.

When Dr. Veatch and I were in the Soviet Union, we had a quite striking experience with our host in Tbilisi, who ran the large medical center there. His wife was a physician, and she died a year before of leukemia, which she had had for five years, and she had never been told of the diagnosis of her disease, which we were quite struck by; and struck further by the fact that her husband, who had known, had said that he wanted to be treated in the same way as well. He said that there is a special fear in the Soviet Union of cancer so that, in effect, that was the one piece of information that the patient was least likely to get. He commented that he thought he could tell a patient that the patient had AIDS, but not that they had cancer. So I wonder if there is that special, almost phobic fear of cancer of a sort that used to exist in this country.

Dr. Qiu: I have two small questions. First, regarding the relationship between the *Jin* and fiduciary relationship, it seems to me that the concept of *Jin* is more basic than the fiduciary relationship. According to Confucianism, it seems that the fiduciary relationship should be based on the *Jin*.

Prof. Kimura: That's right.

Dr. Qiu: So that medicine is at the heart of the *Jin*. My second question is whether you think that Japan will be transformed into a country like the United States, or like Britain, after several generations?

Prof. Kimura: As a Japanese living here in the United States more than ten years, I see more changes here in the United States, with sushi bars and everything. When I came to the United States for the first time more than twenty years ago, there were hardly any Japanese restaurants, and it was a very strange person who went to Japanese restaurants and ate there. The Japanese are not really worshipping at the Shinto temple these days, but there are many foreigners coming and staying in Shinto places. It's a kind of cultural exchange going on.

So it seems to me that the Japanese society is changing radically as you mentioned, but, here in the United States, things are also changing.

But my point is that we usually say in Japan, regarding bioethics, that we need to find a very Japanized bioethics, but I don't agree with that. As a lawyer, I see the violation of the rights of the person as the most important thing. For example, on the subject of truth telling, some Japanized bioethicists would say this is the Japanese way of handling it—not telling the truth can be justified because we are living in Japan. But, many Japanese patients are now saying: I would like to know the results of my diagnosis. So, as a lawyer I see the human rights issue as more important than the traditional Japanese ethical tradition. Maybe I'm too Westernized.

But, now, Dr. Sass asked a question about autonomy. In our Japanese context, we use the word "self-determination," *jiko kete*, which corresponds to the second notion you mentioned. *Jiko* means "self," the same as in the Chinese. The notion of self-determination is rather new, of course, but now it's appearing in newspapers, journals, and on TV, and has become a kind of key word for bioethics. Although we still feel it's a little bit individualistic, I think the situation is changing. The younger generations are catching up with the situation in one word. Rather conservative medical establishments are saying the situation is not going to change, but in the past ten years the first ethics committees and bioethics councils have been established in Japan.

To respond to Dr. Gorovitz's question, every Japanese citizen is covered by National Health Insurance.

Ren-Zong Qiu

The Fiduciary Relationship between Professionals and Clients: A Chinese Perspective

Although there has been no systematic discussion of the concepts of fiduciary, contract, or covenant in China, we can nonetheless find some rudimentary attention to the fiduciary relationship in Confucian ethics and Chinese medical ethics. In what follows, I will discuss the elements of the fiduciary relationship that appear in Confucian and Chinese medical ethics. I will argue that in this historical period of so-called modernization in China, which has been not only the equivalent of the Renaissance, the Reformation, the Enlightenment, and the Industrial Revolution but also the evolution of various professions, it is time for us to embrace the fiduciary relationship as an ethical model which should and could be justified in various professions.

I. The Professional-Client Relationship

In China, there seem to have been at least five models suggested to explain the ethics of the professional-client relationship. They are models of paternalism, friendship, comrades-in-arms, kinship, and serving the people. They can be briefly described as follows:

1. *Paternalism*: In traditional Chinese ethics, paternalism was the ethical model which served as the basis for the teacher-student relationship. The teacher was sometimes called *Shi Fu* (teacher-father). The principle which defines the model is "respecting teachers and

cherishing students." In medicine, the model of paternalism has been passed down from ancient times to the present. One medieval Chinese physician explains his relationship to the patient as follows:

> Medicine is applied humaneness. To see other people suffer rouses compassion and pity within myself. When the ailing themselves cannot make any decisions, I will make them in their place. I always put myself in their place.[1]

This paternalism, however, did not hold in the case of powerful patients such as kings or ministers. When we read biographies of famous physicians in the book of *Historical Records*, we see that those patients always made decisions against their physicians.

2. *Friendship*: According to Confucian ethics, the principles that characterize the relationship between friends are "fidelity," "sincerity," and "reliability." One of Confucius' favorite disciples, Zhen Zi, said that among the things upon which he should reflect every day is whether he was faithful to his friend who came to consult with him.[2] But the inadequacy of the friendship model to the professional-client relationship is obvious because not all our friends have specialized knowledge and expertise to solve our problem when we go to consult with them.

3. *Comrades-in-arms*: After the founding of the People's Republic of China, it was usually said that physicians and patients are comrades-in-arms in the same trench. This model does not accurately represent the relationship, however, because the weapon—medical expertise—is not in the hand of the patient but only in the physician's hand.

4. *Kinship*: Nowadays there is a slogan seen in hospitals or newspapers or heard in the speeches of some officials that counsels physicians to "treat patients as your own kin." However, the physician cannot cry and lament like real kin when the patient dies.

5. *Serving the people*: Some want to incorporate the professional-client relationship into the comprehensive model of "Serving the people" which is typified in the shop assistant-customer relationship. However, the shop assistant in China can refuse to serve the customer. One overhears such exchanges as this: Customer: "Your slogan is 'serving the people,' why are you so rude to me?" Shop assistant: "We serve the people, but not you!"

I agree with Michael Bayles, who argues in his book *Professional Ethics* for the fiduciary relationship between professionals and clients as an ethical model in contrast with the models of agency, contract, friendship, and paternalism.[3] In the concept of fiduciary relationship, the professional's superior knowledge is recognized and thus he is in a more advantageous position. Consequently, he has a special obligation to the client to ensure that the client's trust and reliance are justified. However, the client retains a significant autonomy in decision making and it is the client who gives or withholds his consent to the course of action the professional proposes upon the information that the professional provides.

According to the Confucian perspective, the core of the fiduciary relationship between physicians and patients is the trustworthiness of physicians. A patient enters into the fiduciary relationship with the physician only when a trustworthy physician is available. In general, a patient's choice of a physician is based on either direct or indirect knowledge that the physician is trustworthy. If the patient does not know whether the physician is trustworthy, he or she presumes so. If it turns out that the physician is untrustworthy, the relationship between them will end. The trust of patients depends upon and cannot exist without the trustworthiness of physicians. What, then, is required of the trustworthy physician? One Chinese physician said:

> We only trust and rely on such physicians who have the heart of humaneness and compassion, are clever and wise, sincere and honest.[4]

Another wrote:

> Medicine consists of humaneness [ren] and skill [ji]. Some master the skill and are wanting in humaneness. These are the greedy physicians. Others possess humaneness, yet they lack skill. These are the incompetent physicians. Incompetency and greed are apt to harm men.[5]

The words of these ancient Chinese physicians are in striking consonance with the words of modern medical ethicists.

Humaneness which was characterized in many ways by Confucius and his disciples is the basic concept of Confucian ethics. "Humaneness," Confucius said, "is to love one's fellow men."[6] Mencius interpreted humaneness as the heart of commiseration.[7] He further argued that

> Everybody who sees a child falling down into a well has a heart of commiseration which emerges not because he is a friend of the child's parents, not because he likes being praised by his neighbors and friends, not because he cannot be tolerant of the child's cry.[8]

Humaneness is a virtue that could emanate from inside oneself to all aspects of life: If you have humaneness in your heart, you practice humaneness (*ren*) in the relation with your parents, that is, *xiao* (filial piety); in the relation with your brothers, that is, *ti* (fraternity); in the relation with your children, that is, *ci* (kindness); in the relation with your friends, that is, *yi* (sincerity) and *xin* (reliability); in the relation with your patients, that is, *ci* (compassion).[9] It follows that the fiduciary relationship between physicians and patients could also be based on humaneness.

Two requirements of Confucian humaneness would be helpful to the fiduciary relationship between physician and patient: first, "Do not do to others what you would not desire yourself,"[10] and second, "Help others to establish themselves and have success as you did for yourself."[11] We can summarize these requirements with the phrase: Put yourself in someone else's position. If you do something to the other, you should suppose that you are in his or her position. Then you will be able to understand his or her best interest in terms of his or her value and belief system. Why can one put oneself in somebody else's position? As Confucius said, because "the nature of a human being is similar to the other's, only the nurture makes them apart from each other."[12]

Why should we require trustworthiness of a physician? The ancient Chinese physicians recognized that their responsibility is a very weighty one because the fate of a patient's life or death lies in their hands. If a physician treats patients carelessly or does not use medicine skillfully, as a Confucian physician said, "he will kill even more people."[13] The reason is that physicians have powerful knowledge in their hands. One physician made an analogy of using medicine with the use of soldiers: the decision over life is made in the short span of time between two breaths.[14] Another ancient physician, in an article entitled "Incompetent Physicians Kill Men," warned in a somewhat exaggerated tone that men rarely die from disease, but frequently from medicine that the physician has prescribed.[15]

Heavy responsibility requires a physician to be a virtuous person, the most important of the physician's virtues being to rectify himself. An anonymous author argued:

> The Tao of practicing medicine is that you must rectify yourself before you rectify things. To rectify yourself means to understand principles in order to bring your skill into full play. To rectify things means to treat patient with medication . . . If you have not rectified yourself, how can you rectify things? If you cannot rectify things, how can you cure a patient's disease?[16]

I take "rectify oneself" as a synonym of "subdue oneself." Confucius once said: "Humaneness is to subdue oneself and return to the practice of rites."[17] Although Confucius specifically means to return to the practice of special rites (sociopolitical and ethical norms) of the early Zhou Dynasty, we can interpret it more broadly: Humaneness and rites are two sides of a coin—internal intentions and external norms. So cultivating the virtues and observing the norms are two sides of the professional ethic.

II. Status of Professionals and Their Autonomy

The first thing that Chinese professionals must do under the current circumstances is to struggle for their autonomy in their own fields. History reveals that the professions in China have not been accepted as fully as their Western counterpart. Although the medical profession may have appeared in China two thousand years ago, when the first physicians were separated from magicians and traveled all over the country to serve kings, ministers, various ranks of officials, and ordinary people, the orthodox Confucians fought strongly against the professionalization of medicine. This was well described in Paul Unshuld's book *Medical Ethics in Imperial China*.[18] The Confucians argued that carrying out the principle of filial piety, *each* person should have some knowledge of medicine. In addition, they believed that if medicine were made a profession, medicine as the art of humaneness would be damaged. These reasons given by the Confucians are quite different from those given against the professionalization of, say, science and technology, which were taken as "trivial tricks" that damaged the Tao and man's will. These opponents of professionalization saw Confucianism as an encyclopedic pool of knowledge from which all branches of knowledge and expertise could be derived. For example, if a Confucian had good scores in the Imperial Examinations, he would be appointed a county magistrate, or a city mayor, or a province governor. Because he seemed to be able to manage everything and solve all problems in various fields, he was called "the Official of Father and Mother."

As a result of the broad application of Confucianism, professions such as law, medicine, nursing, research, engineering, and so forth were, it was believed, unnecessary. The only profession accepted by orthodox Confucians was teaching, because Confucianism had to be taught by somebody. Despite this strong opposition from orthodox Confucians, the medical profession has actually existed as long as the profession of teaching in China. However, in the Chinese language there are still no words equivalent to the English "profession" and "professional." Instead, we have only *zhiye* which is equivalent to

English "occupation." "Profession" was, at one time, translated into *ziyou zhiye*—"free occupation," but this is no longer a popular expression, perhaps because professionals in China are not so free.

After the founding of the People's Republic of China, various prospective professionals, on the one hand, were trained in the expanded universities and colleges on an unprecedented scale, but paradoxically, on the other hand, there has been an opposite tendency toward deprofessionalization. The leaders of the Chinese Communist Party needed professionals to help them construct a socialist China, but they did not want these people to have a status comparable to that of Western professionals. The policy of the Party leaders was: "Working people master intellectual work and intellectuals should integrate themselves with the working people." In 1949, the license and degree programs were canceled (the latter was reinstituted in 1956), the autonomy of professionals in their own fields was replaced by the overall leadership of the Party in every institution, the income gap between intellectuals and other people was greatly reduced, and intellectuals were required to do manual labor for a certain period every year. In a criticism of the Soviet Union, Mao argued that one of the reasons that Russia was a revisionist country was that it gave too many privileges to the professionals—the so-called "social strata of high income." Mao said: "The more you read, the more foolish you will be." As far as Mao was concerned, two years of medical study after primary school was sufficient training to become a doctor. During the notorious Cultural Revolution, in a further attempt to eliminate the gap between intellectuals and workers, millions of intellectuals were driven to the countryside or factories to be re-educated by workers and peasants. This, of course deprived intellectuals of the opportunity to engage in their professional activities. One of the major tasks of the Cultural Revolution was "to criticize the bourgeois reactionary authorities," that is, the influential professionals who were taken as a threat to the Party leadership. To this end, teams of workers, peasants, and soldiers were dispatched to every institute or school to take over its administration and management. If anyone was considered to grasp the essence of Marxist-Leninist-Maoist thought, which was called "the universal truth being true of all fields in the universe," this person might be appointed to an important position. It was not the scientific or artistic community, but the Party committee or officials of high rank who decided whose work should be prized or discouraged. Let me provide some examples which reveal the phenomenon of deprofessionalization:

Case 1: A woman medical scientist X returned to China after study in the United States and claimed that she had made a great discovery: she had found a very effective drug extracted from a kind of Chinese herb to speed up the microcirculation of blood. She put forward a new theory of blood circulation to the effect that there is another center in addition to the heart, such that the flow of blood is something like the ebb and flow of tides. The Academic Committee of her Institute (which consists of professional scientists responsible for assessing academic work) said that because her hypothesis required confirmation, she should perform animal experiments with the drug. Upset with the opinions of the committee, X managed to see the then Minister of Health, C, and C told the story to the late General Secretary of the Party, H. C and H supported X, and asked the Academic Committee of the Academy (the Institute is affiliated with the Academy) to promote her from lecturer to professor. Eight members of the committee agreed to promote her only to associate professor. One member supported promotion to professor. After that, the only person who voted for her full professorship was appointed as President of the Academy. X was appointed as Vice-President of the Academy, was given a big apartment and a car, and millions in financial support for her research. This case still causes despair in the Chinese medical community.

I believe that one outcome of this deprofessionalization will be the erosion of a sense of responsibility on the part of professionals. Moreover, the traditional relationship between employers and employees in China is one of superior to inferior, in which the employees should be loyal and obedient to their employer. A conflict of interest situation may frequently arise for physicians who believe that their employer's decision or policy is at odds with the patient's best interests.

Case 2: A former Minister of Education, Z, suffered a myocardial infarction, but was refused admission into the hospital which is assigned to treat officials of higher rank. Z was not admitted because he was labeled as a Capitalist Roader, that is, an official of the Party or Government who was regarded as carrying out a policy promoting capitalism. Z died after receiving no medical treatment. This is one of the most notorious cases that occurred during the Cultural Revolution.

Cases such as this reveal that until they have professional autonomy, physicians will not be able to do what they believe they should do.

Case 3: State policy in China allows only one child per family. In this case, a woman twenty-eight weeks pregnant was admitted for second pregnancy abortion. Some obstetricians refused to perform the abortion because of fetal viability. Others agreed to perform the abortion in keeping with the policy of "One couple, one child."

An interesting development is that in December 1988, the Chinese Ministry of Health laid down and promulgated an ethical code for medical personnel.[19] The code instructs medical personnel to "Heal the wounded, rescue the dying, practice socialist humanitarianism"; to "Respect the patient's personality and his or her rights, treat all equally without discrimination"; and to "Respect the patient's privacy and to keep his or her confidence." Nothing was said about medical personnel's loyalty to their employers—government or otherwise. The question of loyalty to one's employer must, however, be addressed if professional autonomy is to be achieved.

Case 4: A male patient A was treated by physician B for syphilis. After initially lying about the possible source of his infection, A admitted to his physician that he had engaged a prostitute. Prostitution is illegal in China. One day, a police officer came to the hospital and asked the physician and the administrator of the hospital to provide information about the source of A's infection. They refused to do so and yet were not penalized.

During the decades since 1949, China has frequently oscillated between periods of control and periods of relaxation. As a result, the scope of professional autonomy has alternately shrunk and enlarged. Be this as it may, neither hardliners nor moderates have an idea that professional autonomy is a prerequisite for the fiduciary relationship between professionals and clients.

When, as in the cases above, a third party intervenes in or is an integral part of a professional's activity, to whom does the professional give priority in his or her decision making? In other words, in cases 2 and 4, is the government or the patient the doctor's client? In answering this question it might be helpful to distinguish between two cases. First is the case of, say, a civil engineer who is working in or for a department of the government. What the engineer does—for example, build a bridge—benefits all members of the community. In this case, the government, which acts as an agent of the community or in the interests of the common good, is the engineer's client. Second is the case of a physician who is working in a state-owned hospital. In the medical context it is the patient whom the physician treats that enters into the fiduciary relationship. As a result, the patient should be the doctor's primary client. The government could be the physician's client in another context in which the physician, as a citizen or as any other agent, plays a role different from the physician *qua* physician in the clinical setting. In the case of a physician employed at a state-owned hospital, the physician should put his or her patient's interest first.

III. Challenges to the Fiduciary Relationship

In today's China, there are several challenges which the fiduciary relationship between physicians and patients must meet. The first challenge to this relationship is the crisis in the public health care system which covers a population of about two hundred million. Since 1949, the public health care system has provided free medical care to laborers working in state-owned enterprises; all employees of the government, parties, organizations and institutes; peasants in some old base areas of revolutionary wars; and all Tibetan people. The system also covers all prophylactic inoculations for children, although all other care for children must be paid by their parents. During the Cultural Revolution, peasants in some villages established cooperative medical services which became the dominant system of rural health care. After the reform, people's communes were disbanded and the cooperative medical care system collapsed. Since the policy of reform and openness health insurance companies have been set up in some cities. Owners of private enterprises and their workers, peasants who live in villages without cooperative medical services, individual producers, and the unemployed must pay the costs of medical care themselves.

Under the public health care system, all hospitals are graded. Every beneficiary in the system is assigned to a certain hospital, most often to one nearby. If a particular unit of employees is considered important, all the workers in the unit may be assigned to a good hospital. Usually, a unit that belongs to the central government is considered more important than a local unit. In a big city there are three levels (or grades) of hospitals: subdistrict, district, and municipal. Every hospital of high grade is linked up with several hospitals of a lower grade. The latter can transfer the patients they are incapable of treating to the former. In Beijing, the capital, there is another grade of hospital called central grade. Under this designation are the Peking Union Medical College Hospital, the Beijing Hospital, and 301 Hospital (the General Hospital of the People's Liberation Army). If you choose the hospital that you consider best or most trustworthy, but fail to be approved by your assigned hospital, then you must pay all medical costs yourself. Under the public health care system, the demand for treatment always exceeds the supply. High-ranking officials with a blue card have privileges regarding medical care and enjoy special treatment. Ordinary people have to go through the back door or use bribes to be treated by a qualified physician or to be admitted into the hospital on time. If you have a relative, or a friend, or a relative's friend, or a friend's relative, or a friend's friend who is working in a hospital, you are much better off than someone without these connections.

Currently, the government is attempting to reform the health care system by way of the leasing-contract-responsibility program which was very successful in countryside agriculture. Under the program, the government provides a fixed amount of health care yuans (Chinese dollars) to each factory or institute and the more patients a physician treats, the more money he or she earns. Although this program lessens the financial expenditures of the central government, it imposes a heavy burden upon the factory or institute where a patient is working. As a result of this program, there is a kind of trust crisis in the relationship between physicians and patients. If the physician makes an all-out effort in treatment, the patient or relatives wonder if the physician only wants to get more money from the treatment. If the physician's treatment is rather conservative, the patient and relatives wonder if the physician or hospital manager wants to save scarce resources for officials of high rank or other privileged patients.

A second challenge to the fiduciary relationship is the growing pressure on physicians to carry out policies which may damage their clients' interests. A woman with a second pregnancy was persuaded to undergo a late abortion because a second child would result in the revocation not only of the mother's reward but also the rewards of all other members of the factory or institute. Even though an obstetrician refuses to perform an abortion in consideration of the mother's health, the manager of the factory and the representatives of the trade union will beg the obstetrician to give priority to the interests of the whole factory and its workers.

Two questions have been raised regarding the "One couple, one child" policy: (1) Can the policy be justified as a common good? (2) Can the patient's interest be overridden by this common good in the clinical setting? According to a survey, 23.19-29.25% of the urban population and 54.18-74.60% of the rural population favors two or more children.[20] If a policy runs counter to the wishes of so many people, the alternatives will be either the use of coercion to carry it out, or nonenforcement. Between 1971 and 1983, physicians put in 161 million intrauterine devices, removed 24 million, performed 92 million abortions, 51 million tubal ligations, and 23 million vasoligations.[21] The government has not made these statistics available since 1983. In addition, it is difficult to know the extent to which these figures are coercive. However, they do show the scale of physician involvement in solving the problems of birth control. If a physician's concern for the social good is placed above concern for the patient's health, the fiduciary relationship between physician and patient will be violated.

A third challenge to the fiduciary relationship can be seen in the wide application of advanced technology in medicine. Two cases illustrate the problems associated with the use of medical technology.

Case 5: In February 1983, a worker from another province was admitted to a Beijing hospital, complaining of seven months of waist pain projecting to the right leg. He was diagnosed as having bone cancer on the basis of X-ray findings. He refused to undergo a biopsy and was treated with chemotherapy. In November, the glandular cancer cells were found in the stored fluids of the left thoracic cavity. The patient did not respond to the conservative treatment, and his condition declined. He had difficulty breathing, serious pain in his whole body, no appetite, constipation, and weight loss. He requested that his treatment be discontinued but was refused by the physician. On December 6, he committed suicide by hanging himself in the rest room of the ward.[22]

The question raised in the preceding case is whether a doctor's failure to withdraw treatment from a terminally ill patient is ever in the patient's best interest. The following case raises the question whether it is ethically justifiable for a physician to do mercy killing requested by the patient or his or her relatives.

Case 6: On June 23, 1986, a fifty-nine-year-old woman, X, who had suffered for many years with cirrhosis of the liver, was admitted to a hospital in the city of Hanzhong, Shaanxi Province. The diagnosis was: (1) cirrhosis and ascites, (2) coma and liver-kidney syndrome, and (3) serious second to third degree bedsores. After the director of the hospital declared the patient's condition as hopeless, X's son and youngest daughter asked the doctor P to hasten their mother's death. P prescribed 100 mg of pain killer (according to Chinese Ministry of Health regulations, the permitted dose of this medicine is 25-50 mg), which the head nurse refused to inject. Then P asked a nursing student to do it. She dared not disobey his order, but only injected half of the dose P prescribed. At midnight, the patient was still alive, the son and youngest daughter asked the doctor on duty, L, to inject the medicine once again. According to the instruction P left, L agreed and the nurse on duty gave the injection. X died at five o'clock on the morning of June 29. X's other two daughters sued the doctors P and L of murder. P, L, and X's son and youngest daughter were arrested, but released to await trial.[23]

These two cases show that medical personnel are frustrated in the face of dilemmas which cannot be properly dealt with simply by a physician's or nurse's moral intuition. Although more attention is now paid to medical ethical codes and to patient autonomy, it is not at all certain that this is sufficient to guarantee the patient's best interest and the fiduciary relationship between physicians and patients.

If the patient is to exercise his or her right of self-determination, the physician should provide full information about various options and their possible outcomes in an understandable way, and help the patient to make his or her own decision on the basis of the patient's own value or belief system. To do this requires that the physician strengthen his or her sense of responsibility, because it is the physician who is in a more advantageous position—possessing the powerful knowledge and skill of medicine in his or her hand. The cultivation of virtue in physicians, together with the implementation of various normative ethical guidelines and legal constraints, will strengthen the physician's sense of responsibility.

Notes

1. Huai Yuan, *The Thorough Understanding of Medicine in Ancient and Modern Times*, printed in 1936, no publishing company or place of publication given. See also Paul Unschuld, *Medical Ethics in Imperial China* (Berkeley, Calif.: University of California Press, 1979), 102.

2. *The Analects of Confucius*, trans. J.R. Ware; the title of the English translation is *The Sayings of Confucius* (New York: Mentor Books, 1955), 1. My translations in this paper are adapted from the English version.

3. Michael D. Bayles, *Professional Ethics* (Belmont, Calif.: Wadsworth, 1981), 60-70.

4. Yang Quan, *On Physics*, cited from Ren-Zong Qiu, "Medicine—The Art of Humaneness," *Journal of Medicine and Philosophy* 13 (1988):285-86.

5. Shi Zhiyuan, Preface to Xu Yanzuo's book, *Concise Words on the Essence of Medicine*, printed in the period of Jiajing's reign, Ming Dynasty; no publishing company or place of publication given. See also Paul Unshuld, *Medical Ethics*, 109.

6. Confucius, 81.

7. *Mencius*, trans. James Legge; English translation in *The Chinese Classics*, vol. 2 (Oxford: Clarendon Press, 1895), 6.

8. Ibid.

9. See Ren-Zong Qiu, "Medicine—the Art of Humaneness," *Journal of Medicine and Philosophy* 13 (1988): 277-300.

10. Confucius, 76.

11. Ibid., 49.

12. Ibid., 109.

13. Song Ci, *Collected Papers on Redressing Grievances*, cited from Ren-Zong Qiu, "The Art," 285; Shen Jin'ao, *A Book of Respecting Life of Shen's*, (Hubei: Congwen Books), printed in the period of Tongzhi's reign, Qing Dynasty, vol. 1, 1.

14. Ye Gui, *Medical Cases—Guide to Diagnosis*, printed in the period of Dao-guang's reign, Qing Dynasty, Soochow; see also Paul Unschuld, 99.

15. Xu Yanzhuo, *Concise Words on the Essence of Medicine*; see Paul Unschuld, 123.

16. Anonymous, *On Prescriptions of Pediatrics*; cited from Ren-Zong Qiu, 266.

17. Confucius, 76.

18. Paul Unschuld, *Medical Ethics in Imperial China* (Berkeley, Calif.: University of California Press, 1979).

19. *People's Daily*, 12 December 1988, 1; *Chinese Hospital Management* 9.3 (1989):5.

20. This survey made by the Chinese Society for Sociology in 1979; an unpublished report.

21. *1984 Year Book: Health in China* (Beijing: The Press of Health, 1984), 23.

22. *Bochumer Forschungskolloquium zur Biomedizinischen Ethik: Fallstudien für die Bioethische Bewertung* (Zentrum für Medizinische Ethik, Ruhr-Universität Bochum, März 1989), 3.

23. Ibid., 1.

Discussion

Dr. Brock: Another striking feature we found in the Soviet Union was the growth of cooperative in medicine. That is, privately practiced medicine outside of the state. Is there anything like that going on in China, where physicians are seeing patients essentially on a fee-for-service basis?

Prof. Qiu: Yes. Actually, we have a lot of private physicians. And also the government encourages the physicians who are working in the state-run hospitals to do private practice after work times. But, most of the physicians say: "I can't do that because there's no equipment."

Dr. Brock: We couldn't understand why someone would pay to see a doctor after work hours if they could go to see them for free beforehand. And I finally got an answer from a Soviet physician who has been living in Providence, R.I. for a while that, in fact, patients often had to pay under the table to get care during the day.

Prof. Kimura: You mentioned the recent statement of the Ministry of Welfare and Health on the issue of patient's rights. How was it developed? Were there physicians and philosophers and others in various professions involved or just bureaucrats in the Ministry of Health?

Prof. Qiu: I don't know the details, but the Ministry of Health has a committee that advises them in military matters. In this committee there are some ethicists and some economists and some lawyers.

Fr. Langan: I suppose this is more of a comment than a question. I was struck in a way that your paper could be read as an answer to a question Dr. Buchanan put forth about whether we would want to have a profession or not.

I take it your answer is a resounding yes. And that there are many kinds of dangers that have to do not so much with the profession's abuse of its power as with the manipulation of a profession by the government in the political order. I don't know if you want to amplify that or not.

Dr. Buchanan: I think the answer to whether you want to have a profession depends upon what the other circumstances are in society. And I can understand exactly your point that what's needed now in China is sufficient independence for physicians so that they can resist the politicization of medical practice that's been characteristic of Chinese medicine and medicine in the Soviet Union for many years.

But I have first a comment on the suggestion or proposal that you might take back to your medical colleagues. You said that the government had actually encouraged people to go into private practice after regular work hours of service to the National Health System, but that they had no equipment.

The Hungarians have solved this problem—not as far as I know in medical care—but there's a new kind of economic enterprise going on where factories that are state-owned factories during the day are leased out to private enterprise cooperatives at night. And they're becoming quite a threat because they're producing better goods and more of them per unit of time than the state factory system. But it solves the problem of the start-up costs of capitalization because socialist accumulation has provided the fixed capital for these enterprises. And it's a marvelous thing and it could be done, I suppose, with hospitals. They could be kept open other hours.

The other question I had was for Professor Kimura. This is just my ignorance, but were you saying that one hundred percent of Japanese citizens are covered by a kind of national health insurance?

Prof. Kimura: Yes.

Dr. Buchanan: What role, if any, do the corporate employers play in this? I would have thought just from looking at the large role that corporate organizations seem to play in Japanese life as we see it through the media in the United States, that health insurance, like other kinds of benefits, retirement benefits, would somehow be channeled, at least partly, through your belonging to some business enterprise. Is that not the case?

Dr. Kimura: Yes, that's also controlled by the government, but it's not directly managed by the government. Maybe this was not made very clear, but the corporate insurance system is controlled by the government but is paid by the corporations. But we have other systems. For those who retire from the corporation, it would be the government's directly controlled insurance system.

Dr. Buchanan: And unemployed persons are also insured by the government?

Prof. Kimura: Yes.

Dr. Buchanan: So this is similar to some West European systems?

Prof. Kimura: The one big difference is that physicians in the hospitals are not really well paid. They're not really getting an enormous amount of money, even though they're getting some money from outside sources. For example, some may do special surgery for a particular patient, but it does not officially appear in the medical expenditure.

Fr. Sokolowski: I just have a comment about person and relatedness which was in Professor Kimura's paper. I guess it's generally known that in the classical Greek categories, there was no such thing as person. That came in later. And one of the ways it came in was theological. There were other influences too. The notion of a person especially arose in regard to the Trinity in theological terms, and the three persons in the Trinity are essentially related.

But, also, even in regard to Christ as one person with two natures, this Christological controversy, in the Council of Chalcedon and the one before it, Ephesus, Christ was defined in terms of his mother, or vice-versa. There again you had a relatedness built into the theological concept of the person. So, both those trinitarian and incarnational theological controversies involved the person as related.

Dr. Gorovitz: Professor Kimura also mentioned that in Japan there is the mimicking of certain structures like institutional review boards; even though the function isn't the same, the form is; and there's beginning to be some exposure to the bioethics literature that comes from here. I would be interested to know whether there's something comparable happening in China, where you described a very different situation.

Is there interest in Western practices outside the official channels of authority among physicians? And on patient advocate groups, if such things exist? Regarding the scholars that are commenting on the health professions, is there familiarity with Western ways of doing these things and interest in them? And is there communication about those matters?

Prof. Qiu: Of course, we have two kinds of doctors, essentially, but most of them are trained in the West—in the United States, Britain, Germany, Japan. So, yes, they're trained in the Western ways of practice. After they return to China, they have to adjust into that context. They are in communication with their Western colleagues.

Dr. Brock: But I'm interested in the relative economic status of physicians in Chinese society and Japanese society. I was a little unclear because they have these two sources of income. Are they as relatively well off in the Chinese and Japanese societies as they are in this society?

Prof. Qiu: For the physician, the lawyer, and other professionals in China, including professors in medicine or humanities, the pay is about two hundred yuan a month, $58. A worker in a beer factory makes about three hundred yuan a month.

Dr. Brock: And social status? Just to use the Soviet Union again, the social status of professors is probably relatively higher there than here.

Fr. Langan: Not so high as Germany though.

Prof. Qiu: It's different. The social status of professors is not so high. But the lawyer is official, a bureaucrat.

HANS-MARTIN SASS

Professional Organizations and Professional Ethics: A European View

I. Introduction

Ethics and expertise belong together. As citizens we appreciate value-based social, cultural, and political environments; as clients we need professional expertise to support our efforts in reaching goals; as professionals we pledge fiduciary responsibility to customers. Conceptually, we base individual, collective, professional, or political moral actions on virtuous human nature, on a contract between educated persons, or on professional or political paternalistic dominance, depending on whether we find humans by nature intrinsically virtuous or vicious, strong or weak, free or dependent. Concrete moral actions, right conduct, and fiduciary responsibility often are based on a combination of the three, as are codes of professional conduct, systems of law, and models of collective action and decision making in public policy.

The contemporary debate on the foundations of fiduciary responsibility in professional ethics seems to concentrate primarily on the roles of virtue, right conduct, and contract, while ignoring the role which professional associations as corporatist "persons" play in shaping virtues, contracts, and right conduct. In this paper, I will examine the relationship between collective or corporatist "persons," such as professional associations, and individual persons, such as consumers and providers. Although I will address the following issues as they relate

263

specifically to European problems in fiduciary welfare paternalism, they may also be of interest in the American debate: (1) discrepancies between the theory of virtuous or freely contracting individuals and the factual existence of corporatist elements in modern societies; (2) benefits, costs, and risks in professional organizations supporting, shaping, and dominating concepts of professional ethics and expertise; (3) ethics and expertise as two equally important components in expert-client relationships; (4) the dialectics of cultural and technical risk assessment, the role of generalists in expertocracies, and the pressures on beneficence-in-trust to develop into cooperation-in-trust.

II. Changes in Moral Concepts and Survival of Guild Structure

Since the Age of Reason our Western culture has based value-oriented communities and the actions of educated citizens predominantly on the principles of natural virtue or social contract, rather than on codes of conduct or elitist, exclusive, often secret professional guilds or on the paternalism of states or churches. Rousseau, in his famous discourse on the immorality of modern sciences and arts,[1] preached the concept of natural virtues which naturally and originally are given to humans and which have to be protected against the temptations of the modern world; his concept of the "social contract" mirrors the genuine goodness of human nature, stressing that true sovereignty rests in people, not in states, churches, or guilds. From 1751 to 1776, Diderot and d'Alembert published the influential French *Encyclopédie*, which served not only as a critical weapon in undermining the traditional concepts of society, politics, and profession in Europe, but also made public, explained, and described technological, professional, and manufacturing information which had been kept secret within professions, guilds, and private businesses. Diderot wrote that "man is the sole and only limit whence one must start and back to whom everything must return."[2] In 1776, the ideas of free people, free thinking, free trade, and free manufacturing were manifested by such different facts as the "Declaration of Independence" in America, the abolition of torture by Austrian Empress Maria Theresa, Adam Smith's thesis that the wealth of nations can only be based on the market, and the engineering of the first modern machine, the steam engine, by James Watt.

The dream of the Enlightenment movement came true: the construction of societies of free, educated, and responsible men and women, virtuous and contracting freely with one another for mutual benefit where the common good and the welfare of the people was produced by the people, not by states, churches, or associations or guilds. The influential German educator Wilhelm von Humboldt put his critique of traditional paternalism this way: "the government may abstain from paternalism to promote the welfare of the citizen in a positive way and its only goal is to protect the citizen from foreign enemies and from himself; for no other goal may liberty be restricted . . . whoever puts his hope on paternalistic help . . . will also let the fate of his fellow citizen be determined by the same powers. But this weakens civic participation and slows down mutual aid . . . it makes the citizen cold against the citizen, the spouse against the spouse, the father against the family."[3]

In the light of individualistic Enlightenment and post-Enlightenment Western philosophy, stressing equal rights and responsibilities over feudal or corporate privileges, it is surprising still to find corporatist elements in modern society, even reflected in some philosophical and economic writings. For example, in 1821, we find supportive arguments for the role of corporations and associations in society in Hegel's *Philosophy of Right*.[4] Hegel understands the family and the professional association, which he calls corporation, as the two basic moral roots for state and society. Organization or disorganization of the pluralistic society depends on "the sanctity of marriage and the dignity of the corporation." He points out that in large modern states the individual rarely has an opportunity for direct involvement in public matters and state affairs, but that being a member of a corporation allows him to pursue public ethics in addition to private ethics. He emphasizes his general thesis that the individual taking care of his or her needs and goals indirectly produces common goods, but that the indirect production of common goods as a by-product of achieving individual goals is not sufficient. Associations and professional organizations, he says, are a vehicle to transfer individual ethics into the realm of public ethics. The production of common goods becomes "comprehended and reasoned morality only in the corporation (*gewußte und denkende Sittlichkeit*)." Corporations and associations, however, in order not to fall into a miserable guild mentality, need governmental supervision. "Corporations," he says, "are not closed guilds; they represent the moralfication (*Versittlichung*) of the individual profession and its elevation into a circle where it improves in strength and dignity."[5] These paragraphs have been described as a conservative tribute to the old system, not an integral part of the concept of the open and pluralistic society.[6]

The difference between the Rousseauian and the Hegelian approaches is that the first places virtues and professional ethics within the natural goodness of the individual person or some teleological view of the human nature or human good, while the latter places professional values and virtues into a social context in which families as natural collective entities and corporations as socially created collective "persons" create the fabric of moral interaction. Collective "persons" mediate the individual and the general society is not directly made up of unrelated individuals, but constructed out of networks of individuals and their networks.

III. Professional Organizations: Virtuous or Virtuoso?

Guilds were abolished in Britain during the eighteenth century, in France in 1791, and in Prussia in 1807 and 1810. But the principles of brotherhood, cooperation, solidarity, licensing, examining, and monitoring specific knowledge, and expert attitudes survived. Owen, Fourier, St. Simon, and other social thinkers recommended worker's cooperatives for fighting the pauperization of the masses. Arnold Ruge and other liberal Hegelian socialists called partnerships, associations, and cooperatives the most desired form of economic enterprise in a democratic society, avoiding the extremes of capitalism and communism.[7] Catholic, Protestant, and secular movements during the nineteenth century were active in promoting associations and cooperatives for various purposes, from mutual aid to collective bargaining and buying, housing and insurance. The statutory health and accident insurance systems, introduced in Germany in 1885 and based on the principle of mutual aid and solidarity, were political instruments to promote occupational safety and health care; mandatory insurance in areas such as unemployment and social security followed later. The papal encyclical *Rerum novarum* (1891)[8] called for workers' associations and cooperatives as alternatives to capitalism and socialism, and reintroduced the principle of subsidiarity, according to which collective solidarity of associations and cooperatives should take precedence over governmental action in welfare and other social matters. Although we have not yet had a well-rounded debate on the benefits, risks, and disadvantages of state vs. corporate paternalism in pluralistic societies, the philosophy and real existence of corporatist entities might pose a threat to the individual and his or her autonomy to freely contract directly for personal and public goods.[9]

In the Federal Republic of Germany, professional organizations and social interest groups play an eminent role in shaping public policy, professional attitudes, public culture, and provider-client relations. The concept of order politics (*Ordnungspolitik*) was developed in

Germany by Walter Eucken[10] as a direct response to the economic crisis in the early 1930s. It was to this crisis that Keynes responded with a theory of governmental fiduciary paternalism for maintaining employment, interest, and money flow. Eucken's model of avoiding the problems of the market economy and of central planning was based on a quasi-market concept, in which large institutions—associations, unions, corporations, interest groups—not individuals or governments, deal best with economic, technical, and social issues. Order politics has also been called the theory of secondary systems, as it addresses not individual persons as primary players in business or politics, but rather complex and intertwined secondary systems such as health care systems, professional organizations, unions, and special interest groups, in the establishment, protection, and development of political, economic, social, and cultural networks in society. Order politics thus appears as a sort of barter exchange among heavyweight interest groups, who, like the ruling elite in the feudal society, protect their own fiefdoms by negotiating and contracting with others. The goals and interests of order politics are first of all the survival, power, respect, and benefit of associations and collective "persons," and thereafter and only subsequently, the benefits of their particular constituencies.

The rationale for collective and noncollective benefits is clear: collective "persons" are more powerful, longer lasting, and more stable than individuals. They might achieve more goods for those represented by them and do so more easily than individuals could do individually; they bond together individuals with common interests, common enemies, and common values or goals or expertise and make them stronger. The processes of bartering, conflict resolution, and risk reduction become easier as fewer players are involved and, in addition, the interest profiles of collective "persons" might be less complex than those of individual persons.

The return of the guild system in the United States has been described by Garceau,[11] Grant,[12] and Olson.[13] Lawyers may not practice law without being members of a state bar association, and physicians might face, at the least, a genuine economic threat if they are at odds with organized medicine. The self-regulating guilds, based on compulsory membership, provide valuable by-products in addition to lobbying activities; they resemble "miniature governments" because they exercise "all the types of power normally exercised by government":[14] authority for self-government granted by the states; authority to discipline members and to set and enforce standards of ethical behavior; authority and power to defend members in malpractice suits; authority to set standards for academic curricula, for examinations, and direct management of continuous technical education at general or specialized conferences, and publication of politically and professionally influential journals for its members. Olson summarized the benefits of membership in the American Medical Association this way:

> By providing a helpful defense against malpractice suits, by publishing medical journals needed by its membership, and by making its conventions educational as well as political, the American Medical Association has offered its members and potential members a number of selective and noncollective benefits. It has offered its members benefits which in contrast with the political achievements of the organization, can be withheld from nonmembers, and which accordingly provide an incentive for joining the organization.[15]

The corporatist "persons," such as guilds and professional organizations, their members, and the advertisers in the professional journals do well, but are they doing good? The system of the marketplace of corporatist "persons" is a virtuoso system, but is it a virtuous one? Business corporations, professional organizations, organized labor all have or intend to have a corporatistic profile, a corporate identity— and some even hire well-paid experts in public relations to create a corporate logo, maxims of corporate identity, and other tangible or nontangible assets and values for their members and the clients of their members; but what is the role of fiduciary responsibility within the parameters of the corporatistic profile of a professional association? Is it a means to an end, which may be either the survival and benefit of the association or the interests of its members, or is it an end in itself for which the corporatistic structure of the profession is nothing other than a means and instrument to serve the clients better, to provide better and more reliable public and common goods, to strengthen the virtues and the expertise of their members?

Among the arguments against collective "persons" dominating individual professionals and defining the rules of a bartering game in a secondary system, the following arguments have been put forward: individuals might be less powerful in pursuing their interest in values and goods than collective "persons," but who defines these interests and goals, the professional or the association? Collective "persons" might have already divided the cake, leaving nothing to those who do not want to join but have to join in order to become licensed or otherwise accredited. Collective "persons" might abuse their constituency by betraying them and establishing lavish feudal organizations or enjoying the corporatistic power game as an end in itself, not a means for the benefit of members. A collective entity might make unreasonable demands of government or society and thus hurt its own members or damage the smooth functioning of the secondary system of democracy and market. A successful collective entity might produce what has been called social slack, i.e. welfare entitlement that is paid for by others or the taxpayer and that is, in part, wasted or not efficiently spent.[16] A corporatist "person" might also underserve its constituencies when it fights for its own survival, as has been mentioned recently in regard to the workers' unions and the system of unemployment insurance in the Federal Republic of Germany.[17] In these cases, the guilds provide some societal stability, however questionable, at the expense of their constituency. Among the rationality traps in which a corporatist entity might get enmeshed are the following: unions get caught in a conflict of interest to improve the working conditions and wages of their employed members while being pressured to fight for jobs for the unemployed among its members and others; environmental organizations get caught in the trap of having to assess the likelihood of environmentally more appreciable results of research in chemistry and biotechnology while being charged by their constituencies to stop further development of technology in general; health care associations are caught in the trap of having rationally to decide how best to serve the individual patient while being at the same time responsible for the future of the financial system which pays for the system of medical services.

Finally, the flexibility of the quasi-market might cause entrenchment in areas crucial for speedy and good conflict resolution. Examples of this structural stagnation in overcrowded secondary systems of representation are issues of energy and environment as well as issues of cost containment and improvement of social services such as health care. Too many powerful players are interested primarily in protecting their own turf and are willing to compromise cheaply if they can save their power base in the short run.

In the Federal Republic of Germany, so-called Concerted Action (*Konzertierte Aktion*) blue ribbon committees representing powerful special interest groups have been used to solve essential conflicts in particular areas of society, thus replacing the primary political processes of representative democracy. The break-up of Concerted Action committees on social and industrial policy in the 1970s might be responsible for the subsequent reduction of growth rates in the German economy and social networks. The Concerted Action on Health Care in the 1980s was under the chairmanship of the Federal Minister of Labor and represented physicians' associations, insurance associations, drug companies, state officials managing hospitals, unions, and handpicked economists. This committee proposed meager cost-containment recommendations targeting the symptoms, rather than the causes, of cost overruns. All parties involved claimed partial victory and partial loss. The individual patient and the individual physician, however, are worse off than they were before; medical service will not improve, nor will the cost structure of the health care system. As a result of the unyielding attitudes of the corporatist players in the field, essential reforms which might undermine the power structure of some of the players will not occur for a long while.[18]

The moral conflicts in a corporatistic system of representation are threefold: there might be conflicts of interest (1) between the collective entity and its individual members, (2) between the common goods sought by members of associations and the association's own self-interest, and (3) between the official political system of representative democracy, which is undermined or replaced by the sheer existence of corporatist entities charged with authority or exercising authority unchallenged by government, legislation, or citizens.

These structural conflicts exist whether or not a specific corporatist entity is vicious or virtuous. Moreover, given the existence of these entities, who would have the moral authority and the technical expertise to challenge the fiduciary setup of a corporatist "person" which is seen as a trustworthy professional association relative to the public and prospective clients and as a coercive paternalist bureaucracy relative to its members? The public as well as the professionals are aware of the conflicts of interest surrounding the organizational setting of professional associations; this might lead to low levels of public trust and lack of professional moral confidence.

IV. Components of Professionalism: Ethics and Expertise

High levels of technical and moral expertise for the professional and high levels of client and patient trust are preconditions for a technically as well as a morally efficient patient-doctor, consumer-provider, or lay-expert relationship. Ethics and expertise belong together; only together do they constitute true professionalism and provide a morally acceptable foundation for professional fiduciary services. The client or consumer expects not general expertise in scientific or technical matters or general commitment to virtues or moral or religious principles from the expert; rather, he or she expects experienced expertise in making good technical and good moral judgments in concrete cases. The client is not interested in whether good moral judgment is based on religious conviction, utilitarian reasoning, good intention, emotional sympathy, professional rules of conduct, or obedience to the law of the state or the regulations of the professional association; he or she is only interested in good value judgment and value management. Similarly, lay persons are not particularly interested in where academic or technical or vocational training occurred, what the academic curriculum was, or how many publications or patents the expert has, as long as the expert commands the knowledge and skills for good technical analysis, assessment, and management of this particular case. Of course, publications might indicate that a professional commands knowledge, and her church membership or her involvement in volunteer work might indicate her moral commitment; but writers of books can be quite impractical when it comes to real cases and churchgoers might be rather dogmatic whenever concrete moral cost-benefit assessments demand more than commitment to one single eternal principle.

What the client expects and what the good professional should deliver is the experienced judgment and management of concrete cases, using discriminating methods of micro-allocating and mix-allocating technical and moral expertise. This is what Veatch calls "right conduct."[19] Let me explain what I mean by "micro-allocation" and "mix-allocation" of values in professional fiduciary responsibility. We all know that whenever we have to accept concrete responsibility in a situation which requires moral judgment, we seldom face a situation which requires the recognition of one single moral principle. It is the right mix of different moral principles which is needed. In medicine, for example, the principles of *bonum facere* and *nil nocere*, "doing good" and "doing no harm," have to be balanced, as do fiduciary paternalism and the patient's best interest, as defined by the medical profession on the one hand and by the patient on the other. Regulations, codes of professional conduct, systems of law, and rules of the market represent typical elements in the mixed allocation of values for certain scenarios or cases. In medical ethics, moral judgments in the physician-patient relationship have to mix and balance the mid-level principles of professional expertise and responsibility, patient's choice, the patient's best interest, the informed consent principle, and the common good. In clinical human experimentation, moral judgments must balance the principles of no harm, benefit to the patient, benefit to clinical knowledge, and informed consent. Good professionalism requires nothing else than to apply the same methods used in micro-allocating and mix-allocating general scientific information and general technical skills and experience by expert judgment, management, and production.

When applying moral principles in a concrete situation, we want to be aware that these principles have various facets, the same way nails, tools, or pipes have different sizes, shapes, and materials. For example, forms of harm include mild to severe discomfort, levels of pain, forms of stress, and injury, temporary harm, permanent harm, loss of functions, and, finally, death. Forms of benefit include well-feeling, well-being, health; elimination or reduction of risks, causes, symptoms, or side effects; prolongation of life; reduction of suffering; or restoration or improvement or protection of "health" (and again, we have to leave it open what "health" means or, rather, use a more precise word). In addition, forms of consent include informed, educated, partly informed, uneducated, presumed consent, proxy consent, forced consent, and living will. These few examples demonstrate that it is not enough simply to have good intentions to benefit the client, not to harm him or her, and to get his or her consent. The expert has to be as aware of the different aspects of values and their ranking in a particular situation as he or she must be of the complexities and specific requirements of the technical situation. Quite often, moral dissent among those who have to work together occurs not as a result of these individuals having different religious or philosophical positions, but rather, because they are not accurate enough in their moral analysis and assessment of a particular case. The micro-allocation of the autonomy principle, for example, has to assess whether it is used in cases of human or civil rights, legal competence, informed consent, informed decision making, decision under uncertainty, irrational decision, proxy decision, or whether autonomy is to be protected as an expression of religious freedom, freedom of expression, freedom of speech, freedom of research, trade licence, free access to trade, right to be heard, free choice, or the balancing of maternal autonomy against probable fetal rights or rights of the father. The list could be continued, but the message seems to be clear: *ethics without expertise is clumsy, expertise without ethics is blind*. Both the micro-allocation and the mix-allocation of moral and cultural values require skills in a value analysis, value communication, and value argumentation. Poor moral judgment and poor moral management often are not caused by the diversity of world views we hold, but rather, by methodological and argumentative shortcomings that lead to moral malpractice.

Wedding expertise with ethics is a continuing process and challenge, not a one-time assessment. This is evident if we examine the familiar model of ethics committees and review boards. What these bodies actually do is to review a proposal prior to its implementation;

they do not accompany those who ask or have to ask for review; they do not integrate moral expertise into the process of clinical research or treatment of patients. There is no mandated feedback to the IRB after completion of the research, nor is there routinely a system of continuing communication between the committee and the researcher and his or her team. Such a review process is important but insufficient; it has to be coupled with, or in some cases replaced by, a more integrative structure which makes moral assessment an essential, internal, integrated part of the design, assessment, and development of technology. Moral assessment (MA) has to become a part of technology assessment (TA) by active participation of ethics professionals within the press of research and development itself. Good moral assessment cannot be simply reactive or "armchair" review that takes place outside of the practical context. What we need in drug design and drug development, for example, would be a process of professionalization of medical ethics within clinical research, the same way clinical biostatistics has become an integral and essential part of clinical research.

The same is true for all other professions, where specific professional knowledge has to be wed with concrete moral responsibility. The *Classification Scheme for Ethical Statements*, proposed by a working group of the American Association for the Advancement of Science, brings together core lists of moral principles which are either profession-directed, client- or sponsor-employer-directed, or society- or environment-directed, and which have to be addressed in different professions such as engineering, planning, marketing, law, medicine.[20] Alois Riklin, president of the St. Gallen Business School in Switzerland, has encouraged the draft of professional oaths for the business professions, including business administration, political economy, law, and teaching at commercial high schools. The oath of the teacher at commercial high schools, for example, includes the principles associated with the roles of teacher, scholar, and individual person. The oath of the legal professional includes the principles which address the fiduciary obligations of the lawyer, the judge, the legislator, and the academic teacher.[21]

Self-regulation and codes of professional conduct are the two most important instruments to ensure the integration of ethics and expertise by means of professional beneficence. The two other options to ensure moral use of professional expertise are governmental regulation and oversight on the one hand and, on the other, improved cooperation-in-trust between client and provider and education-in-trust of the individual lay person and the public by professionals and professional organizations sharing technical knowledge in nontechnical language.

V. Beneficence-in-Trust, Moral Risk Competence, and Cooperation-in-Trust

Probably the most important challenge to the fiduciary responsibility of experts is the plurality of world views, goals in life, priorities in value preferences, risk tolerance, and risk-assessment competence. While there definitely is a fiduciary responsibility for the expert to make the client aware of the technical positions to promote technical as well as cultural and moral goals in life, only the expert, not the lay person, has sufficient technological knowledge to describe the various ends which can be achieved and the associated technical and moral costs or risks. According to Aristotle, the true master commands various areas of expertise: doing something, knowing reasons why it is done, the way it is done, teaching it, talking about it, and assessing it in the wider framework of the social setting. The last two requirements: communicative skills in describing and assessing techniques for lay persons and general moral technology assessment are, more than ever, required in the fiduciary ethics of most areas of high technology expertise. In medicine, for example, this would mean, the differentiation of four areas of fiduciary responsibility: (1) protection of mental and physical integrity, i.e. preventive medicine; (2) restitution of well-being and well-feeling, i.e. therapy in the traditional technical sense; (3) education about optimal forms of protecting and enriching well-being and well-feeling; and (4) sharing of risk information and promotion of risk competence in health matters.

We have some experience in addressing the benefits and risks of fiduciary responsibility in preventive medicine and in therapy, but how do we assess the responsibilities and limits of health education and health risk education? How can we legitimately criticize or educatively manipulate unreasonable attitudes toward life or health, e.g., drug abuse or other excessive behavior such as overeating, alcoholism, or workaholism? This is part of a wider question of intergenerational fiduciary rights and duties and their limits: how do we better prepare the next generation for a life rich in values, goods, and choices? How may we best use our own set of value priorities and technical skills to prepare our children for a life free of paternalistic dominance, but enable them by means of fiduciary intervention to have the opportunities to reason well, to assess well, to risk well, and to work well? Society in general has not come to grips with its obligation and the limits of fiduciary education; this makes it even more complicated for professionals to assess and manage their fiduciary responsibilities. Three issues are of particular importance in the assessment of fiduciary responsibility:

(A) the professional ethics of those who run professional organizations and who moderate and assess moral obligations in professional life, (B) the difference between technical and cultural or moral risk assessment in professional activity, and (C) the cultured and educated cooperation-in-trust between providers and consumers of professional services.

(A) Professional ethics and professional organizations

What are the specific value components of fiduciary responsibilities or the perceived fiduciary responsibilities of the CEOs, board members, newsletter editors, legal consultants, and public relation professionals who run professional organizations? How do or how should bureaucrats, wielding power by administrative means, and communicrats, wielding power by communicative means in professional organizations, establish, develop, and protect professional values and the professional profile and identity? Will they be guided by what they perceive to be the true professional tradition, by legal or economic consultation focusing on the survival of the professional organization within a corporatist world, or by majority vote of their members? Do the values favored by leaders of professional organizations conflict with those of their members, the lay public, or the common good? What technical, administrative, communicative, and moral skills must leaders of professional organizations have and what skills do they display? We might want to look more carefully into the special ethics of such leadership expertise, which has to be assessed and checked against the benefits and risks of government intervention to establish and protect the moral values important for each professional activity. As it stands now, the consensus is that priority should be given first to professionals and only if this fails, to governmental, judicial, or legislative intervention.

In a society represented by experts, professionals, professional organizations, and the need for interexpert consensus formation, each "expert" has to be also an expert in the field of interexpert communication and expert-lay communication. There might, however, be some tasks which require the special services of "generalists," monitoring, moderating, and mediating not just interexpert consensus formation and optimization of cooperation, but also moral assessment of expert services for the experts as well as for the public and individual lay persons. The rise in employment of professional bioethics consultants indicates that there is a demand for the expertise which is crucial for the moral assesssment of professional services.

The case management approach, as described by Buchanan in this volume, would be a fruitful area for integrating services of professional ethicists or other "generalists." The method used by expert generalists or ethicists, however, will not be that of presenting general statements or confusing deep-think emotions with differential ethics, but of applying the above-sketched method of micro-allocating and mix-allocating moral and cultural principles to specific cases or scenarios. It seems to be a part of the fiduciary responsibility of professionals to be able to assess and to communicate moral risk in his or her professional activity and to cooperate with ethical experts, providing expert assessment and application of general moral principles.

(B) Technical and moral risk assessment

Another problem fiduciary expertise has to face is the difference between technical risk assessment and cultural or moral risk assessment. It is not widely recognized that our individual and collective perception of risk differs from what the technicians and engineers tell us about risk.[22] Individual risk perception and risk tolerance has a lot to do with the priorities of values we set individually for reaching goals in life. Also, the tolerance for risks taken voluntarily is much higher than for risks we are forced to accept. Technical risk perception is a data-based concept of risk while cultural risk perception is a value-based concept of risk. If we see the possibility of high benefits, we will accept higher risks; the benefits might be recreational or professional and might involve money, fun, prestige, or social recognition. But we also share collectively perceptions of risk which differ from technical risk perception. Existing laws, regulations, and attitudes attach different values to protecting life or fighting different types of health risk. We can prevent one premature death by investing $25,000 in cervical cancer diagnosis, $10,000 to $30,000 in colon-rectal cancer screening, $20,000 in improved road signs, $65,000 in rescue helicopters, $90,000 in driver's education, $320,000 in air bag technology, $400,000 in tire inspection, or $300,000 to $200 million in increased safety of nuclear reactors. With no money involved, we could reduce the teenage death rate resulting from drunk driving (over ten thousand deaths per year in the United States alone) by setting the driving and drinking ages at twenty-five years or higher.[23]

Why do we not spend monies more efficiently for averting risks of death or enact regulations that would reduce the death risk at no cost? The reason for not following technical risk assessments is that we personally and culturally have distinct cultural and moral risk perceptions which differ from expert perceptions. But, if we do not want to apply different moral and professional standards in comparable situations, we have to analyze and assess the differences between technical and moral and cultural risk and our individual preparedness for various forms of risk. This is another argument which identifies it as a professional fiduciary responsibility to wed ethical expertise with technical expertise and to educate the public about the advantages and limits of the difference between technical risk and moral risk. The communicative processes of evaluating the moral and cultural risks and benefits of technology, i.e. moral assessment (MA), will have to be incorporated into traditional technology assessment (TA), or better, traditional technology assessment has to become an integral part of an overall moral assessment of technology. Previous generations, in the absence of much technological progress, had a far simpler task introducing traditional values to the following generation. Because technology did not change much, there was no great need expressly to incorporate fiduciary responsibilities into moral assessment or the teaching of moral assessment into codes of professional conduct. Today, the reassessment of traditional values and their priorities in technologically new situations is a challenge for professional fiduciary responsibility.

Studies in comparative cultural history demonstrate that the introduction of more rational and efficient ways of organizing personal, social, and political life comes with periods of rebellion against rationality identified as dehumanizing, machine-like, and barbaric. In Western culture, Rousseau in the eighteenth century was the first, and Hans Jonas, the contemporary German-American philosopher the last person, to present an antitechnological, antiscientific view of the threat to culture and morals by science and technology.[24] These emotional cultural movements rightly perceive the demand for moral and cultural evaluation of the benefits and risks associated with new technology, but they lack the argumentative skill and communicative properties to do so in an adequate way. The technophobic critique of modern technology represents defensive ethics; its thesis is that the means of technological progress outweigh our moral capacity to govern and control the use of technology. Therefore, defensive ethics proclaims the active retardation of technological progress or severe regulation and legislation of technological developments and applications. I see it as a definite fiduciary responsibility of experts and expert organizations to fight technophobic ethics by informing society about reasonable ways to reduce moral and technical risk, and by challenging professionals as well as lay persons to discriminate between value-neutral technology and virtue-based or vice-based applications of technology.

(C) Cooperation-in-trust

Pellegrino and Thomasma describe the fiduciary principle of

"beneficence-in-trust" as indispensable for physicians acting in the best interest of the patient while recognizing the value of patient's autonomy.[25] The same approach can be used in establishing beneficence-in-trust in professions other than the medical. The creation of codes of professional conduct for different professions by Riklin and the draft of a general framework by the American Association for the Advancement of Science have already been mentioned.[26] But professional fiduciary responsibility has to reach out more widely; it has to include lay education concerning technical and moral matters of the technicalities of professional expertise in a nontechnical way. Educating and sharing knowledge, as mentioned, is one of the capacities which, according to Aristotle, makes a person a real master in his or her field. The concept of fiduciary beneficence can be expanded and applied to the wider fiduciary responsibilities of professionals in teaching and sharing moral and technical assessments with individual lay persons and the public. Educating and sharing information with nonprofessionals decreases the exclusivity of professional power and privileged knowledge, information, and skills. Sharing professional expertise in a nontechnical way with nonprofessionals builds trust and improves the educated citizen's competence not only to assess the technical values of professional services better but to make truly informed decisions and to give truly informed consent. Part of beneficence-in-trust has to become education-in-trust of nonprofessionals in matters of technical and moral risks, in a nontechnical way. When used as a utilitarian and pragmatic tool, beneficent teaching of risk competence will, step by step, level the knowledge-based hierarchical differences between experts and lay persons, improve trust, and might finally contribute to a de-hierarchization and deprofessionalization of the competent assessment of moral risk.

Of course, there will be limits to the extent to which technical expertise can adequately be shared with lay persons, but professionals and their organizations have not yet tried hard enough, and the lay people have not yet requested it strongly enough. Such an evolutionary way to share risk information and technical expertise in a nontechnical way is the only tool to *reduce* the need for and the existence of fiduciary prerogatives of experts over lay persons; it also would reduce moral as well as technical and political risks associated with "corporatist persons," basing their authority and power on the exclusivity of technical and moral expertise. Education-in-trust will lead to cooperation-in-trust, a more valuable principle than that of informed consent. Education-in-trust as a long-term process in social and individual education and risk competence is more efficient than one-time, short-term information for a particular case which needs immediate decision. Education-in-trust also is the precondition for what Veatch has called an ethical covenant—the value-based contract between provider and recipient of professional services.[27]

Contracts and covenants have a very poor communicative and moral basis if the partners do not share a minimum of technical information and moral assessment capability. Beneficence-in-trust, when used to share technical knowledge in a nontechnical way, will diminish the unwanted side effects of professionals and professional organizations exercising power by abuse of privileged knowledge and by writing and enforcing self-serving rules of professional conduct. Cooperation-in-trust will develop out of the ethos of information sharing which, since the Age of Reason, has been so important for societies concerned with values and common goods. Beneficence-in-trust may neglect education-in-trust in situations of actual crisis where immediate competent action is required, but will have to put the greatest possible emphasis on beneficent education-in-trust as a general pattern of technically and morally good fiduciary professional activity. The final goal of beneficence-in-trust can only be cooperation-in-trust, dismantling the barriers between professionals and lay persons.

There is no other way to win the future for an increased integration of ethics and expertise than to increase education-in-trust in moral and technical matters, to improve risk awareness and risk competence of the individual citizen and the public, and to enrich professional-lay relationships by moving from simple informed consent and beneficence-in-trust to education-in-trust and cooperation-in-trust. The educated citizen, in the roles of expert and lay person, will have the last word in assessing the moral standards of professionals and professional organizations, because having values, being ethical, and making prudent moral choices is not in the exclusive domain of any particular profession or professional, but is the most valuable resource for educated persons—lay and professional—in building peaceable societies, rich in technical and economic assets and in personal, professional, and common values.

Notes

1. J.J. Rousseau, *Si le rétablissement des Sciences et des Arts a Contribué à Epurer les Moeurs* (Paris, 1749).

2. D. Diderot and J. d'Alembert, *Encyclopédie, ou Dictionnaire Raisonné des Sciences, des Arts et des Métiers*, 35 vols. (Paris, 1751-1780).

3. W. von Humboldt, "Ideen zu dem Versuch die Wirksamkeit des Staates

zu Bestimmen," in *W. von Humboldt, Eine Auswahl aus seinen politischen Schriften*, ed. S. Kohler (Berlin, 1922), 24f., 36.

4. G.W.F. Hegel, *The Philosophy of Right*, trans. T.M. Knox (Oxford: Oxford University Press, 1952), secs. 250-56.

5. Ibid., sec. 255.

6. H-M. Sass, "Hegels Rechtsphilosophie als Strategie pragmatischer Politik- und Rechtskritik," *Archiv fur Rechts- und Sozialphilosophie* 53 (1967): 257-76.

7. A. Ruge, *Die Loge des Humanismus* (Berlin, 1852).

8. Leo XIII, *Rerum novarum*, in *Die sozialen Rundschreiben Rerum Novarum und Quadrogesimo Anno*, ed. von P. Jostock (Freiburg: Herder, 1961).

9. M. Olson, *The Logic of Collective Action: Public Goods and the Theory of Groups* (Cambridge, Mass.: Harvard University Press, 1974).

10. W. Eucken, *Der Grundlagen der Nationalokonomie* (Berlin: Mohr, 1939).

11. O. Graceau, *The Political Life of the American Medical Association* (Cambridge, Mass.: Harvard University Press, 1941).

12. J.A.C. Grant, "The Guilds Return to America," *Journal of Politics* 4 (1942):4, 304 ff., 463 ff.

13. Olson, *The Logic of Collective Action*.

14. Grant, "The Guilds Return to America," 324.

15. Olson, 140.

16. P. Herder-Doerneich, *Ordungstheorie des Sozialstaates* (Tübingen: Mohr, 1983), 26 ff.

17. C. Offe, "On the Vulnerability of Social Policies: Institutional Contexts, Structural Strains, and Populist Politics" (unpublished paper: Wissenschaftskolleg Berlin, 1989).

18. H-M. Sass, "Personliche Verantwortung und gessellschaftliche Solidaritat," in *Ethik und offentliches Gesundheitswesen*, ed. H-M. Sass (Heidelberg: Springer, 1988), 93-112.

19. R.M. Veatch, "Against Virtue: A Deontological Critique of Virtue Theory in Medical Ethics," in *Virtue and Medicine*, ed. E.E. Shelp (Dordrecht: D. Reidel, 1985), 329-45; R.M. Veatch, "The Danger of Virtue," *Journal of Medicine and Philosophy* 13 (1988):445-46.

20. R. Chalk, M.F. Frankel, and S.F. Chafer, *Professional Ethics Project* (Washington, D.C.: AAAS, pub. #80-r-4, 1980), 135-45.

21. A. Riklin, "Der hippocratische Eid. Rede des Rektors anlaßlich der Promotionsfeier der Hochschule St. Gallen," *St. Gallen Hochschulnachrichten* 97 (1983), appendix.

22. H-M. Sass, *Verantwortung unter Risiko: Vom Ethos ordnungspolitischen Riskomanagments* (Alfter-Oedekoven: Koellen, 1986); A. Wildavsky, *Searching for Safety* (New Brunswick, N.J.: Transaction Books, 1988).

23. H-M. Sass, *Verantwortung*.

24. H. Jonas, *Das Prinzip Verantwortung: Versuch einer Ethik fur die technologische Zivilisation* (Frankfurt: Insel, 1979).

25. E.D. Pellegrino and D.C. Thomasma, *For the Patient's Good: The Restoration of Beneficence in Health Care* (New York: Oxford University Press, 1988).

26. Rilkin, "Der hippokratische Eid."; Chalk et al., *Professional Ethics*.

27. R.M. Veatch, *A Theory of Medical Ethics* (New York: Basic Books, 1981), 324-30.

Discussion

Prof. Qiu: In China, the state is the agency that articulates the ethical obligation. In fact, we tried to persuade the professional group to do so, and they declined. In the United States, the associations articulate the only formal codes that exist in pharmacy or medicine. And the state has nothing to do with that articulation, but it does license.

In the United States, you needn't be a member of the professional association to practice in any of the professions we are talking about. The bar is kind of a special case. I gather you still have to be a member of the bar to practice before certain courts. But you can certainly do all kinds of lawyering without being a member of the bar. Most pharmacists are not members of the pharmaceutical association. And something like half, less than half, of the physicians are members of the physicians' organization.

I'm not at all clear in Germany who is the custodian, the trustee that we're talking about. Who has the obligation to articulate the norms and to adjudicate disputes about the norms and administer disciplinary proceedings?

Dr. Sass: You mentioned earlier that you wouldn't trust Dr. Brock to operate on you. In Germany, Dr. Brock could not operate on you because he would not be accepted as a member of the State Chamber of Physicians. Only members of the State Chamber of Physicians may practice medicine.

Dr. Veatch: Is that a government agency or a professional agency?

Dr. Sass: That's a tax-exempt professional organization, a membership organization. But, the government looks very favorably on what the professional organizations do because they do not have to regulate the professional organizations. They are self-regulating. Now, once in a while, a conflict arises. Most recently, with in vitro fertilization, the Federal Chamber of Physicians decided that the professional organizations could regulate in vitro fertilization in the case of married couples.

Now the state says that this is not good enough because they might violate their own rules. In the case of embryo research, however, the state wants to regulate by passage of a law.

Here you see the conflict between government paternalism and professional paternalism. My personal preference would be rather to be exposed to professional paternalism because at least they're experts, while politicians are experts in nothing or everything, and the regulations might not be as precise or well set, or might be self-interested in a way contrary to my own self-interest. But this is an ongoing debate. What is better: governmental paternalism or professional paternalism?

Dr. Meilaender: I would just like a clarification. You said near the end of your talk something about an ethic of trust in education, and that a trust relation would be a necessary prerequisite for entering into some kind of contractual relation. Did I understand you correctly? Would you just clarify that for me?

Dr. Sass: Trust is a precondition for entering into a mutual business or moral contract, a professional, legal contract. But more is required than trust.

You have to be slightly literate in order to know what to do. And I think, when we talk about beneficence-in-trust we should not understand the lay person as, per se, by nature being ignorant. The professional was a lay person prior to his educational process which either by the academic process or learning at the bedside or on the job, by constructing a house, finally, he or she had become an expert in the profession.

Now, going back to Aristotle, it's my thesis that it's one of the duties of a professional to share as much as possible in a nontechnical way the risks and benefits and how the craft works, and what the moral and cultural dimensions of this are. So, beneficence-in-trust cannot take the lay person as someone naturally uneducatable. One of the jobs a good professional has to do from his or her point of view is to share as much as possible technical information and value information on what the outcome of his or her craft may be.

Education-in-trust is not a one-time, two-minute or whatever informed consent thing. And then you get the signature. It's a very long process. And if I am a lay person, this education-in-trust from my doctor, my lawyer, my peer, whoever knows something about things, I will improve in autonomy and self-determination, self-development, and become more risk-competent in other areas of life.

So what I learn probably in education with my doctor might not only help me medically but might help me manage health risks better, and maybe also economic risks or job-related risks.

Dr. Meilaender: Can I just follow up on that? Granting the importance of the claim about education, I guess what I was interested in was trying to connect your claim with some of the things that we talked about this morning and had some disagreement about, because I take it that the business about education is only a qualification that follows after rather a strong claim, namely, that there *does* have to be something special about the relationship established here between a professional and the client. That if the trust to some degree isn't in there, we can't just have autonomous parties contracting and expect this to work successfully.

Dr. Sass: I fully agree with the trust part. If I don't trust you as an expert, I won't believe you and I won't embody the information you give me in my own decision-making process. I would say, well, he taught me this, but I really don't trust him. So I'm not sure. If trust is not a precondition, it's very complicated to assess information you get.

Dr. Brock: This is just a comment. I agree with you about the great importance of improving our capacities for risk assessment, but I would underline how difficult a lot of that is. And there are difficult philosophical issues here in what normative standards we want to use and impose on that process. For example, and there are lots of examples here, in the area of uncertainty as opposed to risk, there's a great deal of controversy about what appropriate normative standards are for making decisions under uncertainty as opposed to risk. If you look at an area of importance to medicine, it seems that people, even when informed that in terms of expected utility they're doing worse, still prefer rescue as opposed to preventive medicine. Now what should we make of that? Has our risk assessment—has risk education failed? Or have we got the wrong standard that we're applying?

Dr. Sass: It's a very complicated question. I feel part of the answer, not the total answer, would be that risk assessment and risk management have disappeared from the public eye. It's now in the fine print of regulations and standards of safety with the Bureau of Standards, and with some agencies. And you and I feel safe in handling machines and going to the doctor, but we're not told about the uncertainties.

The vocabulary has disappeared somewhere because we are so well taken care of by the risk assessors in various ministries, professional organizations, technology assessment groups, consumer groups, and so forth.

As a result of this, when a new technology appears, we, all of a sudden, get very emotional because we do not have the experience in making risk assessment choices.